Praise for *Anything But My Phone, Mom!*

"Cohen-Sandler's research-based guidance is a must-read for parents of teenage girls."

—*Library Journal*

"Sound, reassuring, and practical, Roni Cohen-Sandler's advice helps us stay close to our daughters, even when they seem to be doing their level best to push us away. I'm so grateful for this book."

—KJ Dell'Antonia, *New York Times* bestselling author of *The Chicken Sisters* and former editor of the *New York Times* Motherlode blog

"Roni Cohen Sandler has given moms a reassuring, practical, and compassionate book that we can all see ourselves in and learn from."

—Rachel Simmons, bestselling author of *Odd Girl Out*

"Roni Cohen-Sandler helps moms navigate the challenging terrain of raising resilient daughters during these unprecedented times. Packed with research and practical tips, this engaging book is an excellent resource for moms everywhere who want to make a positive impact on their daughter's life."

—Suzie Pileggi Pawelski and James Pawelski, coauthors of *Happy Together*

PENGUIN LIFE

ANYTHING BUT MY PHONE, MOM!

Roni Cohen-Sandler, PhD, is a licensed clinical psychologist, author, and speaker with decades of experience assessing and treating adolescents and adults, specializing in the issues of women and teenage girls, mother-daughter relationships, parent guidance, and psychoeducational assessments. She has appeared as an expert on *The Oprah Winfrey Show*, *The Today Show*, CBS, *Good Morning America*, and PBS, among many others, and has been featured in print in many major outlets including *The New York Times*, *Newsweek*, *Marie Claire*, and *Teen Vogue*. Along with her husband, she divides her time between Connecticut and Los Angeles.

Anything But My Phone, Mom!

Raising Emotionally Resilient Daughters in the Digital Age

Roni Cohen-Sandler, PhD

PENGUIN BOOKS
An imprint of Penguin Random House LLC
penguinrandomhouse.com

A Penguin Life Book

LIBRARY OF CONGRESS CATALOGING-IN-PUBLICATION DATA
Names: Cohen-Sandler, Roni, author.
Title: Anything but my phone, mom! : raising emotionally resilient daughters in the digital age / Roni Cohen-Sandler, PhD.
Description: New York : Penguin Life, [2022] |
Includes bibliographical references.
Identifiers: LCCN 2021022912 (print) | LCCN 2021022913 (ebook) |
ISBN 9780143135418 (paperback) | ISBN 9780525507086 (ebook)
Subjects: LCSH: Daughters. | Parenting. | Internet and teenagers. |
Resilience (Personality trait) in adolescence. | Mothers and daughters.
Classification: LCC HQ777 .C5965 2022 (print) |
LCC HQ777 (ebook) | DDC 306.874—dc23
LC record available at https://lccn.loc.gov/2021022912
LC ebook record available at https://lccn.loc.gov/2021022913

Printed in the United States of America
1st Printing

Set in Adobe Garamond Pro
Designed by Alexis Farabaugh

All names and identifying characteristics have been changed to protect the privacy of the individuals involved.

For my granddaughter
Olivia Rose, with infinite love

Contents

Part Three

Dealing with Daily Dilemmas 221

Foreword

When my mom's first book came out, I was sixteen years old. My mom had just written a book about mother-daughter relationships during the teenage years.

And I was a teenager.

I was not a well-adjusted, self-actualized, confident teenager (if those even exist). I was a roiling mess of angst, insecurities, and self-doubt. I was deeply enmeshed in that time-honored tradition of adolescence: trying to figure out who I was and carve out my own identity by cleaving away from the maternal figure who had theretofore defined me. I would not be anything like my mother. I would distinguish myself from this dyad. And I would not make this process enjoyable for anyone, least of all my mom. The title *I'm Not Mad, I Just Hate You!* was not a direct quote but it easily could have been.

At the same time, my mom's book, rightly so, was garnering attention and press. "Is it all about you?" people would ask. I should have provided a sound and intelligent response, pointing out her clinical training as a psychologist, years spent accruing expertise, and countless hours of interview-based research. Instead, I would utter a half-hearted "Haha," and when the person turned away, fall upon my go-to reaction: an eye roll honed to practiced perfection. Was I proud of my mom's accomplishment? Sure. Of course. But was I also too wrapped up in myself to be able to separate it from the impact it had on me? Absolutely. Regrettably.

We weathered my teenage years, though they certainly weren't pretty, and once again established the kind of close, meaningful relationship that we both value and cherish. As I became an adult it also grew into more than a mother-daughter relationship; it became a true friendship. The maternal element will always be there, of course, but in addition, we evolved into two women who give each other advice, trade recipes and book recommendations, deliberate over personal dilemmas, giggle over gossip, and ask each other for favors like equals.

Over the years, I've witnessed, firsthand, the depth of my mom's knowledge and veracity of her insight as friends and strangers—always, strangers!—would tell her their stories and ask for parenting advice. I admired her ability to marry firm directives with reassuring kernels of wisdom. She doesn't mince words. She always has the answers. But she also always imparts this knowledge without judgment or sanctimony.

My appreciation and respect could only be intellectual and theoretical, however, until I had children of my own. Five years ago, I met my now-husband, who came as a package deal with a daughter from his first marriage. Suddenly, I was a mother figure. Overnight, I had a wisp of a girl sitting in my lap hunched over a coloring book, refusing to eat anything remotely healthy, and depositing the trash that she always seemed to harbor, like a squirrel, into my automatically outstretched palm. Immediately, my appreciation for all mothers, but especially my own, grew tenfold.

My mom—who delighted over her bonus granddaughter—became my lifeline as I'd text or call about issues big and small. *Is this normal? Is that weird? She's asking for a phone—at eight!—what do we do? She's obsessed with TikTok—help!!! Omg, you're never going to believe the funniest thing she said. . . .*

Instantly, I was part of the tribe, and fortunately, I had the best den mother anyone could ask for to show me the ropes.

At my baby shower in September 2019, my mom brought tears to everyone's eyes when she voiced her fervent hope that I would have the kind of relationship with my baby daughter that the two of us have. Not only do I share this hope, but also add another one: that I will be half the mother to my sweet Olivia that my mom has been and is for me. Having girls of my own has underscored how deeply entrenched, special, and magical the mother-daughter bond truly is.

Our connections to our mothers and to our daughters are at our very core; they are the currents that flow within us. So it is no surprise that the often discomfiting, rocky chrysalis that this dynamic undergoes during the teenage years is universally looked upon with dread. As incredibly lucky as I am to have my mom on speed dial to shepherd me through this process one day, so are her readers. This book is a definitive tome for understanding, surviving, and hopefully emerging gracefully from the teenage years. It is an invaluable resource for mothers of teenage girls; it is also a gift to us.

If you are currently struggling, take comfort in having this book in hand. Also take heart, for I am living evidence that the snarky comments and eye rolls won't last forever. What will is the incomparable bond between a mother and her daughter.

May we cherish all the moments with our girls, even if they challenge us. May we revel in the milestones. May we raise girls who are kind, strong, and emboldened. May we foster a new generation who won't have to bravely admit, "Me too," but rather will boldly declare, "Not me." May we work to shatter the glass ceiling so that they can thrive in an open-air atrium of possibilities. May we do our part to strengthen the collective sisterhood with daughters who understand that empathy and sensitivity—traits often sublimated for more traditional, masculine concepts of strength—are of the highest value, and that our girls' greatest gift is their ability to connect with others and tap into their femininity and humanity. It's what makes us women. We care. We take care. We bring life into the world and then we protect it with a ferocity that is primal and inviolable and glorious.

We are lucky to be mothers. We are incredibly lucky to be mothers of daughters.

With deepest respect and gratitude to my mom, for everything.

Laura Sandler Lekkos

Anything But My Phone, Mom!

Part One

A Different World

Introduction

Mothering Girls in the Digital Age

It's scary because my girls are living in a world I don't know anything about.

—GRETCHEN, MOTHER OF 14- AND 17-YEAR-OLDS

My daughter is growing up so differently in so many ways that I feel like I'm flying blind.

—MIRANDA, MOTHER OF A 16-YEAR-OLD

Does it seem as if your preteen or teenage daughter is growing up in a different universe than you did? When you were her age, you certainly didn't have a personal smartphone or social media accounts. If you wanted to call friends, you used the family landline, hoping your parents or siblings didn't eavesdrop on your conversations. If your mother answered the phone first, she learned whom you spoke to most often—and maybe the identity of your latest crush.

But the digital age is transforming the way your daughter communicates, socializes, and interacts with the world—and, therefore, how you mother her. If you complain that she is constantly on her cellphone, you probably aren't wrong. According to a Pew Research Center survey in 2018, not only do 95 percent of teens have access to smartphones, but also half admitted to being on them nearly all the time—22 percent more than just three years prior to that.

There is no question that ever-increasing technology use is changing young girls' hearts and minds, transforming how they mature, identify themselves, self-reflect, develop social skills, focus, take in information, and learn.

And that's not all. A myriad of other cultural phenomena causes teens to grow up differently today. As many women told me, "younger girls are being exposed to cultural, mental, physical, and social issues, such as cutting, vaping, LGBTQ, depression, suicide, and other problems older sisters didn't have to deal with until they were more mature." Teens are also confronting—and taking on—climate change, sexual harassment, the environment, systemic racism, and other injustices.

Maddie, mother of four, speaks about the impact of teens struggling with serious challenges these days: "There are many rough days with friends going through hard things. My seventeen-year-old has a close friend with severe anorexia. She doesn't know how to help her. Other friends have phone addictions or depression, they're cutting themselves, and another girl's father died of cancer and she's not handling it well. Watching them takes a toll. These teens are dealing with so many burdens every day. Then they come home and unload on Mom."

This generation's unique experiences, vulnerabilities, and opportunities have irrevocably altered raising teen daughters. It is no wonder that mothers I speak with these days are questioning, "Is this normal? This certainly isn't the way it was when I was my daughter's age—and it's so different from her older sister's perspective." You, too, may feel challenged by a whole different set of parenting hurdles than the ones you expected.

Chances are, you are more prepared for the most notorious changes ushered in by puberty. You probably weren't surprised the first time your little girl recoiled from your hug, gave you attitude, or acted testy, challenging, dismissive, or supersensitive. You may have braced yourself for your daughter's sharp criticism—or continual critiques—as soon as she became an overnight authority on everything you wear, do, and say.

You may already have a taste of your daughter's indignation if you try to guide her clothing choices—especially when she's going out. Perhaps you've even reconciled yourself to being the quintessential "embarrassing" mother who single-handedly sends your tween's social status into a free fall—merely by occupying the same space as her friends. Still, even when you think you are mentally prepared, when these things actually happen to you, it can be more upsetting than you'd imagined. If nothing else, mothering teen girls is humbling.

Do you relate to these timeless concerns?

- Does my daughter have enough friends? Or,
- Is her social life distracting her from school and sports?
- Is she too worried about how she looks? Or,

- Why doesn't she care about her appearance?
- Are the friends in her group actually good for her?
- Who *is* this boy she's been "talking" to?
- Is she depressed, or is this normal teenage moodiness?
- What if she's not invited to the dance/party everyone's talking about?
- Why does she flip out when I ask about her day?
- What is she *really* doing online?
- Why are her "friends" leaving her out of plans? Or,
- Could that actually be a blessing?
- Why is she struggling in Spanish/math/English?
- Why hasn't she found a passion yet?
- Should I intervene with her teacher?
- How can I motivate her in school? Or,
- Should I worry about her stress and perfectionism?
- How can I help her through this breakup?
- What can I do about these nightly homework battles?

- Is social media helping or hurting her?
- Why is she in such a big rush to grow up? Or,
- Why is she less mature than her friends?
- Why does she post such provocative photos/videos/TikToks?
- How can I get her to open up to me?

Besides these ordinary worries, on occasion you might be jolted awake at 3 a.m. by the heart palpitations and trepidations that don't dare show up in daylight: Could my daughter be lying to me? Is she drinking/doing drugs/having unprotected sex/behaving in other risky ways I don't know about? What if she gets suspended from school, doesn't get into a good college, or makes a stupid mistake that ruins her life? As you know, these fears are best left nameless. But at least they have been familiar to generations of mothers.

It's the new worries, women I work with in my practice or interviewed for this book tell me, that are taking up most of their mental airspace now: all the different social media platforms cropping up, cyberbullying, school zero-tolerance policies, mass shootings, school safety drills, a plethora of online threats, and the long-term effects of the COVID-19 global pandemic. These are the unprecedented issues that make mothers of this generation of teens feel as if they are venturing into alien territory.

Maternal self-doubt has always been the chief occupational hazard of raising teen girls. As I work with women and girls, present parenting lectures, and conduct workshops around the country, not once in forty years have I heard a mother say, "I never worry about how my daughter will turn out. She has excellent judgment, makes great decisions, and always tells me the absolute truth."

Women often think that every other mother is charting a surer course, raising a more polite, successful, and popular daughter, while they alone are stumbling around in the dark. But nowadays, the challenges of raising technologically savvier daughters are pummeling mothers' confidence as never before. What is the number one cause of maternal angst and mother-daughter conflict these days? My informal poll was unanimous: *screens*—specifically, how much girls are using digital media, when they are doing so, and what they are doing when on devices.

When asked in an interview what motivated her to create the documentary *Screenagers*, physician and filmmaker Dr. Delaney Ruston said it was her own difficulties mothering a twelve-year-old daughter who was "always on social media." Dr. Ruston explained that first she got mad, then she felt guilty, and finally she was at a complete loss. Speaking to other mothers, she realized that dealing with this issue made all of them feel powerless, too.

A school social worker told me about a troubling incident with her smart, articulate thirteen-year-old daughter she lovingly describes as "definitely not one of the cool kids." Unbeknownst to her mother, Madison had created an account on an adult dating app and was "talking with some guy" until she tearfully fessed up. Despite this woman's training and professional experience, she was thrown by confronting her own young teen's uncharacteristic risky behavior.

It is harder to monitor what daughters are doing—both online and in the real world—and therefore to keep them safe. For one, there are fewer opportunities these days for family conversations. With entertainment media now consumed on personal digital devices, teens and parents spend less time watching TV in the family room or going out to movies together. Because most teens listen to playlists or audiobooks through earbuds or headphones, notoriously boisterous family car trips have become more silent.

As Annette describes, "When my three older daughters were teens, they spent car rides fighting about what to play on the radio or deciding if they could tolerate my music tapes. Now all of a sudden when we're together, the girls' ears are plugged up with their own music and they're all doing their own thing. It's very isolating. Everybody's into their own space, their own world. I really hate it."

The main ways your daughter is communicating is further obstructing your information pipeline. Because text messages and social media posts are more discreet and less audible than talking on cellphones, you may get just a whiff of whom she is socializing with, when she is doing so, for how long, and what she and her friends are discussing. Even when teens and tweens are in their bedrooms, supposedly doing homework, they could be "talking" to virtually anyone, anywhere on the planet, about just about anything.

Thanks to this societal shift, another once-premium source of parent intel is drying up. With teens socializing from the comfort of bedrooms, they are 40 percent less likely to get together with friends after school. In fact, today's high school seniors are going out with peers less often than eighth graders did years ago. With parents providing fewer rides, opportunities are dwindling to overhear unguarded teen girl conversations in the back seat.

So how can you stay in the loop of your daughter's social life without violating the sacred trust that binds your relationship? When should she get her first phone or digital device? How can you be up on every new social media platform out there? Does reading your tween's or teen's chat history count as snooping? Is it okay to monitor your daughter's social media posts? Should you ever check her browser history to see what sites she visits?

The good news is, mothering your teen doesn't require being a tech whiz or keeping up with the latest social media apps. Regardless of your know-how, you are still the best person to guide her through adolescence. That is because your unparalleled devotion and attention make you the expert on your daughter—her strengths, vulnerabilities, and needs. For her to become a capable, emotionally healthy, and resilient young woman, she needs you more than ever before.

A close, loving, and mutually respectful mother-daughter connection is your teen's best resource. You are the reliable voice of reason who counters misinformation she gets from the internet and peers. Your strong and enduring bond persuades her to heed your guidance, internalize your values, and avoid squandering your hard-earned trust.

If you are looking for sensible guidance and dependable support through today's rapidly changing and difficult-to-traverse adolescent terrain, this book is for you. While addressing your biggest fears, frustrations, and hopes for your daughter, you will learn about the forces shaping your teen's experience today, the opportunities and challenges she has as a result, and, most important, how you can best nurture her authenticity, confidence, and resourcefulness.

You will benefit from the invaluable insights of women and girls who participate in my research, attend my lectures and workshops, and come to my office for psychotherapy or parent counseling. Over the years, they have taught me much about what makes teens tick, what girls really want from their mothers, and which parenting approaches not only avoid mother–teen daughter estrangement, but also facilitate the most enduring and gratifying relationships.

Being a mother gives me firsthand knowledge of what it's like to raise a teenage girl—the joys, the fears, and the wonders. All these years later, I remember all too well agonizing about what I was doing wrong. Why were teens in my office so eager to bare their souls while my own daughter hardly uttered a word to me? Along with much-relished moments of pure joy, I can also recall the sting of adolescent criticisms, the exhaustion of walking on eggshells, and the guilt of regrettable mistakes.

Just after my first book, *I'm Not Mad, I Just Hate You!*, was published, I remember holding my breath during a *Good Morning America* interview, having absolutely no idea how my then sixteen-year-old, unpredictable, and sometimes prickly teen would respond to Diane Sawyer's questions—on national television, no less! Fast-forward twenty-plus years and my now thirty-eight-year-old, loving, thoughtful, and supportive daughter is not only encouraging me to write *Anything But My Phone, Mom!*, but also offering to pen the foreword.

Watching in awe as my daughter—and our relationship—evolved in ways I never dreamt possible has given me invaluable perspective. Because I have been there myself, I can offer mothers not only infinite respect and compassion, but also deeply felt optimism and reassurance about the blessings of maturation. I can encourage you, too, to find humor in even the most trying moments and, just as essential, in your own inevitable faux pas.

These pages will provide insights into what your daughter is really thinking, give you the real scoop on what motivates her, and debunk myths about what fosters her success. Dialogues demonstrating effective and ineffective ways to communicate will give you tools to skillfully address even the toughest topics. Explanations of why girls stop listening to mothers will point you in the direction of more fruitful conversations. Because raising teens can be a lonely enterprise, anecdotes about other mother-daughter scenarios will both resonate with you and assure you that you are in good company.

Modern neuroscience provides the foundation of fact-based, clinically proven, and practical guidance. What is known about teens and the processes of attention, memory, motivation, and learning will help you to foster the character traits and self-regulation skills your daughter needs for success. Looking through the lens of her growing adolescent brain will illuminate the reasons for previously inexplicable behaviors. You will learn why teen girls who "know better" still use bad judgment and sometimes repeat self-defeating mistakes.

You will even come to appreciate why the threat of being separated from digital devices is the modern teenage girl's notion of the apocalypse.

With greater confidence in handling dilemmas from expected to extraordinary, you will respond more mindfully and effectively. Thoughtful, intentional parenting approaches will help you to achieve your goals in raising your teen, preserve the goodwill in your mother-daughter relationship, and minimize trivial conflict, rebelliousness, and defiance.

At this point you may be wondering, "How am I ever going to know the right thing to do?" Good question. Not all strategies work with every girl. Guidance is rarely cut-and-dried or one-size-fits-all. Situations are complex and nuanced, and daughters vary tremendously. So do families. This book will guide you to consider these variables in making parenting decisions.

The truth is, although raising a daughter can be one of the most deeply gratifying and meaningful experiences, it is rarely easy. A mother's job description may include nurturing, guiding, reassuring, correcting, soothing, teaching, healing, encouraging, cajoling, modeling, indulging, and disciplining. Motherhood is unpredictable and often underappreciated, especially by teen daughters—at least for the next decade or so.

Accept that you won't always know the "right" thing to say or do. For sure, you will find yourself struggling with choices and second-guessing or regretting at least some of them. During times of inevitable stress and fatigue, you may even fantasize about taking a sabbatical or early retirement from motherhood—or maybe just a respite from a particular daughter struggling with a particular issue at a particular time.

But after decades of working with women and girls, as well as raising my own daughter, I can assure you of this empowering truth: even in moments of doubt, mothers are critically important, capable of enormously shaping the young women adolescents ultimately become.

Just your presence in your daughter's life—your willingness to always listen and provide support—lays the groundwork upon which she builds her future. Demonstrations of your abiding love nurture her belief in herself, boosting the self-worth that infuses all her endeavors and relationships. Although girls benefit greatly from close connections with other adults—fathers, close relatives, teachers, mentors, and coaches—mothers are special, uniquely impacting daughters' lives in ways no one else can. But no pressure!

Maybe you're looking for help with specific, hot-button issues that already are causing angst. Your daughter may be frustrating you by acting as if information about her life is classified, on a strictly need-to-know basis. You may be worried that she is being mistreated, experiencing too much friend drama, or posting inappropriate material online. Perhaps you are concerned about her low self-esteem or inability to tolerate frustration and boredom. Tools that have proven effective with a multitude of mothers and girls will allow you to assess what is going on, how well she is coping, when it makes sense to get involved, and how to do so.

Perhaps the achievement frenzy has you dwelling on how your daughter's grades will affect her future. Or you may fear her perfectionism will lead to burnout—or worse. Up-to-date information will inform you about what she needs to thrive academically. The notoriously nerve-racking college process can be reframed as a potentially memorable and treasured time. With these constructive beliefs and strategies, you may watch your teen blossom before your eyes.

It is also possible that you're reading this as the mother of a happy-go-lucky fourth or fifth grader, an old soul who serves as your sidekick in volunteer work, makes her bed every day, and wants to please adults. All is fine now, but other women's rumblings about what's in store for you are giving you heartburn. As your daughter heads into peak puberty, this book will give you the lay of teenage territory. Tips on preventing problems will help you to survive this developmental stage with your mother-daughter relationship—and sanity—intact.

By the last page, you will have answers to some of your most pressing questions: What helps some girls flourish during adolescence, while others are clobbered? What can I do when my daughter is eight or nine so that she becomes resilient? How can I make sure she keeps talking to me? Why do some mothers enjoy their daughters' teen years, while others suffer no end? What ingredients and steps lead to successful outcomes?

Part One prepares you for the adolescent journey. The next chapter outlines the powerful cultural forces that are transforming the world of teens today. An inside look at what girls face every day—academically, socially, and emotionally—will heighten your awareness and empathy for what your own daughter may be up against. An understanding of what truly matters to teens—as well as the impact on this generation's mental health—will make clearer the obstacles your daughter may face in realizing her dreams.

Chapter Two discusses the impact of these societal shifts on families and home life, including the challenges you may be experiencing due to diverse family configurations, intergenerational differences in values, and teen lifestyle changes.

If you are eager for specific guidance, skip ahead. Part Two describes the various skills, personal habits, and personality characteristics your daughter will need to thrive in her future, giving you a vision for what you are hoping to accomplish as you navigate the mother-daughter journey. Next, you'll be given the practical nuts and bolts of how to parent intentionally, mother the daughter you have, do less to achieve more, and facilitate constructive conversations with your digital native.

Part Three coaches you to apply these principles and strategies to specific, everyday challenges mothers find most pressing. You'll get practical ideas for helping your daughter to develop good habits, manage screen time, form healthy friendships and dating relationships, end homework wars, cope with the fallout of divorce, and use the college process to promote her authenticity, emotional well-being, and resiliency.

Your daughter's adolescence is a stage of extraordinary maturation that offers rich parenting experiences. It is an ideal time to harness her youthful optimism and enthusiasm and channel her curiosity.

But realistically, like any adventure, your mother–teen daughter relationship is unlikely to always be smooth. Her development will likely progress in fits and starts, with occasional backsliding. Along the way, there will be unexpected bumps and detours. As with any travel these days, you will need to draw upon reserves of fortitude and patience. Despite moments of delightful spontaneity, much of this journey cannot be navigated reflexively or expediently. Thoughtful deliberation will be helpful at every turn.

But staying the course, being in the moment, and remembering to be grateful for this time with your daughter will hopefully provide unexpected joys and memories to treasure for years to come. Let's begin.

CHAPTER ONE

A Changed Adolescent Landscape

When we give our daughter consequences, we've got to hit her where it's the hardest, and that's the phone. Forget grounding her. Taking away her phone is complete torture to her. She can't live without it. It's as if her father or I passed away. She's sobbing and begging for it back. I literally stare at her with my mouth open and think, "Are you kidding me? You're having a complete mental breakdown because I took your phone away for the night? It's like you're at a funeral. I cannot believe that this just happened." I'm almost sad I got a phone for her.

—CAROLYN, MOTHER OF LIZ

My mom got mad at me for the stupidest reason. She was harassing me about one little thing on my floor and I told her to calm down, so she took my phone away for the night. It's not fair. Why would she do that? I have friends who I

> have Snap[chat] streaks with. I have to keep up with them. I have a 172-day and I have to be on it. Streaks are really important to me. I know it's silly, but it's important to me. She took it away for one night and I almost flipped out. I lost my streaks. It was a rough night. Why doesn't she just ground me? She can't take my phone away. It's a necessity!
>
> —LIZ, 15 (CAROLYN'S DAUGHTER)

The adolescent landscape in which your daughter is growing up is transforming the way she develops, thinks, learns, communicates, and socializes. Much of this probably feels foreign. Yet to appreciate her challenges, empathize with her reactions, and support her emotional resiliency, it is important to know what she and the rest of her generation are up against.

This chapter gives you a chance to step into your daughter's shoes to get a feel for her everyday life. You will learn how changes in middle school and high school environments are shaping girls' academic, social, and emotional experiences; which issues weigh most heavily on teens' minds; why mental health issues are soaring, especially among girls; and what else is contributing to this generation's declining well-being.

Growing Up in a More Nerve-Racking Universe

Although this age group is not immune to the "crises" of social media dramas and dying cellphone batteries, teen girls today are generally more aware of the world beyond themselves. Growing up under clouds of domestic and global threats, this generation cares deeply about socioeconomic diversity, injustice, inequality, poverty, and violence. A *Washington Post*–Kaiser Family Foundation poll found that a majority of teens feels angry and afraid about climate change. The title of the newspaper's magazine article, "The Environmental Burden of Generation Z: Kids Are Terrified, Anxious, and Depressed About Climate Change," speaks volumes.

To their credit, teens today are more motivated to take action. The desire to help extends beyond girls' immediate friends to their communities and the world. One-fourth of young people surveyed had participated in a rally, staged a walkout, or written to a public official about global warming. Some students who survived the Marjory Stoneman Douglas High School shooting in Parkland, Florida, channeled grief into a remarkable national advocacy movement to curb gun violence.

But the cost of heightened consciousness may be skyrocketing distress. The most recent American Psychological Association *Stress in America* survey found that Gen Z adults (ages 18–23) report the highest stress level among all generations. These emerging adults specifically cite the rise in suicide rates (62%) and the #MeToo movement (58%). Young women are particularly affected by widespread sexual harassment/assault reports in the news (67%) and changes in abortion laws (64%). For Gen Z teens, previous sources of stress, which "remain present and problematic," are compounded by the COVID-19 pandemic. This group is "experiencing elevated stress and already reporting symptoms of depression."

Your daughter may also be troubled by current events; a majority of teens reports being extremely upset about the separation and deportation of immigrant and migrant families, a rise in suicide rates, reports of sexual harassment and assault, discrimination against the LGBTQ community, and mass shootings—yes, much of what is in the news these days.

Unlike young women in their later twenties and thirties, teen girls today are retraumatized by footage of hate crimes, terrorist attacks, natural disasters, and school violence that loop endlessly on 24/7 cable channels and cellphone news apps. To get to homerooms every morning, students pass through gauntlets of metal detectors and bulletproof booths flanked by security guards, reminding them that their campuses are vulnerable to shootings. Many teens and tweens reportedly go through school days wondering if they will return home every afternoon and see their parents again.

The year 2018 was the most horrific yet, setting records for school shootings, people shot, people killed, and students exposed to gunfire on campuses. Because my practice is not far from where twenty small children and six teachers were killed at Sandy Hook Elementary School in Newtown, Connecticut, I have seen from the front lines the carnage that such massacres leave in their wake. For years, aftershocks of that 2012 tragedy have been reverberating through heartbroken families and friends in communities surrounding my own.

Efforts to prevent school violence are further traumatizing students. According to *The Washington Post*, in 2018 alone more than four million students endured lockdowns and live shooter drills. Teens and tweens who are sequestered in enclosed spaces are often terrified long after authorities give the all clear to release them. In fact, many of these students develop the same long-lasting post-traumatic symptoms—anxiety, depression, poor sleep, and deteriorating school performance—that crisis teams see after incidents of actual violence.

Girls are also coming of age in the most highly charged political climate of the past half century. Tensions are infused into the air they breathe. Few families have escaped contentious dinner table discussions arising from increasingly polarized and divisive political views. For the very first time in my forty-plus-year career, teens and even tweens in my practice are bringing up issues related to national politics.

When I ask students I evaluate for writing samples, I usually get creative stories or accounts of memorable personal experiences. Arianna, twelve, chose to express concerns about a then-current political event through the lens of a sixth grader's passion for social media. Her essay argued that the Bill of Rights "says we have the freedom to say what we want and post what we want on social media. [The now-former president] is breaking a 279-year-old law by blocking people who criticize his tweets and delet[ing] mean comments."

Arianna's views aside, what is noteworthy is that politics is now in the forefront of a twelve-year-old's mind. Unfortunately, even younger girls are starting to express previously unheard-of global worries. As schools commemorated Martin Luther King Jr. Day in 2020, a mother shared her eight-year-old second grader's writing prompt. In response to "I have a dream that one day our world will________," Kendall filled in the blank with "*be as healthy and will never blow up.*"

Indeed, just when it seemed this generation's worries couldn't worsen, the COVID-19 global pandemic hit. Fears of family members becoming ill and dying, parents being laid off from work, financial hardships, and getting sick themselves triggered or exacerbated teens' already soaring levels of anxiety and depression. According to the CDC, from 2019 to 2020 there was a 31 percent increase in twelve-to-seventeen-year-olds' mental health–related emergency room visits.

Teens' lives were interrupted. Being isolated from peers due to remote learning and COVID-19 restrictions deprived girls of the social support they get from classmates and teachers. The Center for Promise's national survey of 3,300 students found that more than two-thirds of thirteen-to-nineteen-year-olds felt "somewhat" or "not at all connected" to peers. Robbed of rites of passage such as homecomings, birthdays, graduations, and, especially, internships, exchange programs, and first job offers, more than half of teens surveyed reported more uncertainty about their futures.

The Road to Achievement Is More Treacherous

> The competition, stress, and homework workload are out of control. Between work and social stuff, it's an overwhelming avalanche. Teens think they have to get the best grades, the best SAT score, have the best appearance, be the lead in the school play. Some days, the onslaught of pressures comes at them from every direction. It's like an Anxiety-a-Day. It's too much!
>
> —MARGE, MOTHER OF A 16-YEAR-OLD

First, the good news. As far as educational markers go, girls are rocking it. Because they are better able to focus and persist in school, girls not only take more Advanced Placement (AP) classes and higher-level math courses than boys, but also get better grades. Girls score higher than boys on national standardized reading and writing tests. In math and science, they are closing the gap, shrinking boys' previous advantages. Girls also are more involved in high school newspaper, yearbook, and student government activities. Post high school, they more often enroll in—and graduate from—college.

Girls' remarkable progress in achievement should certainly be celebrated. But focusing on the associated risks is equally important. Just because girls can do anything doesn't mean they should expect to do *everything*—or to do everything *well.*

About fifteen years ago, when I was doing research for *Stressed-out Girls: Helping Them Thrive in the Age of Pressure*, I thought academic stress was peaking. In my mind, girls couldn't possibly be any more driven to excel or to craft academic and extracurricular résumés. Surely, I thought, the pandemonium created by striving to become—and to produce—standout college applicants would die down.

But as it turns out, I was wrong. That was wishful thinking.

As highly ranked colleges report steadily declining acceptance rates, the achievement frenzy has only been intensifying. A recent *Washington Post* article, "Early Applications Surge at Prestigious Colleges. So Does Early Heartache," speaks to this truth. With fewer spots available in first-year classes, jobs, and internships, today's candidates—and the schools educating them—feel more pressured than ever. Girls who aim for first-choice colleges are exponentially more panicked about impressing admissions committees. So are some parents.

A high school teacher told me, "For the past three to five years, there's been a huge increase in girls getting anxious and intermittently depressed about school. Getting into college is hugely contributing. I see girls who get perfect scores on their SATs and get rejected from Yale and Dartmouth. You can't even get into a state college now unless you're a stellar student. It affects everyone. I'm worried for them."

Many high schools have become pressure cookers. A deluge of assignments and assessments overly burdens some students, snuffing out gratification from learning. Some teens decide they can't compete and stop trying; others relentlessly push through, fiercely ramping up efforts to excel. In my practice, frantic juniors and seniors insist, "I have to be captain of my softball/lacrosse/soccer team," "I have to do community service," "I have to do SAT classes," "I'm doing so badly; I have a 3.6, so I'm not going to get in anywhere." It is constant.

Stressed girls start to see every test grade as the ultimate judgment of their self-worth. Accomplishments are not relished in and of themselves, but rather triggers to strive for the next, even loftier badge of success. Many teens become too tense and self-conscious to volunteer or ask questions in class. When girls stop feeling smart and capable, too often they shut down and disengage from school.

Monica, thirteen, is among the youngest girls I have seen whose lamp burned too bright. The perfectionism that once drove her to excel, to her parents' delight, became an incapacitating fear of failing. She explains, "All I wanted was straight As. I'd check [her school's online portal] three times a day to figure out what test score I'd need to get an A for the quarter. I'd always be studying. I couldn't miss a day, even if I was sick. I didn't go to the banquet because I wanted to study. But at the end of the year, it became the total opposite. I didn't want to do anything."

Because highly achieving girls want to please adults, they usually hide distress until their missing assignments or unexcused absences become apparent. Learning that daughters are in this predicament, mothers are often stunned, baffled about what went wrong, and determined to correct the problem—whether it is motivation, work habits, social media use, or lack of sleep.

School-related stress is not limited to homework, projects, test scores, and college aspirations. Your daughter may fear being "dress-coded" if her clothing is judged too short or too something else. In the past, students could let down their guard during unstructured periods such as walking in hallways and eating in the cafeteria. But because schools are ultrasensitive to threats of violence, racism, and bullying now, zero-tolerance rules may make your daughter nervously monitor her words and deeds.

Silly comments and pranks that were once chalked up to "kids being kids," potty humor, or unfortunate efforts to get attention are now treated as serious infractions requiring investigation (sometimes by law enforcement). Tweens who are not yet capable of inhibiting off-the-cuff comments, name-calling, or idle threats (e.g., "I'll make him pay" or "I'm gonna kill myself"), whether in school or online, find themselves in hot water, subjected to mandatory suspensions or expulsions, and perhaps in need of legal representation.

When Helena, twelve, got in a fight with a classmate, her mother thought nothing of it. Then the principal called, informing her the other girl's parents had complained that Helena sent "threatening" text messages to their daughter. School policy dictated that Helena be suspended for a week. Confused and embarrassed, her mother worried not only about helping Helena to get past this incident, but also how to prevent anything like it from happening again.

One school morning, Liz, fifteen, realized that someone had hacked into one of her social media accounts and posted antisemitic statements. Mortified and distraught, she fled to the girls' room, where students made fun of her. Liz "lost it," making comments that alarmed her peers, who confided in a guidance counselor, who followed protocol by calling a crisis hotline. Liz was taken by ambulance to a local hospital emergency room to evaluate her risk of self-harm.

If your daughter comes home from school saying she's stressed, her brain is so fried she can't think, or she doesn't feel well, you may now envision a whole lineup of potential culprits. Before she can focus on doing homework or reading textbooks, she may well need a quick nap, a soothing snack, or an amusing YouTube cat video.

Technology's Seismic Effects

> There's this girl nobody likes, and everybody posts pictures of her and says stuff. They Photoshop a screenshot and say she's so fake. It's all under fake names because a lot of people have been expelled in the past for it, so they're trying to be as anonymous as possible.
>
> —DEEDEE, 14

Nothing has revolutionized this generation of girls—or the mothers who raise them—more than technology. Teens and tweens are now consuming a staggering amount of media. According to the nonprofit Common Sense Media's 2019 report, eight-to-twelve-year-olds in the US are using screens for an average of nearly five hours per day. For thirteen-to-eighteen-year-olds, that number grows to nearly seven and a half hours—and that's excluding school or homework!

Vanessa, age sixteen, confirms the accuracy of this stunning statistic.

She admits in an interview, "I'm on my phone 24/7 because I don't want to miss anything. There's this screen thing that tells me how much time I'm on my phone, and I spend seven hours a day. It's really bad, but that's the norm with all my friends, too." She adds under her breath, "Superaddicting."

Ninety percent of teens go online multiple times every day. Nearly half—and far more girls than boys—say they are online "almost constantly," twice as many as just a few years ago. Because your daughter's smartphone is essentially a powerful handheld computer, she can also listen to music; play games; log on to Netflix or Hulu to stream TV shows and movies; access information from the internet; watch YouTube videos; make purchases; and take and share photos—anytime, anywhere, and with the merest touch of her thumb.

To your teen or tween, cyberspace is home. With social networking sites, texting, and video chatting at her fingertips, she expects to connect instantly, with anyone, and literally at any time. In fact, as a digital native who has grown up socializing via texting and video-messaging apps on smartphones, immersed in the world of computers and video-game consoles, confidently navigating a vast range of technologies, she may see this capability as her birthright.

But like most mothers today, you are an immigrant to the digital land. Just like your ancestors who came to America, you're probably daunted—if not utterly overwhelmed—by assimilating and learning the lexicon of the younger generation's language.

This technology gap has created a role reversal. Instead of teaching your daughter, it is usually the other way around. Can you imagine telling her, "Honey, it's high time I got you a Snapchat account!" or "This weekend, I'll show you how to make a TikTok!" or "I'll be happy to help you set up your new iPhone!" More likely, you're asking your teen or tween to teach you these skills—and begging her to be extrapatient with you while doing so.

Despite her superior tech skills, however, your digitally native daughter lacks the background knowledge and judgment to know how, when, and with whom to use them wisely. As she blazes new social trails, she also faces new hazards and unanticipated dilemmas. It is up to you to lead her through uncharted terrain—even if you feel utterly lost, without so much as an old-fashioned road map, let alone updated GPS, to show you the way.

If fears of online risks and conflicts about screen time are robbing you of sleep, be assured we'll get to those issues. But first, it's important to recognize all the advantages technology offers your daughter. From toddlerhood on, apps and programs can teach her highly valuable, educational, and even marketable skills. Now that she is older, the internet provides ready access to a wealth of up-to-date educational information without her having to spend hours in dusty library stacks hunting for rare tomes.

Cyberspace offers an arena for girls to express opinions, ask for help, and get support from like-minded people. Mandy, sixteen, joined a chat group for depressed teens. Many a girl's universe is broadened by learning online of opportunities to volunteer, raise money for charities, and work on political campaigns. Discussing current events on blogs and websites spurred Haddie, fifteen, to become more socially engaged.

The digital world also bridges family members who are separated by miles and generations. Girls forge relationships with aunts, uncles, cousins, and grandparents around shared interests. Teaching older relatives how to text lets families stay in closer touch. This skill proved invaluable during the COVID-19 pandemic, giving many vulnerable grandparents a taste of the connections they craved during a year of otherwise harmful isolation.

Social networking sites and video chat platforms allow girls to maintain contact with friends from whom they otherwise grow apart, such as classmates who move away, camp bunkmates, fellow travelers, and internship colleagues.

Even though teens and tweens communicate mostly via text message and social media, they make exceptions to email teachers. This has opened up a whole new educational channel. Before, shy or self-conscious girls hesitated to ask teachers to review new concepts, extend due dates, or clarify assignments with classmates within earshot. Now, email allows them to quickly and privately ask questions and request meetings with instructors.

Technology is saving many girls in my practice from social isolation. The ease of linking up with peers is expanding the networks of even the most withdrawn and awkward teens. Girls who feel pigeonholed in school have freedom to reinvent themselves and try out different personas in online relationships. With the ability to edit and delete digital messages, tweens interact with less fear of blurting something stupid. Girls of all ages are more confident of crafting witty, clever comments online than when they interact face-to-face.

While it is true that not all technology is bad, technology can be used badly. Just thinking about the potential hazards of technology might cause you to pull out your hair. Is your daughter divulging personal information online or taking other unknown risks? Is she visiting sites that are too mature or even dangerous? And what about cyberbullying, sexting, identity misrepresentation, and vulnerability to sexual predators?

As you try to impress upon your daughter the dangers of posting risqué photos, especially on public social media sites, you may feel as if you are swimming against the tide. With all the pressure on girls today to get attention by presenting themselves as edgy and sexy, how can you convince her to avoid taking or posting revealing selfies—or nudes? How can you impress on her the devastating consequences of such poor decisions without alienating her?

Margaret says, "My sixteen-year-old posts—I guess all the girls do—pretty provocative pictures. She wears low-cut tops and bathing suits, and she's posing in all these different positions. Even her older sister is asking, 'What the heck is she doing? What is she *thinking*?' I understand she's proud of her body—and good for her—but it's not okay to put it out there."

Technology has also ushered in entirely new dating worries for mothers. When Helen was raising three older daughters, now young adults, she says, "I was concerned about them going to a party and drinking too much. Or having a party when parents weren't home. But with Diana, who's just starting high school, I'm worried about keeping her safe from some sort of predator—an adult male, an adult female posing as a teenage boy, a boy in her school—anyone who'll take advantage of her on social media."

Irina is also facing brand-new challenges: "I always envisioned greeting—and, of course"—she laughs—"*interrogating*—nervous teenage boys when they came to pick up my daughter for dates. But for two years now, Nell's had a boyfriend she met online. He lives twenty-five hundred miles away and they've never met in person. How do I know this kid is who he says he is? He could be anybody. They're talking to people they don't know, and you know they're not supposed to, and that's scary. This is so strange to me."

Mothers worry that tech-related mistakes can lead to heartbreak.

This is not an unreasonable concern. Not long ago, I got a call from a distraught mother whose fifteen-year-old, Ivy, sent a nude to a boy she liked. When the two stopped talking, the boy forwarded that photo to every student and faculty member on their private school's listserv. While he suffered no loss of social status, Ivy was subjected to relentless shaming. She was so devastated by her friends turning on her that she stopped going to school and insisted that her family move away. Sadly, I am hearing too many iterations of Ivy's story.

Does this mean you have to use apps to track your daughter's online activities, pinpoint her whereabouts, monitor her driving, and alert you to potentially risky behaviors? Is this what raising a teen has come to?

Other girls endure technology-driven, emotionally shattering episodes through no fault of their own. As Gemma, sixteen, walked home from school, three girls physically confronted her, thoroughly shaking her up. The next day, she saw her classmates clustered around a phone, watching a video of this mortifying incident. Gemma panicked and ran out of school in tears. The aunt who is raising her told me, "This is beyond anything I ever thought I'd have to deal with."

Mothers have always supported daughters embroiled in teen drama—teasing, cattiness, rumormongering, put-downs, and exclusion. But these days, technology is exposing and exponentially magnifying girls' social pain. Embarrassments are no longer limited to fleeting, soon-forgotten encounters on the school bus or in the cafeteria; in cyberspace, humiliations captured on video are permanent, capable of being viewed over and again, forwarded, and disseminated for all the world to see.

Julia, eleven, posted an effusive birthday greeting to a preschool friend who had been distancing herself since middle school. When the girl responded to Julia's heartfelt wishes with deafening silence, Julia experienced the online equivalent of a public slap in the face. When her classmates, siblings, guidance counselor, and parents all saw this unmistakable rejection on social media, Julia felt as if salt had been poured in her wound.

For reasons that we'll get into, cyberspace can give girls license to behave uncharacteristically. It may be hard to imagine, much less to be told, that it is your reserved, kindhearted, and eager-to-please young daughter who is acting inappropriately online.

Carla worried that Penny, her twelve-year-old, was not assertive enough to stand up to savvier sixth-grade classmates. But while monitoring Penny's text conversations, Carla was stunned and appalled by her daughter's inappropriate language, cruel comments, and overtly sexual references. Could her sweet, kind, and caring girl really have written these things? Worse, when Carla tried to have a conversation about this, Penny indignantly accused her mother of violating her privacy and insisted, "Everybody talks like that."

Many teens in my practice confirm what research psychologists are reporting: when social media use goes up, emotional well-being goes down. Overuse can result in addiction, sleep deprivation, learning difficulties, anxiety, and depression. Although girls don't often admit this to mothers, they describe feeling more socially anxious, self-conscious, and vigilant, yet still find it nearly impossible to resist social media's seductive pull.

Some teens get involved in online activities that land them in legal peril, such as identity misrepresentation (pretending to be someone else) and cyberbullying (as perpetrators, victims, or both). In a few well-publicized tragedies, young girls tormented by relentless online cruelty have taken their own lives.

But harmful effects of technology can be subtler. In the past, when Rebecca arrived to teach an afternoon religion class, her eleven-to-thirteen-year-old students were running around outside and playing games. "But now," she says, "they're all lined up on a bench staring at their own devices." Each day, she has to remind her tweens that cell-phones must be turned off and Apple Watches will be confiscated if they so much as look at them during class.

Teens' extraordinary dependency on devices may seem incomprehensible, but it actually makes sense in the context of development. Girls at this age form a clearer sense of who they are, forge more intimate connections, crave peer acceptance, pull away from parents, test autonomy, and manage burgeoning sexuality fueled by raging hormones. This perspective may shed light on your biggest questions about your daughter's relationship to technology.

Why Your Teen Is Glued to Her Devices

Technology instantly satisfies adolescents' universal longings for attention, validation, and connection. Social media apps give your daughter a platform for being noticed and standing out for whichever attributes she values most. Metrics such as the number of messages she gets (and from whom), as well as how many times her posts are viewed, liked, and reposted, may confirm her importance among peers.

Every incoming message is a minithrill. Knowing that friends are thinking about her makes her feel flattered and important, as if she matters, momentarily relieving her fears of being forgotten or excluded. With such powerful confidence boosters, no wonder it may be nearly impossible for her to muster the self-discipline to stop checking her social media accounts, silence her notifications, or turn off her phone. Access to her device provides a perpetual conduit to peer inclusion and gratification.

Why Your Daughter Regresses to Toddlerlike Tantrums If Asked to Unplug

Psychological dependency on devices is bolstered by neurobiology. Sending and receiving messages triggers the release of dopamine, the "feel-good" chemical in the brain. New messages create a buzz. The intoxication she experiences when she hears notifications of incoming messages is as hard for your daughter to resist as highly addictive drugs.

Whether she is in class, asleep in her bed, or banned from devices, when she stops getting messages her dopamine level plummets, her pleasure dissipates, and she suffers a kind of withdrawal. At this point, her cellphone is no longer a merely fun or handy device. Rather, it is a portal to contentment with which she is desperate to be rejoined. Until your teen gets her next "fix"—that is, a chance to see who is thinking about her and what they are saying—she may be as anxious and out of sorts as if she were kicking a chemical habit.

Why Your Daughter Insists on Having Her Cellphone in Social Situations

Like many mothers, it may drive you up the wall to see your teen or tween pay more attention to her cellphone than to the friends surrounding her in real life (IRL). It may be that she's more interested in digital messages—or the people who send them. But it is also possible she is using technology to alleviate social anxiety and awkwardness in face-to-face interactions.

Zizi, fifteen, explains, “I’m uncomfortable being in a social setting without my phone. I feel really awkward because I don’t know what to do with my hands. Even if I’m not using it or it’s in my pocket, having my phone is kind of like a comfort. If you’re in an awkward situation or you finish a conversation and don’t know what else to say, you can pull out your phone and show them something or pretend you have to go somewhere. It’s an easy way out.”

Actually, teen girls are not alone in adopting this strategy; many adults also rely on cellphones to defuse tension or discomfort in social situations.

Why Your Daughter Obsesses Over Her Social Media Posts

In developing a sense of identity, teens often try out various images. Not long ago, girls in middle school and high school spent hours planning outfits, styling hair, and learning to apply makeup, all so they could gauge classmates’ reactions to various new looks when they walked into class or the cafeteria. Now teens look to online metrics for this feedback.

The same girl who wears ratty old sweatshirts, comfy dorm pants, and fluffy mules to my office sweats over crafting the perfect social media presence. This makes sense because a vastly greater number of people see and judge how teens look online. Your daughter knows that anyone interested in checking her out will first look at her profile—perhaps the modern version of a calling card.

In cyberspace, teens can be anyone they choose. Some take advantage by creating avatars that allow them to explore aspects of themselves that feel unsettling, unacceptable, or scary in real life. Others strive to package themselves through online presences that reflect their ideal selves, the people they most want to be, at least at that moment.

With effort, social media posts can satisfy the age-old teenage desire to be seen as fun and popular girls who do exciting things—rather than as "losers with boring lives." As teens put it during a focus group at an independent high school, "It's how you want people to perceive you," "You can be whoever you want to be," and "You can say Tolstoy's your favorite author to look smart, but you've never read *Anna Karenina*." When your daughter tries hard to appear in peers' Instagram posts and garner the most likes for her photos and videos, this is probably why.

How Technology Affects Adolescent Development

Technology is a double-edged sword. While serving teens' developmental needs, digital devices are fundamentally changing the way girls think of themselves, manage emotions, and relate to others. As fast as your daughter can master tech skills, that is how slowly she may be gaining the real-world skills and confidence that foster independence. The following are some of the ways technology may be altering her adolescence.

Increasing Competition

> Social media can be superdestructive. You focus on the likes on Instagram or how many republishes you get, so it's damaging to some people. A lot of my friends have to go to therapy for it if they don't get a certain number. It really bothers them. "Why is this person getting so many likes and I'm not?"
>
> —MIRABELLA, 16

Social media exacerbates the self-consciousness and competitiveness young women already experience around their looks. Pru, fifteen, says, "In high school, everyone tries to be the most popular, wear the best clothes, and look the best. It's always been like that, but now it's amplified because you see what people are posting and it's always perfect." Sadie, fourteen, adds, "Social media is giving you another way of comparing yourself. It's adding to the pressure to be somebody else—idealized and perfect. You can't see anyone's flaws. They're all filtered out."

Social media is cranking up the volume on teen girls' harsh internal self-critique: *Am I attractive/popular/interesting enough? How do I compare with everyone else?* Marketers are exploiting the biggest vulnerability of this demographic with a glut of apps that optimize images.

A simple Google search yields the top ten options, which promise to "impress your friends" by producing "the carefully crafted selfie," "the glamorous selfie," and "the artsy selfie." Your daughter can airbrush her way not only to perfect skin and body proportions, but also enviable moods (e.g., kiss, cute, seduce, fierce, smirk). With a keystroke, autofilters can turn her into an online "hero," "belle," and heaven knows what else.

The mother of a college first-year told me, "Last week my daughter went away for the weekend with friends, and I just saw what she posted on Instagram. She's standing on the beach between her two best friends. It's her face, but not her body. She edited the photo so she had a flat stomach. It broke my heart. I tried to talk to her about it and she went ballistic on me. She kept screaming, 'You don't understand the pressure!'"

Girls are consumed not only by what they should post, but also by what they see friends doing online. Social media dramatically increases girls' fear of missing out (FOMO). "It shows you what everyone's doing and when they're doing it," Marguerite, thirteen, tells me, "so it's a much more stressful environment." It is the rare teen girl who can resist feeling envious or left out in the face of visual proof that peers are having fun without her.

Georgie, fifteen, says, "Seeing people on social media doing things together that you're not part of can lead to a lot of jealousy issues. You can see people's locations. I'm grounded right now and there's a party at the beach today and a ton of my friends are going and I really want to go. I'll look at the maps on Snapchat and see them all there." Nia, seventeen, relates: "If you're home, you torture yourself by seeing where people are. You're, like, 'I wanted to go, but I wasn't invited.'"

Undermining Self-Reflection and Authenticity

What you want people to know on social media is all a facade.

—FRAN, 16

Technology makes it astronomically harder for teens to develop insight into who they are, identify their feelings, and pay attention to the inner voices that guide behavior. External noise is distracting. With constant ringtones, buzzing, vibrations, chimes, and other digital notifications, it is rare for girls to create the peaceful space that facilitates self-reflection.

Crafting a social media presence hardly encourages insightfulness or authenticity. In fact, it is an invitation to pretend, to present superficially appealing but fake personas. As girls spend angst-filled hours cultivating images of perfection, they present ideal—that is, *false*—selves rather than discovering the genuineness that lies within.

The chasm between teens' and tweens' authentic experiences and what they post online is poignantly illustrated in the film *Eighth Grade*. The painfully awkward, self-deprecating thirteen-year-old protagonist, Kayla, posts motivational videos on YouTube that advise peers how to combat insecurities—the very ones she suffers during the last week of middle school in a succession of cringeworthy peer interactions. Desperate for validation, Kayla ends each advice video by asking her few viewers to like and forward them.

The wider the gap between your daughter's public and private personas, the greater the risk to her well-being. To appear as someone else, she suppresses, if not extinguishes, her true self and genuine voice. A well-examined inner life is a far more accurate and dependable source of validation. In contrast, a quest for likes can subjugate her true values and interests. Relying on feedback from social media users who could be fickle friends or cruel strangers makes her too vulnerable.

Trouncing Self-Esteem

> A lot of my friends care about what others think of them and it affects their self-image. If you're susceptible to peer judgment, social media can make you feel bad about yourself.
>
> —SARALYN, 17

With girls barely reading for pleasure nowadays, they may be less exposed to memoirs, biographies, and autobiographies of accomplished women worthy of emulation. Teens are instead comparing themselves with social media influencers, reality-television actresses, and YouTube stars whose name recognition gives them enviable power and wealth. Unable to compete with social media personalities' millions of followers, girls can feel demoralized. Yet they are basing notions of success on narrow, unreliable, and arguably meaningless measures.

Exacerbating Social Anxiety

When it comes to social anxiety, digital devices are a mixed bag. On the one hand, your daughter's cellphone can be a lifeline assuring her she has friends who care about her. Yet always being on the alert for the next incoming message induces a state of hyperalertness. Studies show that people who relentlessly scan devices for new messages—referred to as "constant checkers"—are significantly more stressed than those who don't.

Think about waiting eagerly to hear from someone. No matter what else you are doing, repeatedly looking at your phone will probably distract you. When a new message comes in, your hopes soar, only to sink again if it was not from the person you expected. Now imagine how a teen girl would ride this emotional wave, with her hormone-fueled reactions, desperation for peer contact, and still-developing coping skills.

With digital communication, teens today expect friends to instantly read and respond to messages. This assumption is ingrained. If there's no immediate response, girls are anxiously preoccupied. Why isn't her friend answering her text? Could something be wrong? Is her friend mad at her? And if the shoe is on the other foot, your daughter may fear that not responding right away to a friend's message could make the girl angry or cause a fight.

Because text messages are usually brief and highly abbreviated, misunderstandings easily occur. Plus, without nonverbal cues such as facial expression, tone of voice, and inflection, it can be hard to judge whether messages are sincere, sarcastic, condescending, or ironic. This is why misinterpretations of digital communication so often spark teen girl drama.

Girls also feel anxious and out of sorts when devices that light up, vibrate, or buzz interrupt what they're doing in the moment. That's because happiness research demonstrates unequivocally that almost regardless of what people are doing, being focused and engrossed leads to greater contentment. Distractions reduce that satisfaction.

Finally, a lack of control over online privacy can also trigger teens' technology-induced anxiety. Although your daughter is in charge of much of her own social media presence, she may be upset if friends or acquaintances post photos or videos of her without first asking permission—especially if she is tagged, thinks she looks unattractive, or is acting inappropriately. Plus, a sense that everyone else seems to know her business can make your teen feel rather helpless.

Stunting Social Intelligence and People Skills

Mothers I speak with are increasingly concerned about girls interacting primarily over devices rather than in person. While these teens may be connecting with greater numbers of people, the quality of their connections is different. Without the intimacy of real-life, face-to-face interactions, the ability to develop fundamental social and communication skills diminishes.

Schoolteachers are seeing such tech-associated social problems in the youngest students. Ann tells me kindergartners brought up on screens "don't know how to play with each other. In the art room, I have them sit in a circle and teach them how to look each other in the eye and say 'Hi, my name is ___. What is your name?' They don't have basic skills like how to sit still in a circle and be mindful of students sitting next to them."

Among teens, empathy is taking a hit. In the past, girlfriends spent countless hours talking together while hanging out in their bedrooms. These spontaneous conversations encourage empathy; when girls are attuned to each other's facial expressions and similar nonverbal cues, they are likely to imagine how the other feels. Speaking on devices, however, many of which preclude picking up on body language, facial expressions, voice tone, inflection, and gestures, it is harder for teens and tweens to read friends' thoughts and feelings.

These days, many teens and tweens are even uncomfortable speaking on the phone. Samara says, "If we ask our daughter to make a phone call, she says she doesn't know how to talk to the person. We say, 'What do you mean? You have perfectly good conversations with your friends all the time.' She says, 'Yeah, but we're texting.'"

Aisha similarly tells me, "My fifteen-year-old is losing the ability to communicate face-to-face because she's buried in her phone. When she's in her room studying, I hear her talking to friends. They're using FaceTime. But actually, her phone is off to the side, so they can't actually see each other's faces. They're just talking in their [respective] bedrooms."

With more teens shopping online rather than in malls, girls are also having fewer interactions with salespeople. Without practice, they are not learning to maintain proper eye gaze, project their voices, and ask assertively for what they want. Zoe tells me, "We were in a crowded Dunkin' Donuts the other day and I asked my daughter to get me creamer. She said, 'Excuse me' in the quietest voice. I told her, 'You gotta talk loud!' Same thing in restaurants; servers can't hear her because she's so timid."

Increasing Loneliness

According to Cigna's Loneliness Index Report, more than half of Gen Z teens report the sense that (a) people around them are not really with them, and (b) no one knows them well. With fewer in-person interactions, teens get less peer empathy and emotional support—and therefore may be lonelier. Jean M. Twenge, a psychologist who researches the effects of media use on well-being, finds many links between a lack of real-life social interactions and feelings of isolation among young people. In fact, the highest social media users report the most loneliness.

Causing Trauma

Whereas digital natives' online fearlessness is commendable, even enviable, it can also cause accidental trauma. Dana, fifteen, a tech-savvy and avid blogger I saw in therapy, trembled as she described visiting a familiar site and being stunned by a child pornography video suddenly popping up. Days later, she was still struggling to shake disturbing, graphic images from her mind.

Technology is also exponentially magnifying the fallout of whatever mistakes girls make. In the past, the humiliations of foolish actions and rejections were limited by friends' memories and overshadowed by the latest gaffes capturing peer attention. But today, with smartphones turning everyone into a videographer, your daughter's worst moments can be immortalized in online posts, causing her seemingly eternal shame.

Cyberbullies are sending messages that are astonishingly cruel. Girls in my practice have been told: "You're so ugly," "Nobody likes you," and, most horrifically, "Why don't you just kill yourself already?" To most teens and tweens, let alone the most vulnerable, such words are among the most brutal imaginable, designed to inflict maximum pain.

Dousing Creativity

Just as solitude is required for self-reflection, it is mandatory for creativity. Girls who journal; write nonfiction, poetry, or songs; sketch, draw, or paint; practice calligraphy; sculpt; or take photographs have to tolerate quietude and being alone. To access the inspiration within her, your daughter must shut out the noise of the world around her.

A teacher describes the lengths she and her colleagues go to encourage middle school students whose creativity is threatened by digital overstimulation:

> Kids are growing up faster than previous generations and can access just about anything on the internet. They're exposed to things we never dreamed of. They're so overwhelmed with information to sort out that they don't get a chance to quiet their brain. With the constant stimulation, they come down to art class and have to be chilled down. If they're still hyper, I have them sit down outside the door. When that calming comes, they're invited into the

classroom. If they become hyper again, I turn off the lights and ask them to rest their heads on their desks and stay quiet. They have to drown out all the noise to hear the voices in their heads, their imaginations. They can listen to their own thoughts again. Once they do, I can hear the exhale.

Reducing Mental Health and Well-Being

Statistics consistently indicate declining mental health in this age group. A recent Gallup poll found the highest rate of stress and worry among young people in at least a dozen years. According to a 2018 Pew Research Center study, 70 percent of surveyed teens said anxiety is a major problem for their generation. They mostly blamed pressures to get good grades, do extracurricular activities, and fit in socially.

Rates of depression are also soaring. A 2019 study published in *The Journal of Abnormal Psychology* found that between 2009 and 2017, depression rose by more than 60 percent among teens ages 14 to 17 and 47 percent among 12- and 13-year-olds. This is a remarkable increase—and girls are hit hardest. Between sixth and tenth grades, rates of depression doubled for boys but tripled for girls. Last year, one in five teen girls had an episode of major depression.

Research increasingly finds links between media use and well-being. After technology entered the scene, there was a sudden decline in teens' reported self-esteem, happiness, and life satisfaction. Again, girls are disproportionately affected. Negative social media experiences are associated with a threefold risk of developing depression and other emotional problems.

In the decade from 2007 to 2017, the Centers for Disease Control and Prevention (CDC) reports that youth suicide increased by 56 percent. It is now the second-leading cause of death in teens. The jury is still out on whether media use is contributing to these skyrocketing rates. But this much is clear: desperately unhappy teens can go on the internet and social media to get explicit, step-by-step instructions on how to end their lives. Young people can also go online to buy guns, a highly lethal means of self-harm that is now responsible for more suicides than homicides.

Cutting and other forms of self-harm are on the rise for girls, as well. According to the CDC, self-inflicted injuries have remained stable for boys, but rates among girls ages ten to fourteen nearly tripled, causing the steepest increase in emergency room visits.

It can be difficult to spot mental health issues in teens and tweens. Especially when girls are highly competent and performing well, it is hard for adults to imagine that degree of invisible pain. Belle tells me, "My thirteen-year-old suffers from anxiety, but nobody in the world would know. Angela is a straight-A student, she just won the scholar award in her school, and she's in her element speaking in front of three hundred people. But she's irrational and anxious about little things, like going to the dentist's office or even hearing the siren of a police car or fire truck."

There are many accomplished girls like Angela who hide their distress well. While working on this book, I read *The Washington Post*'s profile of a twenty-three-year-old superstar whose life may serve as a cautionary tale. Despite her extraordinary outward success—she earned perfect SAT scores, spoke fluent Mandarin, attended elite schools, was first-chair violinist in her high school orchestra, and became an Olympian silver medalist and three-time world champion cyclist—this young woman chose to end her own life.

The suicide note she wrote shortly before her death suggests that beneath her ferociously competitive spirit were unmet—and, perhaps, unrecognized—cravings for basic nurturance: "I only ever truly desired Love. Kindness. Understanding. Warmth. Touch." Her family, who reportedly conveyed that failure was an impossibility and crying was a weakness, may have prioritized her achievements over her emotional well-being.

Teachers are increasingly spotting red flags for mental health problems in the classroom. Melody tells me, "A group of incredibly smart students were having conversations over FaceTime and warning each other about who was cutting. The origin was one student who was bending the metal strip around her pencil and cutting herself in class. I noticed another student become very distracted, but only when I pulled her aside did I find out why. This is a good kid; I didn't know she had problems."

The trends teachers are observing coincide with statistics. Marlee says, "In the last three years, there's been a dramatic increase in my students' anxiety. A startling number of students have been avoiding school, cutting, having suicidal thoughts, and making suicide attempts. It's hard to know what to do." Lee agrees, "Teachers who have been teaching even longer than me are seeing the same thing. There's a lot more pressure. Anxiety is tremendously increased."

With more students struggling emotionally, the impact on classmates is growing. Tori, who teaches middle school, says, "They're dramatically affected. In class the other day, I saw a bunch of students looking at this one girl's arms. She wasn't cutting in school, but they could see marks and it distracted them. They were worried and concerned. It interfered with their focus—and their education. It becomes a crisis that the [school] team has to address."

Struggling with so many more emotional problems while growing up, it is easy to see why college students are in worse psychological shape than ever before. A 2018 National College Health Assessment found that in a twelve-month period women reported feeling hopeless (57%), overwhelmed (90%), very lonely (67%), very sad (73%), overwhelmingly anxious (70%), and so depressed it was difficult to function (45%).

New students are inundating and exhausting universities' mental health resources. Supply closets are being converted into treatment rooms. Many college students tell me of having to wait weeks for initial appointments at counseling centers, and then being limited to only a few visits. Crisis management is more available than ongoing psychotherapy.

* * *

Knowing more about the transformed landscape your daughter is navigating these days, you can better anticipate the preoccupations and worries she may bring home with her. How will all this affect your home life? How might evolving and complex changes in the composition and dynamics of modern families affect your teen's development—and your parenting? The next chapter gives you insights by zeroing in on these new challenges.

CHAPTER TWO

New Challenges at Home

> This year when I came home from college for Thanksgiving, it was me, my mother, my stepfather, my five-year-old half brother who they had with IVF, and my twin ten-month-old half brothers who they had with a surrogate. Also, my father's birth mother and aunt. He doesn't know them, but I found them with 23andMe and invited them. At that dinner, that's when I came out to my family.
>
> —JAMI, 18

The family your daughter is born into greatly affects how she feels about herself growing up. Much of the information she uses to form a strong, positive identity—a key adolescent developmental task—comes from experiences within the family. Your teen's earliest interactions with you, her other parent, and siblings determine to what degree she feels protected, safe, and valued. She also learns how people in intimate relationships treat each other.

Your daughter's awareness of her family history and where she comes from gives her a better understanding of who she is—and why. Her assessment of whether she lives up to family expectations shapes her self-esteem. She may question, for example, if she fits in and is as smart (or attractive, talented, and accomplished) as her siblings. Your teen may wonder if she is a valued and important member of the family as she is, or whether she has to work harder to prove herself—or, worse, will ever be seen as good enough.

This chapter highlights how cultural changes are transforming what transpires at home. What do families look like these days? How are new, more complex configurations of modern families and teens' birth histories shaping identities and self-esteem? How are this generation's beliefs and attitudes impacting parents? What are teens looking for at home? How can your family interactions empower your daughter to become her best self?

More Complicated, Messier Families

These days, your daughter may be growing up within a far different family structure than you did. In 2019, about 15.76 million children lived with a single mother. You may be raising a teen alone, as part of a heterosexual or lesbian couple, or as someone unmarried, separated, divorced, or remarried—perhaps more than once. You may even be bringing up a teen girl as her aunt, grandparent, or other relative.

The permutations of modern families are endless. Your daughter may be growing up among one or more blended families. She may have stepparents, half siblings, and stepsiblings, among other relatives.

Because parents and other close relatives are potential role models for teens, these variations make establishing an identity less straightforward. With whom do girls identify? Those with biracial or multicultural backgrounds may struggle to feel as if they truly belong in any group. If you and/or your daughter's other parent are immigrants, will your teen adopt your ways or assimilate into the culture in which she is raised? Sasha, seventeen, speaks for many girls when she says, "My mom was an immigrant, and her parents were immigrants. We had different lives. She had a restricted upbringing and no freedom. I want to stay out, like my friends do. It causes a lot of problems in our family."

With far more babies conceived through assisted reproductive techniques such as fertility drugs and IVF treatments, it is thornier for teens to gauge how they stack up. Some girls have biological, surrogate, or adoptive mothers, not to mention whole siblings, half siblings, and adoptive siblings with whom to compare themselves. I am also seeing a sharp increase in teens who are parts of multiple births—not just twins, but now also triplets and quadruplets. The dynamics of these sets of siblings greatly complicate the process of growing up.

Even trickier, some girls find out they do not share DNA with one or both parents. One set of fraternal twins I evaluated, for example, was conceived from their mother's eggs and sperm from different donors. Despite being twins, they were actually half sisters. Another teen learned of the opposite: she was the product of her father's sperm and an egg donated by a family friend, making her biologically unrelated to the mother who carried and raised her.

While mothers may feel uneasy or threatened when daughters they are raising search for biological relatives, the wide availability of home genetic kits is helping curious teens who were adopted or conceived through fertility treatments to investigate family origins. Tina, fifteen, says, "Last year, I found my birth mother and half sisters on Facebook. I contacted them, and I've corresponded with them ever since."

Some teens are surprised or unsettled by newly discovered information about their families and themselves, leading them to reassess fundamental beliefs. Caren, eleven, asked her parents to see a therapist. Having just found out that she was adopted at birth, Caren is furious and hurt that "my parents lied to me for the first decade of my life. How can I ever trust them?"

Joni, seventeen, however, is thankful she "knew from day one that I'm adopted. It would've affected my head if [my adoptive parents] didn't tell me from the beginning. I have a whole new identity, a whole new life. I'm grateful that my birth mother wanted me to have a better life." Getting to know her birth mother and half sisters has been powerfully validating. Joni's face lights up as she says, "My birth family is really proud of me."

For some girls, knowledge of their roots guides adolescent decision-making. Nora, eighteen, says, "I've always been curious about my birth parents. I first talked to my birth mother when I was nine and met her at seventeen." For Nora, this was life changing. After dismissing her adoptive parents' warnings about substances, she says, "Knowing my mother's history of being a meth addict, there's a higher chance of me getting addicted. I'm not interested in trying drugs now."

Shifts in Family Life

As you've surely noticed, families these days bear little resemblance to the classic TV sitcoms of yesteryear. Remember when mothers served dinners wearing dresses and heels; well-behaved children sat still, quietly finishing everything on their plates; and sage fathers doled out measured advice about using good manners, fessing up to misdeeds, and telling white lies? Fast-forward to today, and you may marvel at how different things are around your kitchen table.

Topics of Discussion

Whenever you get together for dinner, you may see a chance to catch up on what is going on in your daughter's life. But if she is reluctant to talk about herself or feels compelled to discuss what is happening in the world, suddenly you might be conversing about the latest mass shooting, political scandal, heart-wrenching story, or social controversy in the news.

The attitudes and fears your daughter brings home can surprise and fluster you. Her choices may give you pause, if not ulcers. You may be taken aback by her sudden mindfulness of what is politically correct and the pronouns she insists that you use. Your teen or tween may ask probing, often provocative questions at the dinner table. She may not hesitate to express strong opinions and call out family members, including—or especially—you. Brace yourself.

As girls today grow up in a more global, diverse world, they are demonstrably more inclusive and tolerant than previous generations. In a survey of new college students, as many as 77 percent of women report being able to see the world from other people's perspectives, and 80 percent accept people with different beliefs. When your daughter's passions are aroused, don't be shocked if she accuses you of being prejudiced, rigid, or judgmental in your thinking.

Harper, fifteen, articulates what many girls her age think when she tells me, "This whole generation is starting to become more aware, and the parents aren't really there for them. I have very different views than my parents. My parents believe what they believe. I don't. And that causes a lot of fights." With this in mind, these are some controversial topics your fervent teen might raise at the dinner table—or when you least expect it.

THE #METOO MOVEMENT

News stories about powerful men who have been caught up in the #MeToo movement are keeping these issues in girls' minds. Many are discussing what constitutes sexual harassment, consent, and other tricky topics. Teens' curiosity and resolve to delve more deeply has forced mothers to confront family secrets or unspoken histories. These are often difficult conversations.

As examples, a fourteen-year-old in my practice found out that her highly successful, divorced father was not laid off due to downsizing, as she had been told, but rather summarily fired after he had a brief affair with a subordinate. A fifteen-year-old finally learned why her mother has had a strained relationship with her grandparents: they hadn't protected her from ongoing sexual abuse during childhood. Another young woman, age twenty-three, struggled with a brother who, as a teen, "went to jail for molesting our younger half sister."

LGBTQ ISSUES

According to the Pew Research Center, one-third of Gen Z teens—far more than millennials, Gen Xers, and boomers—know someone who uses gender-neutral pronouns. No wonder so many mothers name LGBTQ issues as among the biggest challenges in raising girls today. If daughters are not questioning their own sexual orientation or gender identity, they most likely have friends who are.

LGBTQ issues are driving painful wedges in girls' long-standing friendships and family relationships. Like many of her generation, Bess, fifteen, is a fierce advocate for inclusiveness. She tells me, "I want to go to all the Pride marches. I don't identify with that, but I'm for it. But my parents get upset. It's against our religion. But I believe in it and it's important to me. Whenever I see stuff like that it makes me superangry and I just want to go to it and be a part of it."

BLACK LIVES MATTER

With many schools closed or held remotely during the COVID-19 pandemic, teens were more tuned in to the demonstrations that erupted after George Floyd's death in protest of his and other Black people's treatment at the hands of police. Because girls today are often being educated in more multicultural environments, many white teens home from college or boarding school began wondering about their nonwhite classmates' experiences, and even questioning whether they, too, might have inadvertently treated peers with prejudice. Many teens were likely traumatized by repeatedly viewing video footage of George Floyd's death, but this country's racial reckoning may have especially compelled Black, Indigenous, and girls of color to become activists. Certainly, the ensuing shift in public sentiment and controversies over race, police reform, and other issues have prompted much discussion among teens and families.

RELIGION

In the process of figuring out who they are, girls often reexamine their beliefs in religious tenets and devotional practices. Like many teens, Maija, fifteen, is struggling to reconcile personal views with the lessons of her parents and Sunday school teachers. She describes her quandary: "I believe in religion. But a lot of things could be changed. Some religious laws should be changed. Sometimes I really don't believe that our religion is right. I don't want to believe in this, but at the same time this is how I was raised—and I want to believe in it."

Girls who become more religiously observant than parents present different challenges at home. Mona, mother of two teens, tells me, "I'm not sure why, but suddenly my girls are insisting on keeping strictly kosher and eating only kosher meat when they're out. They want to observe even minor Jewish holidays. That's made me rethink how I've always done things. But family is important to me, so I've had to make a lot of changes."

POLITICS

In the past few years, politics has become a deeply divisive issue for the entire country as well as for individual families. Perhaps you are among the women who have resorted to declaring a moratorium on political discussion just to get through holiday dinners without heated and unpleasant arguments. As your daughter matures, she may become pricklier and more vocal about political positions that resonate with or directly affect her, provoking more clashes at mealtimes.

Tara, sixteen, is an only child who tells me, "My parents are conservative—Republican and pro-life. I don't believe that women should be treated the way they are, and I don't think the [then] president is right in a lot of what he does, and I barely know that much about politics. But I don't think it's right. I'm more feminist, and I express my opinions a lot with my family, and they just don't want to hear it. They're not going to change their opinions."

GUN LEGISLATION

Many teens growing up with school shootings advocate for stronger and more protective gun laws. Yet this position may run counter to long-held family values and traditions. Kendra, fourteen, explains, "My dad is pro-choice with guns. I don't believe that people should have guns they don't need, like military guns. You can have one gun; that's fine. But there should be screenings, a long process to get one. My parents have very different positions. My father is like, 'Nope, I have my opinions. That's it, we're done here.'"

Homework Wars

Two cultural trends—the achievement frenzy and soaring technology use—have conspired to make the hours between dinnertime and bedtime the bane of many mothers' daily lives. I constantly hear, "I dread nightly homework battles," "Most evenings are superstressful," and "The fight to get them to shut off electronics and get into bed is an absolute nightmare."

This is a challenging time of day, period. With extracurricular activities, sports, tutoring, test prep commitments, and enrichment programs going into the evening hours, by the time girls get home and grab something to eat they are running on fumes. And this is after grueling school days, when teen brains are already so fried that they practically need rebooting.

Before tackling more mentally strenuous tasks, what teens and tweens crave is time to "chill." Thinking they are pros at multitasking, some girls try to connect with friends on social media or watch videos while doing homework. You, on the other hand, know it is impossible to focus on two tasks at once—not well, anyway. But, again, choosing to intervene to get her to prioritize better, finish her work more efficiently, and go to bed at a reasonable hour may ignite a firestorm that only makes the situation worse.

If you track her use of screens and threaten to confiscate her cellphone, your efforts may be met with irritation, if not fury. The later it gets and the more exhausted you both become, the more tension you may feel sizzling in the air. Conflicts and arguments over homework usually backfire by zapping the motivation and energy your teen needs for her work. If this sounds like the scenario in your house, know that you are not alone. This is an epic problem.

Bedtime Hours

Hardly a week goes by without a major news report on how sleep deprivation harms teens and tweens. Getting fewer than the recommended eight to ten hours per night predisposes girls to illness by suppressing the immune system. Too few zzzzs impairs learning by disrupting vital memory consolidation that occurs during sleep.

Besides, as you may have observed, exhausted daughters have fewer inner resources to manage feelings and impulses, making them crankier, more emotionally reactive, and apt to use poorer judgment.

For these reasons, parents have always been worried about teens' sleep. But lately, more young people are describing how hard it is to get enough rest and, as a result, the mind-numbing fatigue that builds throughout the school week. Sadly, this problem is now trickling down to younger girls. For the first time, fifth and sixth graders in a series of wellness workshops I conducted recently brought up sleep concerns.

Asked why they got too little sleep, girls cited three main reasons. One, they won't go to bed until finishing all homework. Two, they get into bed, but can't fall asleep because of minds that keep whirling and refuse to shut down. Thoughts (Did I do everything I was supposed to? Did I forget anything? Am I prepared for tomorrow? Did I study enough for my test?) agitate them further, preventing the relaxation needed to nod off. Three, girls delay going to bed to find time for what they most crave: watching videos, checking social media, and messaging friends.

Between disagreements about priorities, ingrained habits, and academic deadlines, it is not surprising that sleep issues frequently spark family conflict in the evening hours.

Hanging at Home

Teens and tweens today are a different breed than they were even a few years ago. Specifically, tremendous shifts in how this generation is choosing to spend spare time may be radically altering your home life. Although your daughter may not say this in so many words, what she needs from you and the rest of the family may utterly surprise you.

According to research by the brand innovation firm The Family

Room, a greater focus on stress, worrying about college, preparing for success, and making parents proud have for the first time in thirty years caused young people to give up on just being kids and going outside. Poignantly, what matters most to teens these days is well-being; their core desires are "feeling safe and content in my home," "knowing that my family understands and appreciates me," "trusting my parents," and "knowing that my parents trust me."

Young people express a greater need for external support in navigating a world they see as more judgmental, less safe, and lonelier. To counter such feelings, Gen Z teens are looking for consistency and predictability. They are seeking what The Family Room's founder and CEO, George Carey, calls "emotional sanctuaries." Practically speaking, to satisfy this need, your daughter and other teens are looking to families to provide secure, comfortable home lives.

Many more young people these days are focused on family traditions. In my practice, teen girls are suddenly craving family movie nights with popcorn and childhood board games. They look forward to cheesy holiday rituals—and, remarkably, are even willing to pitch in to make them happen. Unless forced to miss out on a much-awaited concert or friend's birthday party, girls don't even mind being grounded—though they'd have to deny that if asked.

Despite the innumerable ways the COVID-19 pandemic interrupted this generation's adolescence, surveys indicate a possible silver lining: 68 percent of teens said that quarantining at home made them feel closer to their parents.

With Gen Z teens more anxious and fearful of safety, there is also less risk-taking and rebellion going on. Fewer in this age group are drinking alcohol, using illicit drugs, or getting pregnant. Instead of going out to parties, your daughter may be content just staying home, socializing from her comfy bed. She can get food from the fridge rather than trek to the local diner. She can order clothes and school supplies online instead of shopping at brick-and-mortar stores.

* * *

Because of reluctance to venture out in the world, nearly 30 percent of high school seniors today don't have drivers' licenses. This is a radical shift. For the last four decades, teens in my practice counted the days until this rite of passage, begging parents to take them to the DMV the moment they became eligible for learners' permits. Waiting an extra day or two was inconceivable. Nothing made girls feel more grown-up than shiny, laminated tickets to freedom.

In a departure from this norm, so many sixteen- and seventeen-year-olds have been reluctant to learn to drive in the past few years that it is parents who are nagging daughters to go online and sign up for DMV permit tests—often without success. For teens, there is little incentive. Some girls are too anxious to take on what they see as the overwhelmingly scary responsibility of operating a vehicle. Others simply have no burning desire to leave home.

* * *

Now that you have reviewed how cultural changes are impacting teens, families, and home lives, it is time to embark on your mother-daughter journey. Part Two gives you the practical know-how, the guiding principles and parenting tools, to navigate more smoothly and effectively. The pages ahead provide strategies for remaining close with your teen, fostering reciprocal trust and effective communication, modeling a healthy relationship, and nurturing the skills that prepare her for success now and in her future.

After debunking well-accepted myths about success, the next chapter charts your course by giving you the real scoop on the traits and personal qualities today's teens need to thrive. To learn more about the transformative combination of emotional resiliency, self-control, responsibility, social perceptiveness, resourcefulness, and grit, read on.

Part Two

Navigating the Mother-Daughter Journey

CHAPTER THREE

Flourishing in Her Future

> My daughter, Jordan, was at college for only five weeks when she called me, sobbing and asking me to come pick her up and take her home. She insisted she was in the wrong place. I found out that she was upset because she wasn't getting along with her roommate and did poorly on her first paper. This seemed to me like the normal stuff that freshmen stress about, but Jordan refused to stay. So I had to fly out there, help her pack up her things, and bring her home.
>
> —JOHANNA

Women like Johanna have called my practice more in the past five years than in the previous thirty-five-plus years all together. It's concerning. The discovery that daughters are not making it in college not only upsets and alarms mothers, but also catches them off guard. It is easy to miss red flags signaling that teens lack skills to manage on their own, especially when there may be an unconscious desire to avoid even peeking into that particular Pandora's box.

For many mothers, successfully launching daughters into young adulthood is the ultimate goal. Finalizing college plans usually brings relief beyond measure. Getting past the onerous pressures of junior and senior year frees up women to indulge in pleasant fantasies of girls blossoming on campus, excelling in studies, participating in meaningful activities, perhaps becoming leaders, and making lifelong friends. Who would want to rock that boat?

When teens leave home only to boomerang right back, distraught families are usually mystified. Why wouldn't girls who have had every educational opportunity thrive in college? What has gone wrong—and what will fix the problem? Where would daughters flourish? These are the questions families who seek psychoeducational assessments want me to answer.

The reasons girls do not adapt well—academically, socially, and/or emotionally—are always unique and complex. Yet one theme regularly emerges. What is jeopardizing young people's well-being and success, causing them to abandon college dreams and return home, is an underdevelopment of fundamental inner resources.

This notion may challenge your beliefs about achievement. Many daughters and parents think success and happiness hinge on where students go to college. With this mindset, the focus of high school is ensuring girls' applications are impressive enough for them to be admitted to highly selective future alma maters. But this is a myth. What really threatens eventual success is not ten or thirty SAT points, plus or minus half a point in a GPA, or even having to attend "safety" schools.

What matters is whether teens can adjust to campus life, solve problems that arise, manage living independently, and take good care of themselves—wherever they go to college.

This chapter outlines the character traits, inner resources, and pragmatic skills your teen needs throughout high school, college, and beyond. You will learn how her growing emotional resiliency, self-discipline, self-awareness, and empathy facilitate greater academic and social success; why perseverance, optimism, gratitude, and curiosity foster her creativity and problem-solving; and how strong executive functioning skills promote her productivity.

Resiliency

Transitioning from the structure, predictability, and security of home to the freedom, stimulation, and even chaos of dorm life can be hugely challenging. Now add higher academic expectations, new and more intense social demands, and a multitude of potential distractions and temptations. It makes sense that the best predictor of your daughter's success in college is not the strength of her high school academic records. It is her emotional readiness.

The American Psychological Association defines resiliency as "the process of adapting well in the face of adversity, trauma, tragedy, threats, or significant sources of stress." Resiliency, along with grit and perseverance, are among the noncognitive factors and character traits that researchers like psychologist Angela Duckworth are finding predict success far better than IQ. "Grittier" students are more likely to finish college, advance to the Scripps National Spelling Bee finals, and earn higher GPAs at Ivy League universities.

Resilient teens adjust to new situations, stay positive, handle pressures, overcome challenges, and rebound from mistakes and difficulties. At college, thriving might entail dealing with incompatible roommates, a friend who abuses substances, being closed out of required courses, or not getting bids from sought-after sororities. Resilient girls bounce back from a first test grade of C—or perhaps A minus—determined to improve on the next exam.

The trouble is, this generation is already struggling with adaptability. The teens in my practice who drop out of college are part of a national trend. According to the UCLA Higher Education Research Institute's *The American Freshman* surveys, from 1985 to 2017 female college students have been reporting worsening emotional health compared with their male counterparts. In this same time frame, the gap between incoming women and men who are "frequently overwhelmed" by everything they have to do tripled, with more than half of freshman women now lacking confidence in their ability to cope. The American College Health Association's survey finds that within the previous two weeks, almost 60 percent of college women felt overwhelmed.

Besides having supportive parents, close relationships with other caring adults, and good peer friendships, resilient girls boast the following internal strengths.

Managing Stress

This generation, growing up with already high levels of anxiety about achievement, getting into college, and global issues, may be ill prepared to cope with further stress. Students with overwhelming pressure may be crippled by tension, panic, indecisiveness, or cloudy thinking. Feeling helpless and powerless leads to despair, which causes further fears of performing poorly, which erodes confidence. This becomes a classic vicious circle.

Resilient teens, on the other hand, use inner resources to manage adversity so they don't become overwhelmed or immobilized. A positive mindset about stress liberates and empowers, as psychologist Kelly McGonigal describes in her TED Talk, "How to Make Stress Your Friend," which has been viewed over twenty-six million times. This shift in mindset is essential to success.

Instead of interpreting physical symptoms as threats, resilient girls see stress arousal as the body's natural way of preparing them to function at their best. They reframe self-defeating thoughts (e.g., "I'm totally having a panic attack," "I can't possibly do well," "I'm gonna be in such trouble," "I'll never get into college") into motivating self-talk (e.g., "I'm breathing faster so more oxygen gets to my brain," "Now I'll have more energy," "My thinking will be sharper").

Empowering beliefs keep girls from enacting negative self-fulfilling prophecies. Rather than expecting to bomb tryouts, tests, auditions, and recitals, confirming their worst fears of failure, adaptive teens learn to think of nerve-racking challenges as opportunities to demonstrate the skills they've developed through vigorous work and tenacity.

To combat sky-high, destructive levels of pressure among undergraduates, colleges are offering stress management events and programs. Students are given smoothies and stress kits that include crayons, markers, candy, inspirational quotes, and stress balls. Instructions on contacting counseling centers are included in case more help is needed. Campuses provide nap pods, petting zoos, neck massages, and certified therapy dogs during study and exam weeks.

Relieving stress allows students to become more resourceful and effectively solve problems. Success begets even more success. That is not just because self-defeating cycles are broken. It is also because managing stressful situations well actually rewires brains, and these structural changes lead to better coping in the future.

Using MRIs to study youth living in violent Chicago neighborhoods, Northwestern University psychologists imaged the brains of resilient twelve-to-fourteen-year-olds. These tweens and teens were no less anxious or depressed. But higher levels of functional connectivity in their brains enabled better self-control. This skill, in turn, helped them to choose healthy rather than risky coping behaviors.

Learning from Setbacks and Failures

As Michelle Obama famously said, "Failure is an important part of your growth and developing resilience. Don't be afraid to fail." Resilient girls are more adept at dealing with mistakes and setbacks along the road to accomplishment. Unfortunately, the media bombards teens with far different, misleading, and harmful notions. "Reality" television shows glamorize cutthroat competition, distorting expectations about what it takes to succeed. YouTube influencers convey that exposure and viral recognition are tickets to wild, overnight success.

Young people growing up with these models of achievement may have trouble buying into the need for hard work and persistence. They may not accept that doing poorly or even messing up badly on occasion is inevitable. Because of the intense achievement pressures described in the last chapter, in fact, girls often fear that just one wrong move will extinguish their hopes. This mindset is incompatible with viewing failures as the seeds of future victories.

Intolerance of mistakes has become a generational vulnerability. According to *The American Freshman*, only 56 percent of college students accept errors as part of the learning process, and just one-third take on challenges that scare them. Take a moment to let this sink in: two-thirds of students are so afraid of making mistakes that they won't take academic risks in college. But if growth is the goal, the most comfortable route is usually not the best route.

If your daughter is a high achiever, you may believe she is inoculated against fearing obstacles and setbacks. Actually, the opposite may be true. The higher your teen's or tween's personal standards and the more eager she is to please, the greater may be her dread of failure.

As many middle school and high school teachers describe, it is the intelligent, high-flying students who are most often flattened by setbacks. Farah says, "They're not accustomed to struggle. It was always easy for them, so they can't tolerate not getting good grades. If they get a ninety-one instead of one hundred on a test, they think they're in trouble. They have no resiliency. They're despondent and can't cope." College often exacerbates this mindset.

Teens arrive on campus with academic stress already baked into them. Ambitious girls often feel compelled to prove themselves all over again with college classmates they see as just as smart, if not more talented, than they are. So if your daughter's grades drop in her first year, which is typical, she may feel disappointed in herself, insecure about her abilities, or ashamed that she failed to live up to your expectations.

When I speak about the value of risking failure and persisting in the face of obstacles, the timeless adage "nothing ventured, nothing gained" often makes sense to students. But what always resonates are stories of famous people who suffered spectacular failures prior to achieving extraordinary successes. I describe A-list movie actors, for example, who washed dishes or wore chicken costumes on the streets of Hollywood before catapulting into stardom.

It is hard for teens to believe that many of their favorite authors struggled to get published. It is impossible for them to fathom that if J. K. Rowling and Theodor Geisel had not persisted after dozens of demoralizing rejections by publishers, they would never have gotten to read Harry Potter and Dr. Seuss classics. Girls are utterly shocked that Oprah Winfrey's first manager not only fired her, but also told her she didn't have what it takes to be on TV.

Colleges are now invested in teaching students that making mistakes and failing are both a fundamental part of the learning process and an inevitable, invaluable part of growing up. Through workshops, online programs, and events, faculty members share what they learned from personal self-doubts, professional failures, and social missteps. Supportive videos, TED Talks, and audio clips are offered. Teachers now assign undergraduates papers about fiascoes in school, friendships, and personal lives. "Best Fail Ever" stories line the walls and bulletin boards of some campus buildings.

The most academically rigorous colleges have developed initiatives to promote campus collaboration over competition and to emphasize the value of mistakes over perfectionism. At Smith College, there is a "Failing Well." Stanford University offers the Resilience Project; Harvard University a Success-Failure Project; the University of Pennsylvania's program is called PennFaces; and Princeton University created the Perspective Project.

Intrinsic Motivation

If aiming for perfection harms learning, what about just trying to earn good grades, win awards, and get into elite colleges? All these goals may sound good. But new research on motivation and achievement suggests a self-defeating downside.

Students who focus on these external markers of accomplishment to demonstrate they're more competent than their peers are *performance-oriented*. They attribute success to intelligence, not to effort—a belief that puts them on precarious ground for learning. That is because if these girls don't do well, they have to conclude they're not smart. To avoid looking or feeling stupid, failure is avoided at all costs. To avoid failure, students don't take risks; unless success is assured, they won't even try.

Unfortunately, more and more teachers are seeing the fallout of performance-oriented mindsets in the classroom. Charlie tells me, "Students' love of learning is dissipating because of the focus on grades and external rewards. They're used to being given things and are praised for mediocre progress rather than having to work hard for something. At first, I couldn't put my finger on it, but that's why I'm finding it harder to motivate students intrinsically."

Sheralynn, who teaches in a large public school system, tells me that eighth-grade term papers often reveal students' mindsets about achievement. "It's unpredictable who gets into it and does a great job, but it's not usually the top students." Nancie agrees, "Students who are not the highest achievers feel freer to pick a topic they're interested in, not what their parents tell them to research or what they think the teacher wants."

High-flying students who focus on getting good grades, on the other hand, often choose topics based on what they already know. Nancie explains, "Kids who get one hundreds may not have that freedom because they're afraid to take risks. They become little robots and it breaks my heart." Taking the easier, safer route ensures short-term, external rewards but is less likely to build the intrinsic motivation, grit, and problem-solving girls need to thrive in the longer term.

Mastery-oriented students, on the other hand, focus on the *process* of learning, the experiences along the way, rather than on end goals and rewards. When frustrated, the adaptive beliefs that (a) failure is valuable and (b) they can change outcomes with effort inspire girls to shift gears, find new solutions, and improve. This winning trifecta of hard work, perseverance, and dedication is what psychologist Angela Duckworth calls "grit." According to her research, far more than talent, stick-to-it-iveness predicts which students commit to doing whatever it takes, for as long as is necessary, to achieve.

Students with grit are more motivated by intellectual curiosity and a genuine desire to learn. Nan sees this mindset paying dividends in the classroom: "Some of the most amazing eighth-grade presentations come from the most surprising students. They get excited about it and have a real desire to challenge themselves." Choosing a topic that sparks their interest, these teens get caught up and run with it.

Self-Discipline

Most people equate intelligence with academic success. But here is a remarkable fact: self-discipline counts twice as much as IQ. Christa, eighteen, exemplifies students who crash and burn despite intellectual giftedness. Because she coasted through high school, she had little idea of how to study in college. With lengthier reading assignments, Christa grew bored, daydreamed, or tuned out. Although she thought she had an attention deficit, her problem was poor self-discipline. She never learned how to make herself do what she preferred to avoid.

Brooklynn, seventeen, who came to see me because she was at risk for not earning enough high school credits to graduate, described a classic scenario: "I can't push through boredom and do what I'm supposed to. I feel like I should just switch off daydreaming. I'm causing myself so much grief. I can see it, but I can't do anything about it. It's so frustrating."

Few teens and tweens today have the self-restraint to avoid the omnipresent lure of screens, which has become a technological black hole. Kim, fifteen, says, "Before I do my homework, I go online just to check my messages and the next thing I know it's been an hour." Rashida, thirteen, cannot turn off or ignore her cellphone's notifications, so she ends up "looking at my friend's Instagram posts and funny YouTube videos. It's a modern time suck."

In my experience, many students who lack self-discipline get through high school only because of tremendous scaffolding. But relying excessively on extra help, tutors, executive functioning coaches, constant parental reminders, and morning wake-up calls prevents teens from developing the self-regulation skills they need to function on their own. In college, these girls struggle to replicate previous academic successes. Used to being propped up, they flounder when left to fend for themselves.

Resilient teens, on the other hand, prevail not because they are the smartest or highest achievers, but rather because they can self-regulate emotions and behavior. When self-disciplined girls prefer not to do something, they marshal resources from within to make themselves do it anyway. They persevere through frustration and boredom. They resist momentary distractions, no matter how appealing, to refocus on goals.

Resilient girls use self-discipline to resist self-defeating temptations.

Faced with deadlines or exams, they stay in and work instead of going out and partying. They cope with inevitable urges to procrastinate by forcing themselves to knuckle down rather than checking out social media or going on online shopping sprees. Instead of giving in to the desire to sleep in, students who thrive manage to get themselves up and out for morning classes.

Managing Emotions

> So much is going on. I have so much pressure. I freak out and stress in a big classroom. How am I supposed to get this done? I don't know how to do it, and I see my teacher working with someone else. What if I have a question?
>
> —BEATRICE, 14

> I never want to get called on. I don't like being the center of attention. I hate presentations.
>
> —CLARISSA, 16

The value of emotional self-regulation can't be overemphasized. Your teen's awareness of her emotions predicts her happiness and academic success, her resistance to anxiety and depression, her productivity at work, and even whether her future marriage will last. A meta-analysis of studies consisting of more than 42,000 students from 27 countries found that higher emotional intelligence is associated with better grades and achievement test scores.

Girls who are attuned to their interior lives and can stay in charge of emotions—even when stirred up—are three steps ahead of the pack. This vital inner resource helps maintain a sense of personal agency and stability, especially in situations when emotions run high. Conversely, teens who struggle with self-management are at the mercy of mercurial, overpowering moods. As you can imagine (or have seen firsthand), this vulnerability compromises success in school, at home, and with peers.

Thora, sixteen, who is perpetually in trouble for skipping classes and missing assignments, insightfully describes how emotional dysregulation affects her: "The more stressed I am in my personal or home life, the worse my work production is. If any emotion is too strong, I avoid going to classes all day. I shut down as a person. It's hard for me to tolerate distress. It's hard for me to get beyond my feelings."

Avoidance is a common coping strategy among girls like Thora, who struggle to manage discomfiting feelings. They steer clear of emotionally arousing people and situations, such as hard classes, chaotic cafeterias, or anywhere conflicts might arise. But momentarily escaping fears only reinforces them. Avoidant teens don't get to practice tolerating and working through negative feelings, which is necessary to develop resiliency.

This has become a challenge for girls who enjoyed remote learning during the pandemic. For students with social anxiety, COVID-19 afforded a year's respite from feeling nervous when they had to show up in school for classes. Alexandria, fifteen, tells me, "I like it much better this way. I want to keep doing remote school." Although she knows that it's in her best interest to face and conquer her fears, she is in no rush to do so. Avoidance feels much better.

Feeling socially anxious in school can be torturous. Thirteen-year-old Aurora's preoccupation with her mental state keeps her from being fully present. She says, "I'm sitting in class and I have to use the bathroom, but I don't want to draw attention to myself and stand up because I know people would look at me. So I just stay at my desk." Clearly, this predicament is in itself distracting. Willow, sixteen, whose powerful feelings breed rumination, says, "During class, I go over situations or conversations in the past and change them completely into what I wish they had been."

In my work with families, I often have to explain the inextricable link between emotional management and achievement. It can be hard to appreciate that girls who cannot keep feelings in check—but instead are at the mercy of their emotions—are less capable of focusing on learning and performing at their best.

Typical challenges in the classroom can seem insurmountable. Agitated or despondent girls can't stay seated, take part in discussions, volunteer answers, ask questions, or collaborate with peers in class. Some can't even *get* to class. Learning that her special education case manager had a conversation with her mother, for example, seventeen-year-old Lorene was so overwhelmed by anger and embarrassment that she skipped her next subject and hid in the girls' restroom to try to collect herself.

Mental health issues also can wreak havoc on motivation, energy, and work effort. Constance explains, "I might get so anxious about a project that's due that I have to take a break. And then I might forget about it. With my depression, I lose my motivation for it. I know I should do this, but then the other half of me is, 'You have no motivation. Don't even bother.'"

Janelle, eighteen, puts it bluntly: "Being depressed and a teenager at the same time doesn't go well. You're sad and you have this overwhelming feeling in your chest. You have other responsibilities like homework and projects, too. That gets intertwined and makes your life a living hell."

Ever-present cellphones are also thwarting the development of emotional resiliency. Teens and tweens who are upset about social incidents, disappointing grades, or clashes with teachers often text or call mothers from school bathrooms. Dumping problems makes girls feel better in the moment, but does nothing to teach them how to manage painful feelings.

The repercussions can continue in college and beyond. After I presented a lecture about stress and emotional resiliency to faculty and staff at a midwestern university, a department chairwoman shared a memorable anecdote. She had just visited a first-year medical school class that got back their first graded exams. When the period ended, a female student ran up to the instructor, a cellphone in her outstretched hand, breathlessly telling her, "My mother wants to talk to you."

Instead of unloading on mothers, teens can learn to sit with and increasingly tolerate distress. A discouraging exam score, for example, might spur girls to start studying earlier or to use better strategies next time. Feeling offended by a friend's weird look or snarky comment could encourage reflecting on what might have prompted those reactions. Dealing on their own with upsetting situations, teens can discover the benefit of positive self-talk in which they remind themselves of past successes, strengths, and supportive people in their lives.

Character facilitates emotional regulation. Optimism and gratitude counteract negative thinking, disappointment, and immobilizing helplessness. Curiosity alleviates boredom. Tenacity helps to push through frustrating problems that might otherwise seem overwhelming.

A fascinating study demonstrates how character strengths such as kindness, courage, and wisdom promote teens' success. Researchers randomly assigned ninth-grade literature students to two groups. Both read *Romeo and Juliet* and *The Scarlet Letter*. One class included a positive psychology component; teens explored the strengths of main characters and had to do three loving things for someone else. Three years later, at the end of high school, students in the character-oriented class had better social skills, a greater love of learning, and higher grades than the control group, which had just read the two books.

Executive Functioning Skills

Strong executive functioning (EF) skills are an invaluable asset for teens. Overlapping with self-discipline and self-regulation, executive functions refer to higher-level cognitive abilities that enable adapting, planning, and solving problems according to the demands of specific situations. Located in the frontal lobes, executive functions serve as the brain's CEO.

EF has cognitive (thinking), emotional, and behavioral components. Unlike students with poor EF, who repeat ineffective strategies or shut down when initial strategies don't work, teens endowed with effective EF flexibly shift gears to generate, implement, and self-monitor new solutions. Skilled teens can follow directions, think abstractly, and make good decisions. They grasp main points of stories and generate ideas when writing papers.

Emotionally capable girls can tolerate frustration, accept constructive criticism, abide by rules, manage anger, comply with adults' instructions, and resist becoming argumentative. Behaviorally adept teens act age-appropriately, check impulses rather than starting tasks rashly, and restrain themselves from blurting the first thing that comes to mind. These girls generally can remain still, stay in control, obey adults, and work at a pace that minimizes unnecessary mistakes.

Teens with strong EF skills need little or no adult scaffolding to manage everyday lives. With orderly bedrooms, they don't spend time frantically looking for favorite sweatshirts, AirPods, keys, and cellphones. If these girls borrow clothes, they remember to give them back—in good condition. They keep track of time, don't drag their feet, and are habitually punctual.

In school, they are seen as capable, well-organized, independent learners who manage schedules and due dates, start studying well before exams, and turn in assignments when they're due. These girls monitor ongoing work and correct errors. Thinking ahead, they anticipate obstacles and find ways around them.

Clarissa, sixteen, epitomizes such a capable teen. She not only earns good grades in higher-level junior classes, but also juggles multiple after-school activities and a demanding sport that requires twice-daily practices. Her parents are in awe of what Clarissa accomplishes, all on her own. Fiercely self-reliant, she dislikes accepting help. Her seemingly effortless ability to get the job done prompts her parents to dub her "a self-cleaning oven."

In contrast, girls with poor EF skills aren't terribly productive. They have trouble making decisions and carrying out plans. These teens show up late to class, forget necessary materials, and are surprised by tests and quizzes. While their active participation and insightful comments give teachers the impression that they are smart and engaged in learning, these girls' work output tells a different story.

Because teens with poor EF work inefficiently, even simple tasks that peers accomplish easily feel onerous. They have trouble starting and finishing homework. Jess, fifteen, explains, "I have full intentions. I sit down at my computer with the essay in my room and I literally sit there for four hours and do nothing. I've completely wasted my time. It won't even be started. The more energy it takes, the less chance I start it."

For these reasons, girls with poor EF are often called spacey, underachievers, or absentminded professors who don't live up to their potential. Like Jess, girls who can't achieve their own goals or meet the expectations of parents and teachers feel helpless and inadequate.

Social Perceptiveness and Interpersonal Skills

In today's world, collaboration is fundamental. For young people to be successful, they need to get along with others and maintain intimate relationships. In middle school and high school, interactions with classmates greatly affect how well students learn and perform.

The prerequisite to social perceptiveness is self-awareness. Teens who are attuned to their own emotions can more easily imagine how others feel. Awareness of how their behavior impacts others encourages self-control. Yet developing self-awareness is another hurdle for this generation. Looking within requires solitude.

Psychologist Sherry Turkle, who for thirty years has been studying the effects of online connectivity on adolescent social development, speaks of "the essential connection between solitude and conversation." She writes, "In solitude we learn to concentrate and imagine, to listen to ourselves. We need these skills to be fully present in conversation."

As discussed earlier, communicating on devices doesn't provide practice in perceiving others' thoughts and feelings. Gen Z teens have less experience picking up on and interpreting subtleties and subtext. This is problematic; an estimated one-half to three-quarters of communication is nonverbal, especially among teen girls.

Your daughter will need strong interpersonal skills for the future. When she interviews with internship directors, college admissions officers, and prospective employers, she must be comfortable in her own skin, make appropriate eye contact, and come across as interested and engaged. Many positions these days specifically require good people skills.

Girls who thrive on campus create relationships that become supportive communities away from home. As research demonstrates, even one caring friendship can make all the difference. But more than a third of undergraduates who seek counseling do so because of relationship problems. The perception of not belonging is a catalyst for failure. Loneliness often triggers a downward spiral in girls who eventually drop out.

Undergraduates who have trouble making friends often self-isolate in their dorm rooms. Because they have no one to sit with, they skip class, gradually falling hopelessly behind in academic work. Lacking social support, students are more inclined to turn to unhealthy coping strategies, such as eating junk food alone rather than more nutritious meals in dining halls. To self-soothe, girls sometimes overeat, fast, or misuse substances, which of course creates more problems.

Collaboration

Now more than ever, succeeding in school and work requires collaboration. In the classroom, girls who work well with peers do better academically. With an ally, teens and tweens feel more at ease. If they are absent or confused about an assignment, they have someone to ask for clarification. In contrast, social discomfort dampens motivation for group projects, which many schools emphasize. In fact, they are the bane of students who have trouble relating to and getting along with peers.

As Cora, fourteen, describes, "If my teacher tells the class to pick a partner and I don't like anybody, I just stay at my desk and don't say anything. And I kind of keep my head down and hope to God that nobody comes up to me. But if someone does come up to me, I just kind of say, 'Okay, we can be partners,' even though I don't want to be."

Girls benefit from being able to work well within pairs or groups. Having a partner boosts motivation to get work done. If not for their own benefit, teens at least want to be fair to classmates who are relying on their contributions. Kaitlyn, fourteen, says, "Even though I don't care that much, the project doesn't really matter to me, another part of me is saying, 'You shouldn't let her do all the work.' So I end up doing the work."

Later on, getting along well with colleagues and clients is central to young women thriving in the workplace. Articles in business journals and mainstream media describe that it is becoming harder to find candidates who have the "soft skills" required for many jobs. Human resources personnel observe that young people today have more trouble reading people, which prevents them from demonstrating empathy and developing trust. In fact, young employees are getting fired and being replaced by older workers with natural people skills.

According to professors at the University of Pennsylvania and California State University, social isolation in the workplace disadvantages workers. Loneliness weakens performance for two reasons: One, lonely employees are less committed to their jobs, which reduces the drive to work hard. Two, because coworkers see lonely employees as less approachable, they are less likely to exchange vital information and resources.

Self-Advocacy

It is a truism that in life, things do not always go smoothly. As adults, we know that people misplace important paperwork, miscommunicate or give flat-out wrong information, make unfair decisions, and renege on promises. This can happen to teens in classrooms, during college visits, at sports tryouts, and when being interviewed for sought-after internships and jobs. That is why girls who can express their needs to authority figures are generally more resilient and successful.

Good communication skills and confidence enable teens to self-advocate with parents' input. Letitia describes what it looks like when girls feel less empowered and capable: "My sixteen-year-old daughter puts up roadblocks with her teachers, especially this one social studies teacher she's convinced doesn't like her. When I talk to her, she says, 'He's not going to listen to me' or 'It's too late!' or 'He won't care.'"

This self-defeating attitude prevents girls from speaking with teachers who grade midterms incorrectly, coaches who renege on promises, college registrars who close them out of prerequisite classes, deans who turn down requests for dorm changes, and bosses who don't provide the training, raises, or promotions they offered.

Imagination and Creativity

After the pandemic, there is an even greater demand for creative jobs in product/app, branding, marketing, and online user experience design. To thrive in these industries, young women can't merely follow instructions to reach a specific goal. Solving novel problems requires considering multiple possibilities and experimenting to discover what works best. This can be a lengthy process. To succeed in creative jobs, it is necessary to embrace the uncertainty of working without instant answers—and, of course, to persevere with uncertainty.

Two aspects of the adolescent experience program girls with exactly the wrong mindset for creative jobs. The first is panic about being wrong, making mistakes, and failing. The second is intolerance of being alone. Teens today have too little of the peaceful, solitary time that is mandatory for sparking the imagination. If girls are to access creativity and find innovative solutions to problems, they have to be comfortable reflecting and generating ideas from within.

Life Skills and Confidence

Although physiological factors are causing girls to enter puberty earlier and making them look physically mature, the activities of today's teens are less adultlike than in the past. A meta-analysis of studies demonstrated that in the thirty years from 1976 to 2016, significantly fewer teens have been working for pay, going out without parents, dating, driving cars, drinking alcohol, and, yes, having sex. At home, girls are not doing as many household chores that, while teaching skills, nurture lifelong values of contributing, responsibility, and self-discipline.

The fact that IQs have been soaring is attributed to increasing academic rigor. But middle schools and high schools are offering fewer classes in life skills (personal finance, home economics, etc.). As a result, teens are more likely to go to college without knowing how to set up and work within a budget; do laundry; keep dorm rooms or apartments clean; and balance school, social, and self-care responsibilities.

Extracurricular activities pursued just to get into college don't prepare them. On the other hand, babysitting, dog walking, waitressing, scooping ice cream, and other after-school jobs may not impress admissions officers, but they do endow girls with a work ethic, confidence, and collaborative skills. Because young people are depending upon adults long after they should, colleges around the country are rectifying undergraduates' life skill deficits by offering classes in "adulting." The response has been overwhelmingly positive.

• • •

Fortunately, there is much you can do before your daughter leaves home. Arming her with skills that foster competence and confidence may require reexamining long-held beliefs. The next chapter discusses the principles of parenting intentionally, which will allow you not only to develop a close, loving relationship with your teen or tween, but also to encourage her to become a sensible, perceptive, and resilient young woman who can take good care of herself, make good choices, and accomplish her goals.

CHAPTER FOUR

Parenting with Intention

My neighbor's recent outdoor concert to celebrate the release of her twenty-six-year-old daughter's first CD was not only a musical delight, but also a heartwarming glimpse into a loving mother-daughter relationship. Between these women there was remarkable ease, obvious affection, admiration, and good humor. When Kate sang her original songs, Natalie became transfixed, her face transformed by unmistakable, pure joy. There was no doubt that this mother was kvelling, the Yiddish term for feeling extraordinary pleasure and bursting with pride.

As I sat in that lush, fragrant garden, savoring Kate's soulful voice, it struck me that this is what every mother hopes for: seeing her daughter using her talents, doing what she loves best, and authentically expressing her truth, surrounded by supportive family members, friends, and community—all while delighting in the intimacy of their mother-daughter relationship. What more could a parent ask for?

Well, you might be thinking, a road map for getting to that point would be nice.

This chapter gives you guiding principles for developing a close, trusting, and enduring mother-daughter connection that research and experience suggest will best usher your teen through adolescence as well as create a foundation for your future adult-to-adult relationship.

What You Can't Control

Realistically, you won't have complete control over how your daughter turns out. If only! Her infancy probably served as a crash course on the limits of your maternal clout. If not, her teen years probably will. From the outset, it is important to accept that although you are a powerful force in your daughter's life, you are not omnipotent. Other factors, many beyond your control, will contribute to the young woman she becomes. This reality may be scary, humbling, liberating, or possibly all of the above.

Like all children, your daughter is born with a particular temperament. How she is wired predisposes how she thinks, perceives the world, learns, and responds to people. Some girls come out of the womb exquisitely sensitive, hot-tempered, and impulsive; others are easygoing, imperturbable, and cautious. Your daughter may start out of the gate at a crawl or a gallop. If you have two or more daughters who couldn't be more different, you're probably already sold on Mother Nature's supreme influence.

Depending on your daughters' diverse strengths, challenges, and personalities, you may be a different mother to each. Sally, mother of sixteen-year-old fraternal twins, tells me, "One of my daughters is überresponsible and can find her way around any city by herself, while the other has her head in the clouds, can't remember to turn off the stove, and has to ask people how to get around her own high school. They need entirely different mothers."

Once your little girl enters school, any illusion of control dwindles with each successive grade. Random happenings—both positive and negative—can affect her sense of security, acceptance, contentment, and confidence. Whether each year is wonderful or turns her life upside down depends on the intermix of students in her classes, whether her teachers are warm and supportive or critical and harsh, and if her friends are loyal or not.

As you're mothering your daughter, life happens. Many women I speak with in my office, at speaking events, and during interviews share stories of being diagnosed with breast cancer and other life-threatening illnesses during girls' adolescent years. Other moms undergo painful treatments, emergency surgeries, and months of grueling recuperation and rehabilitation. Some women are psychiatrically hospitalized for bouts of mental illness. These stories illustrate that when highly stressful life events are handled thoughtfully, mothers can foster daughters' capacity for compassion and resiliency while growing closer to them.

Evelyn, for example, tells me that when her daughter was in fifth grade, "my breast cancer recurred and Lisbeth saw Mom lose her hair, get sick, and stay in the hospital for weeks at a time." Her voice trembles as she recalls, "Lisbeth thought I was going to die. She was there and saw all of it. She watched every horrific bit of it." Evelyn and her husband vowed to always be direct with Lisbeth. While giving her age-appropriate information and honest reassurance, they admitted what they didn't know. Lisbeth, now seventeen, says her mother's illness inspired her to go to nursing school—and to get serious about the high school science courses she needs to apply.

Life also happens to girls themselves, sometimes from the moment of birth—or even before. Many mothers today go through months or years of uncomfortable, expensive infertility treatments. Multiple women told me that conceiving their daughters took ten years of in vitro fertilization. Others had high-risk pregnancies, gave birth prematurely, or had gravely sick newborns whose survival was uncertain. These traumatic beginnings fundamentally shape mother-daughter bonds.

Julietta tells me that thirteen-year-old Gianna is "spoiled because she is an only child and I was told I wouldn't be able to have a baby. I had so many complications that I was in the hospital at six months and stayed there until Gianna was born—at thirty weeks and 3.8 pounds. It was a struggle to have her and carry her. We both almost died. By rights she shouldn't even be here."

As a result, Julietta acknowledges, "It makes me give in to her more than I should. But when Gianna gives me attitude, I have to step back and remember that the reason she's fighting me so much now is that she had to fight from the beginning. Her feistiness is actually a strength."

Life events that imperil your hopes for your daughter can make you feel utterly helpless. Serious or chronic illnesses, learning problems, family turmoil, traumas, and other disruptions of childhood can affect her cognitively, socially, and emotionally. Ambitious high school students may fall ill, preventing them from taking college entrance exams. Injuries may steal athletic hopes. Harper, sixteen, was an elite gymnast anticipating college recruitment—and a likely scholarship—until complications from foot surgery dashed her (and her parents') dreams.

You may see collateral damage, as well. After several concussions forced her to stop playing soccer, Fiona, fifteen, missed getting together with her teammates after practices, games, and dinners. She felt isolated, withdrew to her room, and became more anxious and depressed. Her mother struggled to find an activity that could help Fiona reconnect with her peers: "We sent her on a mission trip to build schools in South America with money we didn't have."

Principles of Intentional Parenting

Fortunately, there is much you *can* control in raising your teen or tween. You can provide the experience and support she needs to become an authentic, emotionally resilient, self-disciplined, and interpersonally skilled young woman. This is, of course, a tall order. Winging it and hoping she turns out okay is too big a risk. Instead, a thoughtful, proactive, flexible, and knowledgeable approach is called for. These are the elements of parenting intentionally.

Self-Awareness

The most essential tool in your parenting toolbox is self-awareness. It is crucial to appreciate how your own family background and home environment shaped the mother you've become. Did you grow up experiencing harsh conditions, frequent moves, or poverty? Are you still grappling with strict religious, moral, or political beliefs that were indoctrinated in you? Whether you were raised by a struggling single parent; an unpredictable, volatile alcoholic; or a narcissist who always came first greatly influences your approach in raising your own daughter.

Working with women and teens, I see time and again how maternal self-awareness can prevent lifelong heartache. Too many adults—in every stage of life—still struggle with fallout from troubled mother-daughter relationships. Even decades later, devastating disappointments, unresolved conflicts, neglect, and mistreatment continue to erode emotional well-being. Such experiences weigh on women like a heavy, uncomfortable coat.

Wanda says, "I think my mother was insecure and competitive with me. She had a hard time complimenting me. We had horrible conversations. Her hurtful words were so powerful, I always have them in my heart and head." When I ask Wanda what she is doing differently with her three nearly grown daughters, she says, "Think before you talk."

Rosie, who suffered from low self-esteem and body image issues throughout her life, tells me, "My mother was very hard on me, very critical. I always reached out to try to get her encouragement and approval. But I'd always be disappointed in her reaction. I'm the most accomplished of my siblings in terms of career, which always made me wonder why she had this animosity toward me."

Reflecting on what you bring to mother-daughter interactions—feelings, idiosyncrasies, internal conflicts, and so forth—pays dividends by minimizing unhappy misunderstandings and needless conflict. Being open to acknowledging and apologizing for your part in difficulties between you and your teen demonstrates the collaboration, give-and-take, and cooperation that are the fabric of all healthy relationships.

Even if you are not inclined toward introspection, when your daughter thrusts a metaphorical mirror in your face you will be forced to confront your habits and quirks. Girls are usually delighted to "help" mothers improve by pointing out not only flaws, but also any inconsistencies between words and actions. Your astute tween or teen will make you walk the walk. To prepare for this eventuality, do some reflection by asking yourself the following questions.

HOW SENSITIVE AND REACTIVE ARE YOU TO FEELINGS?

Because of upbringing and/or temperament, some women's discomfort with the emotional realm makes them avoid feelings as if they were toxic. If your MO is keeping peace at all costs, you might extinguish even a flicker of irritation before it can erupt into anger, let alone a heated conflict.

If this is your emotional style, you probably already know that burying feelings is neither authentic nor healthy. For one, emotions provide valuable information that prompts making positive changes. Suppressing feelings is also exhausting, a waste of energy that could be used more constructively. Plus, unless unpleasant emotions are addressed, they are wont to chafe, fester, and erupt unproductively.

Or perhaps your family doesn't hold back on emotions. In your household, whatever feelings parents and teens have are expressed spontaneously, continually, and sometimes loudly. As Marcie describes, "We're all yellers. Lots of times we're all screaming at once. In one second, though, it's done. We love each other like nothing else. That's the dynamic in our house."

As a general rule, aim for moderation—neither a reflexive nor a restrictive approach to managing emotions. This optimizes communication and enriches mother-daughter relations.

DO YOU ENCOURAGE YOUR DAUGHTER'S AUTONOMY?

Despite knowing that teens need to grow up, it can be hard for mothers to cede the involvement and authority that have been part of their maternal identity for more than a decade. Edith, a single mother, took pride in being able to help her daughter solve whatever problems arose in her life. But now that her twenty-seven-year-old still lives at home, she says, "Maybe by always fixing things for her, I gave her the message she couldn't do it on her own."

Carolina, on the other hand, respects that her teen and tween daughters "want their space. My sixteen-year-old is pulling away from me and wants her independence. It's hard for me, even though I know it's normal. I want to stay connected and know what they're up to. I think back to when I was a teen, and then I can remember why my girls are doing what they are. It also makes me appreciate when they go out to lunch with me."

DO YOU GET UPSET ABOUT TRIVIAL THINGS—OR FOR NO APPARENT REASON?

When you speak to your daughter, does the conversation start out about one thing and quickly escalate into an argument about something else entirely? Do you find yourself getting more riled up than you know deep down is warranted? Noticing this is a great first step. Next, try to figure out what it is that's *really* bothering you.

In my experience, the top culprit in such scenarios is usually fear. Maternal anxiety is rampant these days. The most recent American Psychological Association *Stress in America* survey found that 70 percent of parents say family responsibilities are a significant source of stress in their lives. Against a backdrop of life-and-death fears and sharply increased pandemic-related stress about tweens' (76%) and older teens' (67%) schooling, everyday worries about girls' safety and other catastrophes have become surefire catalysts for more extreme reactions.

Jessie, fifteen, tells me, "I asked my mom if I could go to the movies with my friends Friday night. She started yelling about how it was too late and the theaters are too dangerous on Friday night. What? She really thinks I'm gonna die if I go to the movies at the mall? She kept saying we should go to a Saturday matinee, which I'm not. That is so weird. I told her that she was totally overreacting and she didn't like that. She totally freaked out."

Being Present

When you practice intentional parenting, you commit to making your best effort to be present—physically and emotionally—when your tween needs you most. This isn't always easy. Women are busy. You may be taking care of several children; a spouse or partner; aging or ailing parents; employees; and coworkers, friends, or siblings who need support. In the best of times, juggling all these responsibilities may make it hard to give your daughter the attention she would like. As Suzan describes, "Lots of times when my fifteen-year-old wants to talk to me, I'm holding the baby, trying to get two little boys off to school, and rushing to get to work."

But it's important to pay attention when your tween may be most vulnerable, such as in the after-school hours. After holding it together during a long school day, behaving as teachers expect and navigating complex social dynamics, girls return home eager to exhale, shed their facades, and be truly themselves. But still-unprocessed thoughts and emotions from daily experiences swirl in their heads, leaving them feeling out of sorts or overwhelmed—precisely when homework responsibilities loom.

This is when your daughter's worst impulses may come to light. Teens "in a mood" often take out distress on the mothers whose emotional support they need. As you well know, your tween might roll her eyes in disgust, slam her bedroom door, or hurl accusations (e.g., "You're the worst mother ever" or "You don't understand anything" or "You're so clueless"). If anything, this might make you *less* eager to be around her. You could, in fact, be tempted to send her to her room—or to take shelter in yours.

And yet, ironically, this is when your daughter is most desperate for your emotional presence. Her irritability and unreasonableness are signs of pain. Despite teens' and tweens' professed desire for autonomy, many also have competing needs for mothers' nurturance. While answering your questions monosyllabically and rejecting your advice outright, your daughter may crave the hot cocoa or favorite snack you make for her. If you are still at work, calling to say hi and check in can similarly assure her of how important she is to you (even if she doesn't act like that when you call).

As the one constant in her unpredictable, often turbulent teen world, your daughter counts on you as her ballast. She depends on you to provide reality checks, help her disentangle confusing thoughts, and ease overwhelming feelings. When you don't give up on her despite her carrying on, acting obnoxiously, or goading you into a fight, you prove—more convincingly than any words could—that you can see and trust in the essential goodness within her.

Being physically present does not guarantee emotional availability, as a colleague and I witnessed while having lunch. A woman with a cellphone pressed to her ear came into the café with a girl who looked about eight, presumably her daughter. Over the next hour, the woman continued to talk on the phone while she ordered, ate, and paid the check. She was so engrossed in her call that she was oblivious to the little girl getting up from the table and amusing herself by spinning around the restaurant.

Mothers, being all too human, cannot always be present—physically or emotionally. On occasion, urgent matters or your own emotional state will distract you. This is not problematic unless it becomes a pattern—or goes unacknowledged. Apologizing for not giving your daughter your full attention and telling her when you will be able to do so makes her more likely to think she matters to you.

When I think of mothers with an unwavering presence, Emily comes to mind. She showed remarkable grace throughout her sixteen-year-old's lengthy mental health crisis, remaining closely connected and attuned to her daughter. When Anabel's social life, emotional stability, and grades started to crumble, she became increasingly hostile to her mother. Accusing Emily of giving her no space and always badgering her with questions, Anabel declared she wanted to live with a friend rather than be in the same house as her mother.

Although terribly confused and hurt, Emily stayed the course. She was careful not to intrude into Anabel's room or insist that her daughter come out to speak to her. But Emily never withdrew. She regularly knocked on Anabel's door to check on her, ask if she could help, or offer something to eat. This went on for weeks, with no sign of a thaw in Anabel's icy stance.

Then, out of nowhere, Anabel announced in therapy that she and her mother were getting along well. This coincided with Anabel's recognition that her emotional demons were draining her coping reserves. She was able to admit that the urge to self-medicate with alcohol and drugs had become too overwhelming to resist. Finally ready to address her problems, Anabel knew in her heart of hearts she could count on her mother to help. Instead of denouncing Emily as the enemy, Anabel embraced her as the ally she had been all along.

Had Emily reacted angrily, chastised her daughter, punished her, or withdrawn during this long process, things might have turned out badly. Anabel almost certainly would have used her dwindling emotional energy to fight back rather than to address her own mental health. But Emily's steady love and presence freed Anabel to look inward instead, which jump-started her recovery.

This is how, through the power of attentive, intentional mother-daughter relationships, women can be beacons for teens who stray off the path of personal and emotional well-being.

Conveying Values

Now more than ever, young people have to depend on parents to convey values that help them put things in perspective. Teens who turn to peers or the internet for information are exposed to a tsunami of material that can be exciting, confusing, or downright disturbing. What these sources rarely provide is moral guidance. Maryanne, an art teacher and mother of a teen daughter, describes seeing increasing evidence that this is what her students need:

> "I gave them an assignment to use Google Images to find pictures of someone they look up to. I was expecting basketball stars, or maybe celebrities. What I got were YouTube stars. Kids watch video after video of YouTubers glorifying

> negative things, like eating something and throwing up. They're distorting the values that parents and educators are trying to instill."

As a mother, you are instrumental in setting standards for your daughter. Personal and family values shape your expectations, including what you praise, what you criticize, and how you respond to disappointing behavior. One woman told me, "What I'd really like is a good filter to know: When do I take something on? What is something I should be concerned about and put my energy toward? And when do I just let go?"

The priorities you bring to parenting your teen are that filter. Clear-eyed values are the North Star of intentional parenting, a reliable reference point guiding your decision-making when you're confused or fear you've lost your way. So take some time to reflect on and clarify your principles.

You probably want to stay close to your daughter, get along well with her, and keep her safe. Most likely, you want her to have a joyful, fulfilling life and enjoy healthy relationships with people she cherishes. Maybe you'd like her to pursue passions and find gratifying work. Beyond that, you may envision her as kind, gracious, strong, and independent. You may prioritize personal qualities such as hard work, trustworthiness, assertiveness, compassion, self-confidence, resourcefulness, social savviness, wit, spirituality, generosity, tenacity, or gratitude.

What have you learned from your own mother, aunts, teachers, grandmothers, and other female role models that you hope to emulate with your daughter? Conversely, what would you prefer to do differently? Could your hopes for her arise from your own unfulfilled dreams, past disappointments, or lost opportunities? Can you relegate less crucial or relevant concerns to the back burner, or perhaps let go of them entirely?

Think about where you stand on controversial issues. What are your beliefs about teens using alcohol and other substances? Do you expect your adult daughter to be a teetotaler? When do you believe it is appropriate for your teen to date? How do you feel about sexual exploration and premarital sex? How would you respond to your daughter announcing an unplanned pregnancy?

Being crystal clear about your positions is crucial. That is because if you try to promote values you don't truly believe in, it won't work. Your daughter will sense your ambivalence and your arguments will be ignored. Losing credibility with her will weaken the potency of any convictions you advocate in the future. At the same time, your beliefs may change. Your teen's maturity, persuasive new information, and changing circumstances could at some point convince you to tweak the moral equation you use to guide your parenting decisions.

If this is the case, be truthful about what made you change your mind. Hearing your reasoning will model for your daughter how to sort through her own values. She will appreciate your openness to rethinking and shifting your position. Don't worry about her seeing you as flip-flopping; teens and tweens can differentiate between mothers truly having an epiphany versus "caving in" because they're too tired to argue or too afraid to make daughters unhappy.

Self-Care

When you think of parenting intentionally, the need to take care of yourself may not even register on your radar. But mothering a teen is a time-consuming as well as physically and emotionally strenuous endeavor. As

Pamela put it, "Tolerating all of what teenagers are doing—the back talk, the persistent 'Can I go downtown after school?'—can wear you down. Her needs, her tone, and the urgency of it all, it's exhausting."

Like many women, you may find it hard to compartmentalize. Whatever bothers you about your daughter—her attitude, her worrisome dejection, a failed class, or a wretched breakup—hangs over you, crowding out everything else in your head. That is, you obsess. Even a minor argument with your teen or tween could haunt you for the rest of the day or rob you of desperately needed sleep.

As families live farther apart and connect with fewer neighbors, women are increasingly isolated from potential supports. By the teenage years, playdates are a thing of the past and there are fewer school or sport events where you can mingle, commiserate, and swap info with other mothers. Plus, in this intensely competitive environment, some parents whitewash problems that could damage girls' reputations or status for college and internships. All this encourages you to imagine it is only your own teen who struggles with challenges.

For all these reasons, seeking support and taking care of yourself are not luxuries, but necessities. If reaching out to a local friend feels uncomfortable, confide in someone from childhood or college who lives elsewhere. Or a reassuring sibling, parent, aunt, or cousin whose judgment—and discretion—you value. It can be liberating just to put your concerns, fears, frustration, sadness, or self-criticism out there. Aired in the light of day, things seem less formidable than when kept under wraps. Most likely, you will learn that your most shameful maternal thoughts, feelings, and transgressions are rather ordinary, if not universal.

Women who choose self-care over self-sacrifice are best able to hang in there when daughters go through difficult times and need them most. Replenishing your inner resources helps you to stay engaged when, for instance, your daughter goes to battle with you to figure out what she really believes; she feels so unlovable that she becomes demanding to test your devotion; or she clings to you as her rock when her world feels like it's falling apart.

Giving yourself permission to practice good self-care is like putting on your own oxygen mask first. Carve out time to nourish your soul, whatever this means to you: socializing, pursuing hobbies, treating yourself to a bit of pampering, traveling, reading, meditating, or exercising. It might not take much for you to feel refreshed. When my infant daughter was colicky for five months, an hour wandering the aisles of the local super-drugstore was soothing beyond reason. Whatever works for you, go for it.

Modeling Healthy Relationships

Perhaps the most important element of intentional parenting is creating a healthy relationship with your teen or tween that not only will help her flourish during adolescence, but also will become her template for connecting with friends, teachers, romantic partners, and future colleagues and assistants. You'll likely want to demonstrate how she can be authentic and comfortable in her own skin, empathize with others, and express genuine feelings. By setting reasonable boundaries in your mother-daughter relationship, she'll also learn it is okay to expect reciprocity—as opposed to always gratifying others' needs at the expense of her own.

Consider this, as well: If your daughter has children of her own someday, how would you like her to raise your future grandchildren? What do you want to show her now, by example, about how to be a mother?

For relationships to thrive, both parties have to be committed to doing the work. But in the case of mothers and teenage daughters, mothers bear more responsibility because they are the adults. In my clinical work, I see that when girls are unilaterally blamed for problems arising during the teen years, everyone suffers. This is why women who model healthy relationships for daughters have to be scrupulously self-aware, receptive to feedback, accountable for their own missteps, and able to modify their behavior when necessary.

Nan recognizes that her knee-jerk reactions can harm her daughter. "When I get frustrated with her, she always says, 'Mom, are you okay? I'm sorry.' But I have to tell her, 'No, no, you're okay. I'm the one who's sorry.'" By taking responsibility for her part in tensions rather than allowing her daughter to take all the blame, Nan is inoculating her daughter against the destructive belief that she is not—and never will be—good enough in her mother's eyes.

Self-reflection takes courage; it is often hard and sometimes painful. As you read about what constitutes healthy relationships, be honest about the things you need to work on. Habits are hard to change, so set small, achievable goals and feel good about accomplishing them. Also practice self-compassion; beating yourself up over slipups helps no one. Like all humans, you are a work in progress. Following are some of the key elements of healthy relationships that you can demonstrate to your daughter by example.

GOOD COMMUNICATION

The ability to converse with others—to listen attentively and to express thoughts effectively—is at the heart of strong and satisfying personal and work relationships. As you know, these skills take practice. Think of every conversation throughout your daughter's teen years as a potential learning experience—for you as well as for her. The talks that make you feel best and most assured ("Yes! I nailed this!"), as well as the most exasperating and soul-depleting exchanges ("Will this *ever* go well?"), are all opportunities to refine communication skills.

HAVING A VOICE

Since you would like your daughter to learn how to articulate her thoughts, concerns, and desires to people most important to her, she has to practice with you. Be prepared for whatever pops out of her mouth. Unlike when she was seven, it may not be that you're the best, prettiest, and nicest mother in the world. Instead, what your teen or tween might be eager to express is her displeasure with you or the decisions you make about her life.

How women respond to girls speaking their minds varies tremendously. If your mother interpreted your complaints or protests as disrespectful back talk or your parents ruled with an iron fist, intolerant of perceived challenges to their authority, you might reflexively view your teen's words as unacceptable. That could make it hard to reframe her comments as positive signs of sharpening her observations, opinions, reasoning, and communication skills.

Talulah, mother of a fourteen-year-old, says, "I work hard to have a different relationship with my daughter than I had with my own mother. We have most conversations in the car, where there's less eye contact. She challenges me, but in a good way. Like, 'Why do you do this, or that?' I'm glad my daughter feels comfortable asking me why she can't go to someone's house. It's not a disrespect thing. It's normal and healthy. These questions help my daughter to grow."

Verbally abusive behavior, on the other hand, should neither be ignored nor condoned. Differentiate developmentally appropriate and desirable behavior—challenging why you made certain decisions, voicing her views, pointing out what you did that upset her—from what is off-limits. Whether it is swearing, raising her voice, name-calling, getting in your face, or telling you to "shut up," draw a big red line in the proverbial sand to make clear what is not okay for you.

EMPATHY AND VALIDATION

Think about your most treasured relationships. The special closeness and trust you enjoy are probably based on mutual understanding, empathy, and respect. Constructive criticism is offered lovingly and tactfully. With these select people, you can be yourself, share your innermost feelings, and expect to be supported, not diminished.

These are, of course, the same ingredients of healthy mother-daughter relationships. Admittedly, it is challenging to sympathize with teen girls who are being difficult or acting up. When daughters experience mothers as lacking empathy, however, they feel utterly invalidated. Nothing more powerfully undermines their sense of self as well as connections with mothers.

Consider these exchanges:

> **Daughter:** I can't take this. We had so much work put on us today, on top of what we got all week, and

I can't possibly get it all done. I don't know what I'm going to do.

Mom: I'm busy, too. I did the cleaning. I grocery shopped. I made dinner. And I did my paying job. You've got it so much better than I do.

Daughter: You just don't understand what it's like to be a teenager today!

Mom: But I do! I've been through this before.

Daughter: No, you haven't! You had a pager! You didn't have what I'm going through. You didn't have social media, the same pressures, the same ideals that you're supposed to live up to. Never mind—

OR

Daughter: It was an awful day, Mom. I'm soooo stressed I don't know what to do. I'm superanxious . . .

Mom: You're too young for that. When I was your age, I was superhappy.

Daughter: You didn't live through the generation I do, Mom. There are different problems and different solutions. Obviously, you don't realize that. Just forget I said anything!

For mothers, a daughter's distress elicits all sorts of reactions. Worry or anxiety may prompt you to jump in to fix, or at least ease, her problems. You may want to reassure your teen—and yourself—that her experiences are perfectly normal, no different from other girls her age. The trouble is, this approach deprives your teen of support and commiseration. Worse, she may think you are minimizing or dismissing her feelings because you find them unacceptable or she's wrong to voice them.

Girls react far differently when mothers respond empathically:

> **Daughter:** I can't take this. We had so much work put on us today, on top of what we got all week, and I can't possibly get it all done. I don't know what I'm going to do.
>
> **Mom:** I'm sorry you had such a bad day. Stress is awful. Do you want to talk about what happened?

OR

> **Mom:** Sounds like you've got a lot on your plate right now. How can I help?

OR

> **Mom:** What can you do right now to relieve some of the pressure?

AUTHENTICITY

Because you want your daughter to be herself in relationships, to be genuine rather than a chameleon who tries to please others, it is important to model authenticity. Yet it is also hard to be completely transparent. To keep the peace and avoid making waves with a moody teen, you might be overly accommodating or walk on eggshells. Expressing dissatisfaction or irritation can seem a fool's errand if all you will get for your trouble is a daughter stomping off in an angry huff. Besides, who can blame you for just wanting your daughter to like you?

But when other people may be unwilling or unable to be honest with her, she has to count on you for feedback. Expressing your disappointment or displeasure in her attitude and/or behavior promotes her growing understanding of right and wrong, teaches her what does and doesn't serve her well in relationships, and guides her to become her best self.

Granted, telling your teen you're unwilling to jump through hoops to fulfill her every desire will probably displease her. But if she is unreasonably demanding in relationships, who else will tell her that her overentitlement is off-putting? Plus, if you don't want other people to ask too much of your daughter or to take her for granted, it is wise to model for her how to set these limits.

Chrissie told me a rather classic story about her teen, who "excels in mommy manipulation; she knows every button to push." During her nightly meltdown about homework, Lydia, fifteen, told her mother, "You *never* help me!" Although Chrissie knows this is untrue, the accusation nonetheless hit a nerve because she feels guilty about having to travel for work. So, although she had been looking forward all week to her one yoga class, Chrissie skipped it.

This sort of emotional blackmail helps neither mother nor daughter. Chrissie resented being manipulated and missing her class, and Lydia was rewarded for shirking her work and acting in a controlling manner. Being a good mother does not require dropping everything and neglecting yourself. It may be exceedingly difficult to give yourself permission to honor your own needs and set limits with the daughter you adore. But remind yourself that saying no teaches a lifelong lesson that I find women and girls often need to learn: it is perfectly okay to honor your own needs along with attending to others.

Besides, by your daughter's adolescence, if not before, it is pointless to repress or disguise your true feelings. Girls are gifted at intuiting them. Neurobiological research tells us that in early to midadolescence, teens are maximally sensitive to facial expressions of anger and fear. When your daughter accuses you of "yelling," even when you speak in a perfectly calm, even voice, she is responding to your underlying mood more than to your words. Plus, it is counterproductive to deny what your daughter accurately senses. To facilitate her developing good people skills, you want to teach her to trust her own perceptions.

APPROPRIATE BOUNDARIES

In all healthy relationships, individuals are separate rather than enmeshed. A *Wall Street Journal* article recognized that what often undermines mother-daughter connections is women blurring the boundaries between girls and themselves. When I was interviewed for this piece, I emphasized that what gets mothers in trouble is seeing daughters as extensions of themselves rather than as separate and unique individuals.

As a mother, respecting boundaries means that you differentiate your daughter from yourself. You recognize that her thoughts, feelings, and experiences are not necessarily yours; conversely, you don't assume that she sees the world as you do or shares all your beliefs. This is not the case for Raina, seventeen, who says, "I can't figure out my personal issues until I'm out of the house. Some were never brought up, and others I was told I have that I don't actually have."

In your teen's peer relationships, healthy boundaries translate to having empathy for friends, but not taking on their troubles as if they were her own. Candace, a high school junior, describes difficulty drawing these lines: "When my teammates were going through horrible things, I'd skip the game because I was too stressed until I knew they were okay. If my friend at school is sad, I immediately skip class and see if they're okay. I can't get on with my own stuff until they've made peace with it."

Seeing your daughter as her own person may seem easy. But when powerful feelings infuse mother-daughter relationships, boundaries can be blurred and perceptions of situations may become distorted. During a class meeting, Thea, fifteen, told me, "My mother has a problem because I have kinda long sideburns. She keeps telling me to shave them or people are going to make fun of me." Thea knows that when her mother was her age, peers ridiculed her for being awkward and funny looking. "But," Thea says, "I just don't care what people think. I wish she would stop making this such an issue."

Audrey, a more self-aware mother, shared a poignant story of having to repair her relationship with her thirteen-year-old daughter after overidentifying with her. "When Dana's two best friends excluded her from their plans, her heartbreak became my heartbreak," she admits. "It became very personal to me. I needed to make everything better, but at first I didn't know that I wasn't helping my daughter."

Because Dana's pain became her pain, Audrey was unable to see what her daughter really needed. She says, "I tried to make her feel better by saying, 'Oh, we all go through this,' and 'I think it was mostly the field hockey team that they invited.' But it didn't work because she knew better. She told me to stop making excuses for her friends and to stop pitying her. Then I called one of the girls' parents and that backfired terribly. My daughter stopped talking to me. She wanted me to leave her alone. That's when I knew I had to switch gears."

After soul-searching, Audrey reestablished healthy boundaries and revised how she approached her daughter's problems. She was able to explain to Dana, "My heart was breaking because I knew yours was. It wasn't pity; it was hurt because I knew you were hurt. I just wanted to take away your pain. I know you just want those girls to be nice to you again, and so do I. How do you want to move forward?"

TRUSTWORTHINESS

Trust is central to the mother-daughter bond and to all healthy relationships. Questioning whether your teen is honest with you can send your maternal anxiety into the danger zone. After all, how can you ever be assured of her safety and well-being? But to encourage your daughter to (a) tell you information you may not like, and (b) come clean about her regrettable decisions, you have to demonstrate that you, too, are trustworthy.

Jordana describes the fine line mothers often walk: "My daughter was reluctant to tell me that her group has been avoiding our family friend's son because he's always vaping. She was afraid I'd reveal that to his mother and she'd become a social pariah for tattling. I feel conflicted because it takes a village, and I want to be protective of other kids the way you hope other mothers would look out for your girls. But I'm so thankful she could tell me."

Teens courageously reveal info about themselves or friends only if they don't have to worry about how mothers will react. Do you say the first thing that comes to mind, or think carefully before responding? Are you likely to flip out, or keep your composure? Raise your voice, or speak softly? Criticize and punish her, or nonjudgmentally discuss the situation?

Melanie, seventeen, spoke in therapy about finally confiding to her mother that her boyfriend had become overly controlling and pressured her to do things sexually that physically hurt her: "My mother didn't say how awful that must have been or ask if I'm okay. She just started yelling at me about what was wrong with me that I would let some loser treat me like that. I felt even worse about myself after I'd told her. I knew it would be a mistake."

Thorny issues are best handled with kid gloves. The more you can demonstrate that you will react to upsetting information with calmness, diplomacy, respect, and your daughter's best interest in mind, the more likely she is to confide in you. Be up-front about whether you can keep what she tells you confidential—or specify what you will divulge and to whom. Including her in this process minimizes the chance of her thinking you betrayed her by going behind her back.

When Alyce, thirteen, told her mother that a classmate was being bullied on social media, she begged Rochelle not to tell anyone. But Rochelle explained that cyberbullying is a serious problem, and that she was proud her daughter was brave enough to get help for the girl. Wisely, Rochelle asked what Alyce was worried about. She was then able to reassure her daughter that when reporting this to school personnel she would not give Alyce's name.

Treasuring Your Time Together

Finally, parenting intentionally means taking a step back now and then to be grateful for the daughter in your life. It's too easy to get caught up in day-to-day routines and challenges and forget to spend enjoyable time together. With the serious issues you may think you have to focus on, it can be hard to remember to laugh. Trust me, despite days that go on forever and phases you fear will never end, the adolescent years go by in a flash. Soon enough, girls go off to college, move across the country, and eventually start families of their own.

That is precisely what happened, in fact, with my colicky baby girl. While I now treasure our adult-to-adult relationship, I'm also grateful to look back and relish memories of our weekly mother-daughter breakfasts and special travel adventures during her teen years.

Don't Take It Personally

No matter how diligently you strive to be an ideal mother, it is a given that you will fail. As a wise training psychologist once told me, "Even the perfect mother stinks." The reflection you did throughout this chapter will hopefully give you a better idea of the strengths you bring to the mother-daughter relationship as well as what might be improved. This knowledge allows you to consider valid criticisms while not taking to heart the meritless barbs of testy teens.

Remember that distressed girls often use mothers as scapegoats. Even if you *were* perfect, she might still point out, noisily and unashamedly, all the ways you disappoint or infuriate her. Keep in mind that girls are hypersensitive to their mothers' behavior during these years, especially around friends. Fears of being judged by their mothers' actions can result in hyperbolic reactions or interpretations. A sense of humor can be your lifeline.

Chloe, fourteen, told me, "My mom and me went to the mall today with my friend and my mom was singing and dancing and talking to herself—in PUBLIC! And she's so loud! I'm like, 'Mom, please just calm down. Everyone's staring and thinks you're crazy.'" More likely, Chloe's mother may have hummed a few notes under her breath. Someone may have smiled in greeting. But in front of her friend, Chloe perceived—and reported—this as if her mother had been performing in a flash mob for Glee in the middle of the mall.

Although being the target of your teen's wrath feels awful and unfair, it's actually a huge compliment. I'm not kidding. If she didn't feel secure in your absolute love, your daughter would not have the luxury of taking such liberties with you. Meanwhile, be content with doing your best, and accept that what your best looks like varies from day to day—and sometimes from moment to moment.

• • •

Now that you're more familiar with parenting intentionally, it is time to zero in on the daughter who will be your traveling companion throughout this journey. What does she bring to the relationship? The next chapter discusses the art and science of truly knowing—and coming to terms with—who she is at her core. Reconciling any differences between your ideal teen and the daughter you are raising forges a trusting, empathic, and nonjudgmental connection. Not only will you get along better with her, but also you will encourage her to become the most authentic, healthiest version of herself.

CHAPTER FIVE

Mothering the Daughter You Have

It's hard as a parent to help girls become what you would hope they will be. You have to accept their weaknesses. Instead of "this is how it has to be," you have to be a lot more flexible.

—FRAN, MOTHER OF GWEN, 15

There's such a narrow range of what's acceptable now. But my kid is who my kid is. I'll try the best I can. If you're always pushing for something else, you're invalidating who girls are and they have more mental health issues. They'll grow up thinking they're not good enough as they are.

—MAUREEN, MOTHER OF CHARLIE, 17

Kids who are more successful have a sense of themselves and good self-esteem. You can't control peers, or whether a

> teacher takes a shine to your daughter or has it out for her. There are many different factors. But parents have to do their part. If you don't take her where she is, nothing else is going to work.
>
> —SUZETTE, MOTHER OF LORNA, 16

A mantra for raising authentic, socially skilled, and emotionally resilient girls might be: "Mother the daughter you have." No principle is more vital for daughters to grow up feeling known, validated, and loved for who they really are. If, instead, mothers hold girls to idealized or unrealistic ideas of who they *should* be, teens grow up not feeling truly seen, heard, or understood. Worse, they believe their true selves will never be good enough.

Like all mothers, you probably have hopes for how your daughter turns out. While she was still in utero—or maybe even before that—you may have envisioned how she would look, the personality she would have, and the milestones you would share with her. After she goes through puberty, the image in your mind of your daughter as a young woman has likely come into even greater focus.

There is nothing wrong with having dreams for her, so long as you recognize they may not be realized—at least not right away. As teen girls try on various identities and demonstrate growing independence, you may see a chasm between the daughter you've imagined and the one who sweeps past you on her way to school in the morning. Wait, booty shorts? Multiple chains? Kohl-rimmed eyes? And what about that attitude?!

This chapter is filled with stories of women who had to work hard to mother the girls they had. But by remaining open to observing the iterations of your teen's constantly evolving self, there is less temptation to judge and thereby interrupt her maturational process. Your daughter will be freer to blossom into the best expression of herself, and you can take pride in the well-grounded, genuine, and self-assured young woman who emerges.

Becoming Herself

As teens form a clear, stable identity, they continuously test out and refine ideas about who they are and who they want to be. These days, girls have the added challenge of reconciling personas created online with more genuine identities developed through real-life interactions. It is fortunate that you can greatly affect this fundamental developmental process.

Your daughter can become authentic when she is free from pressure to measure up to an idealized version of herself, let alone someone else entirely. When she feels known and understood, she is more comfortable sharing what is truly in her heart and mind. When she trusts your enduring acceptance, your teen becomes secure in who she is. This strong and accurate sense of self infuses her with empowering self-confidence.

Girls whose mothers have clear-eyed visions of who they really are don't have to fear being rejected or losing support. Basking in mothers' unconditional love protects them from aiming for false perfection—that is, always being good and nice, never angry or jealous or selfish. These daughters are less inclined to go through the motions, creating faux selves in the hopes of making themselves more acceptable.

Authentic teens learn to be in touch with the thoughts and feelings that reside within. Rather than needing to please others, they look inward to honor the inner voices that serve as spokesgirls of their consciences—and behave accordingly. Differentiating what feels right from what does not sit well with them, they act according to their values. Genuine, confident girls resist peer pressure because they are secure enough to risk others' displeasure.

Feeling sure of who they are helps teens develop and navigate healthy relationships. Their interactions are real. Rather than becoming manipulative or passive-aggressive when they feel slighted or hurt, authentic girls explain what is bothering them and ask directly for what they need. This approach obviates much of the rumormongering, backbiting, and other underhanded aggressive relational tactics that spawn teen social dramas.

In contrast, parenting the ideal teen you have in mind not only chafes at the mother-daughter bond, but also sets up girls for a whole host of emotional difficulties. To make adults proud, some teens pretend to be the people they imagine parents and teachers want them to be. Rather than explore what actually intrigues them, they act interested in topics and activities that bore them. Inauthentic teens essentially live a lie.

Feeling like constant disappointments—and sometimes unlovable—some girls begin to dislike and disparage themselves. Often, these teens become rebellious. In their minds, since they can't be the daughters their mothers want, they might as well stop trying. Or they go out of their way to become the exact opposites of the perfect teens they believe mothers envision. All these strategies promote disingenuousness. None serve girls well.

Walking a Fine Line

For sure, parenting the daughter you have is easier said than done. There is a fine line between encouraging her to become the best version of herself and pushing her to be someone she is not. When you encourage your reluctant teen to try out for the volleyball team, socialize more, or run for student government, it is often hard to know whether you are helping her to overcome impediments to growth or pushing her to do something that goes against her grain.

Similarly, it can seem like a dereliction of your motherly responsibilities to sit back and do nothing when your teen says and does things that are unusual, unexpected, or unacceptable. When pointing out her shortcomings, are you helping her to improve—or imposing overly specific, rigid ideas about how she should look, act, feel, and love? At what point does constructive criticism become mothering the daughter you *want* instead of the one you actually *have*? The key to making these judgments is being scrupulously self-aware of your own biases and goals.

Ilana learned from her work as a school psychologist what not to do with her own teen: "Parents push kids in different directions because they aren't insightful about their own needs and desires. They get pressured by other parents, and then pass that onto their kids, adding another layer to their stress." As she raises a sixteen-year-old, Ilana says, "I try not to get caught up like the parents who have to get kids into a top school. That's a setup. Where my daughter goes has to be good for her. That's what she needs to feel successful."

Deviating from Family Scripts

Familiarity can make parenting easier. You may find yourself unconsciously echoing your parents' words or expecting your daughter to follow the same path that you, her other parent, or her siblings took during adolescence. Of course, pleasant deviations from the norm are usually welcomed.

Zizi says, "My youngest daughter is an old soul. Compared to her sisters, who were so challenging I thought they'd send me to an early grave, she's strange and different—but a really welcome change! She's not a risk-taker and accepts her responsibilities. She cleans the kitchen before I even come home from work."

Rather than lumping your teen with her siblings, recognize her uniqueness. When describing her girls' approaches to schoolwork, Erika does not expect them to have the same styles. She tells me, "My older daughter is a perfectionist. She's quick, exacting, has a good memory, and loves working hard. My younger daughter is hard on herself, but more relaxed and easygoing and amenable. She has to work harder because things take her longer and she wants to do well."

Some families take this too far by assigning daughters overly distinct nicknames such as the Sweet One, the Smart One, the Messy One, and the Funny One. But monikers are limiting. Young women describe being unable to live up to such narrow expectations or unwilling to be constrained by labels they have outgrown.

Rebecca, nineteen, tells me, "I used to be supermessy. It's true, my room was a disaster. My stuff was all over the place, I had clothes on the floor, and I could never find anything. But once I got to college, it was different. I had a roommate, so I tried to be more neat. I started being organized, and now I love having a system for where everything goes. But my mom treats me like I'm still ten years old and a total mess."

Mothering the daughter you have goes beyond not comparing her with siblings, friends, and classmates. It means not judging by past behavior, defeats, or mistakes, but rather always looking with fresh eyes to mother the daughter you have in every moment. This mindfulness gives your teen freedom to grow. Acknowledging her improvements reinforces them.

Unspoken or unconscious expectations often become problematic. Your family may have rigid ideas about where everyone should go to college, which majors are worth pursuing, and the careers that are acceptable. There may be carved-in-stone standards for behavior at home and in public. A tacit yet ironclad list of requirements may restrict whom teens may date.

Mona, the mother of two grown sons and a daughter in college, tells me, "I wasn't at all prepared for the new boyfriend Vanessa brought home from college last weekend. I was utterly shocked when I saw him. His hair is bleached blond and he has tattoos completely covering one arm." In this family, the unspoken norm was a more conservative style of dress. Mona says, "Vanessa's previous boyfriends were preppy, like her brother." Fortunately, she was able to counsel herself to take a deep breath and get to know Vanessa's boyfriend, rather than react to his unexpected appearance.

It is harder when stakes rise, particularly in matters of education. I often see high school juniors and seniors who feel tremendous pressure to attend relatives' alma maters. The desire for girls to follow family scripts overrides consideration of their true capabilities and needs. This is when a mismatch between the ideal daughters mothers envision and the ones they actually have can be harmful.

Margo, sixteen, told me her parents "really want me to go to the college my father and sisters went to. Going to all the football games as a family is a big deal. My father's up at the school a lot because he's on some committee." Margo's credentials gave her a good shot at getting in. But although she enjoyed family traditions, she was self-aware enough to know this wasn't the school for her: "I'm not really into football games. I'm just not a rah-rah person. It's a big school, too, and a small school where I can get to know my teachers helps me do better."

Looking for a Mini-Me

Sometimes the daughters mothers hope for are essentially clones of themselves. This is understandable. It is human nature to be more comfortable with what is familiar. Yael describes this poignantly: "When my first daughter was born, I felt like I had known her all my life. With my second daughter, I feel like I've been getting to know her every day."

Unless you are scrupulous, mismatches in mother-daughter interests, temperaments, or goals can intrude upon parenting in big and small ways. You may prefer an outgoing, bubbly, and energetic girl who gets involved in everything and makes friends wherever she goes, but instead have a shy introvert who chooses to cozy up to books rather than people. In the reverse, if you believe your daughter should be studious, you may get upset because she always wants to make social plans.

This dynamic played out in Suzette's relationship with her daughter, Lorna, during middle school. Suzette told me, "It drives me to distraction that my twelve-year-old constantly asks for playdates. She can't be alone, and that makes her way too dependent on other people." Plus, Suzette was afraid that Lorna's need to constantly socialize would hold her back from the intellectual pursuits that were prioritized in her well-educated and accomplished family.

But when Suzette denied these requests and tried to convince her daughter that solitary time was necessary for success, Lorna felt criticized. In a joint session, Lorna spoke of feeling hurt and confused. "What's so bad about me wanting to see my friends?" she asked. "Isn't it normal for middle school kids to hang out with friends?" And she reminded her mother, "It isn't like I don't do my work. I'm in the highest math and just got picked for a special science program."

What this tween didn't know is that her mother's beliefs had little to do with her. When Suzette was Lorna's age, she had struggled at an elite school in which she was marginalized and bullied for being on scholarship. To prove her academic worthiness, Suzette hunkered down with her books. In fact, she credits this coping strategy for creating the gratifying life she now enjoys as an adult. When Lorna didn't show this same resolve, Suzette became alarmed.

Girls who are not carbon copies of mothers can be more difficult to understand, relate to, and raise. Ginny recognizes that she and her tween's disparate styles make her job harder: "Sometimes my daughter doesn't go through routines efficiently, and I don't always deal well with it. I get frustrated because she doesn't take the initiative to get ready for softball practice. But I need to be more patient and handle it better."

Callie, too, is aware that she has to take responsibility for getting through the day with her thirteen-year-old: "My daughter has attention issues. She drives me insane because while she's organized about sports, in the rest of her life her head could fall off and she wouldn't notice. I'm type A, which is a huge conflict for us because she takes forever to get herself ready. I give her tools, but she's not able to use them yet. She drags herself. When I get frustrated with her, I feel bad. I'm the adult. I have to meet her in the middle."

More significant differences raise bigger challenges. Eva's insight, mindfulness, and effort bridged a potentially troublesome chasm with her fourteen-year-old daughter. Eva sought my help, in fact, precisely because she feared her "force of nature" personality could damage Theresa's sense of self along with their mother-daughter relationship.

Eva is an accomplished professional in a highly competitive, male-oriented field. She attributes her success to a capacity to instantly see the big picture, identify relationships and patterns, and confidently make rapid-fire decisions. Her daughter, Theresa, is cut from an entirely different cloth. She is a clever girl who processes information slowly and therefore doesn't work well under pressure. She turned down placement in an accelerated science class.

Eva and I explored what she might inadvertently model for her teen. She was aware that Theresa might get the impression her mother's fast-paced style and occasional impatience was a rebuke of her own slower pace. Eva was determined to avoid Theresa interpreting being different from her mother as being inferior. When Eva told me that she was trying to "find activities we can do together that won't highlight our disparate strengths," I felt optimistic about where this mother-daughter relationship was headed.

If you think life would be much easier if only you and your daughter were more alike, be careful what you wish for. Being *too* similar can be just as troublesome. As you know, we are often irritated by traits in others that we most dislike about ourselves. Marilou says, "I definitely see things in my fifteen-year-old that I know come from me, like when she's stubborn or short-tempered. We don't get along because she learned that from me."

Bridging Gaps

Whatever differences exist between the daughter you observe and the daughter you might have envisioned having, the following strategies can help you come to terms with them so your relationship stays intact and she is free to become her most authentic and confident self.

Focus on Inner Strengths

With the notorious ups and downs of adolescence, your daughter's moods, attitudes, friendship statuses, and grades are likely to vacillate. So will various personas she briefly takes on or fads she momentarily adopts. If you react to each and every blip, you will quickly become emotionally exhausted, your daughter will think you are scrutinizing her under a microscope, and your home will become a minefield.

During this time of rapid transformation—and sometimes upheaval—it is better to focus on your daughter's inner strengths. These traits and characteristics that remain more stable over time are better predictors of her future success. When you acknowledge her assets, you powerfully validate them. Plus, your daughter feels known and appreciated.

Rather than zeroing in on how she falls short of your expectations, catch your daughter being someone you like. Tell her how much you admire her persistence, unflappability, and open-mindedness. Notice when she is nonjudgmental, warm, loving, and astute. Compliment her insightfulness, sensible decisions, and listening skills. Relish her fun-loving, adventurous spirit and unique take on the world. All this lets her know you value who she is.

Tolerate "Negative" Feelings

Girls are undeniably more pleasant to be around when cheerful, sweet, curious, grateful, and jubilant than when frustrated, anxious, envious, resentful, petulant, irritated, or furious. But all these emotions are a part of the human experience. How you respond to so-called negative feelings affects how your daughter grows up thinking of herself.

Despite this culture's strides, there is still a double standard for women who express anger or hostility. Whereas aggressive men are seen as assertive and strong, women are labeled strident or even crazy. In school, boys who engage in spirited debates with teachers are praised for participating in class, while girls who do so are seen as argumentative or disrespectful—and are more apt to be disciplined.

Your daughter should know that she does not always have to be cheerful or nice. You shouldn't expect her to be because that would be unrealistic and inauthentic. Working with Alexis, sixteen, I saw that her parents felt differently. Both had been brought up in traditional, conservative families that demanded children's respect, unquestioning obedience, and perpetual gratitude. If Alexis was sad or in a bad mood, her parents thought she didn't appreciate the life they had given her. They interpreted typical—and reasonable—teenage requests as evidence of rude, spoiled, or overly entitled behavior.

Like many teens who crave the love and approval parents withhold, Alexis tried doubly hard to be good, polite, and compliant. She inhibited assertiveness and buried all "undesirable" feelings underground. But by not allowing herself to have—much less to express—emotions that might anger or offend her parents, Alexis couldn't acknowledge all parts of herself. She was unable to embrace her whole self, flaws along with strengths, warts as well as gifts, which is necessary to function as a well-integrated, authentic person.

Manage Different Emotional Styles

Whereas some people react to problems by thinking things through, others react emotionally. This can make it hard for mothers and daughters to be in sync. Identifying and managing different emotional styles can help. Carrie, who knows her hotheadedness can overwhelm her teen, says, "My daughter takes on my stress and emotions. I try to be open and honest, but I can't expose myself too much, like how angry I am sometimes, because I don't want her to get upset. Her eyes well up and I think, 'That's not fair. What have I done?'"

The opposite is also true. Women who are even-keeled can be irritated by teens getting stirred up about minor issues. Sasha, whose daughter gets worked up about minutiae, says, "She's so dramatic telling me the details around her problem, it's like noise. I'm exhausted from hearing it but still don't know how to fix it. I have to tell her, 'Hon, we need to get past the clutter of all this drama and get to the situation so we can find a solution.'"

Expect Her to Develop in Her Own Time

Except for infancy, at no time in your daughter's life will her development be as rapid as during adolescence. She may seem to change by the day. At times, you can practically watch her blossom. Alternatively, if you're not seeing the maturational spurt you expect, you may be frustrated by your teen seeming to be stuck in old habits or behaviors that you think she should have outgrown. You may be waiting impatiently for signs of growth.

This is a good time to remind yourself that your daughter's development is not on a timetable. Don't give up. Difficult stages *will* end and she *will* change. Meanwhile, it does no good to compare her with the ideal adolescents in your mind or in real life—such as older siblings, cousins, or close friends.

As I always advise parents, "Never say never." The twelve-year-old who is practically a caricature of tween self-centeredness may suddenly become exquisitely compassionate and caring. The sullen thirteen-year-old may surprise you someday with her sudden quick wit. The fourteen-year-old who mercilessly teased her babyish younger sister may turn into her biggest defender. The fifteen-year-old who exhibits zero self-awareness may someday become so insightful and wise that all her friends seek her advice.

Although you may worry if your daughter's classmates are more academically or socially advanced, keep in mind that every girl develops at her own pace. The brain continues to mature throughout the teens and mid- to late twenties. Some girls don't blossom until college or even later. At some point, your daughter will be capable of the higher-level analysis, concept formation, critical thinking, and organization that eluded her in the younger grades.

Mothers of daughters who are wired differently or have disabilities know this all too well.

"Lindsay didn't get invited to birthday parties," Iris tells me. "She had a very difficult time socializing. Nobody accepted her because she was different. Her sensorimotor difficulties made it hard for her to know where she was in her body. She was so loud and hyper that it was hard for kids to understand her behavior." During the teen years, Iris's worry intensified. She says, "I tried to get Lindsay to have friends and to make friends. I so badly wanted her to be normal."

Once she was assured that her daughter "was going to be okay," Iris recognized her earlier error: "She's socially awkward and different, but my lack of acceptance with where she was in her development was what most harmed her. In retrospect, I realize that Lindsay had been picking up on my anxiety. It made her feel worse about herself, about not having friends."

Lindsay agreed. She told me about withdrawing to her bedroom to avoid her mother's pointed questions about who she sat with at lunch and if she had a partner for a school project. Lindsay had allies in school, which was all that mattered to her. Her mother didn't realize that Lindsay had little need for companionship. She preferred being alone, doing her own thing, rather than hanging out with peers. In fact, she admitted, "I have to work myself up, like once a month, for spending a day with friends. It's exhausting."

With her own anxiety waning, Iris was able to take Lindsay "wherever she is at. I nudge her to expand her skills at her own pace, according to what she wants and can tolerate." Lindsay is grateful for her mother's change of tack. She says, "My mom going along with what I want to do and not trying to make me different is making life easier for both of us."

Meet Her Halfway

Perhaps you love nothing more than taking in an opera or ballet, enjoying Renaissance art, and listening to jazz, but your daughter is passionate about rap, heavy metal, or boy bands. By all means, invite her along on a visit to a museum or performance. But be mindful not to make your daughter concerned about disappointing you if she doesn't become an avid fan of your favorite artist, dancer, or musician.

Show her you value her individuality by meeting her halfway. Sample her interests. If you listen to recordings of her favorite artists or take her to a concert, ask her to explain what she likes about the music. Plan an outing to the record stores she combs for her vinyl collection. Ask if you can watch her at the skateboard park to see what she finds exhilarating. Take her to browse the vintage clothing stores she loves; you may get a kick out of finding an unexpected treasure, too.

Expand Narrow Definitions of Success

Although mothers' visions of success usually come from a loving place, based on wishes for daughters to live their best possible lives, fixed or narrow ideas still encumber girls. It is hard for teens to gratify mothers' desires while also attending to their own.

The frenzy around achievement makes it hard for parents to accept that some students don't excel in high school. I am often asked to evaluate "underachieving" teens or tweens to determine if learning disabilities or attention disorders are at the root of disappointing grades. Many turn out to be perfectly fine students who perform on par with their aptitude. There is nothing to correct or treat. The only problem is expecting these girls to be straight-A students.

Some aren't cut out to thrive in traditional educational settings, but shine in the real world. These teens learn best not from books, but from hands-on experiences. Despite struggling academically, they get along well with classmates and teachers. Supervisors in part-time jobs and volunteer programs give them rave reviews. With freedom to be true to themselves, these girls find meaningful, enjoyable jobs that draw upon their strengths.

Amelia, fifteen, a personable and bubbly teen, was universally adored at her rigorous high school. She enthusiastically participated on school committees and in various clubs and extracurricular activities. Amelia was a star athlete in several sports. What came less easily to her was schoolwork. Language processing difficulties made it hard for Amelia to grasp concepts and integrate material when taking tests and writing papers.

Despite her struggles in school, I assured Amelia's parents that with her extraordinary people skills, appealing personality, and strong work ethic, she was sure to flourish in life. Meanwhile, Amelia's cognitive and learning profile suggested she would not thrive at the demanding liberal arts colleges her parents hoped she would attend. I recommended a career-oriented program that offered hands-on experiences for her to learn marketable skills.

Resist Urging Her to Specialize Early

Seeing a daughter develop her niche reassures you that she can stand out, compete, and succeed. It also relieves you from feeling responsible for finding her a passion. This is why many parents today make sacrifices and drain financial resources so girls can dance six days a week, travel with elite teams or orchestras, or take private voice lessons.

If your daughter does not have a passion, you might offer a veritable smorgasbord of tempting activities in the hope something appeals to her. Problems arise when teens turn up their noses at these choices. Or when they politely nibble, but don't partake wholeheartedly. Or when girls are initially enthusiastic, but quickly lose their appetites.

A more harmful scenario unfolds when teens go along with the interests others suggest. Friends in middle school might persuade girls to try a sport or activity. Parents fully support that. But when the commitment or competition becomes too much or the sport loses its luster, girls feel stuck. Quitting raises fears of disappointing coaches, teammates, and parents who invested money in fees and uniforms, and time chauffeuring to practices and games. So girls go through the motions, keep up the charade, and miss out on new opportunities that truly excite them.

Besides, early passions may not pan out. In his book *Range*, David Epstein argues that people who ultimately succeed usually experiment before narrowing their focus. Elite athletes, for example, first try other sports. Acclaimed musicians learn to play various instruments. Specializing too early in a career may backfire, too. Despite initially earning more money, such employees are more likely to quit. For all these reasons, pressuring teens to prematurely find and prioritize passions can be counterproductive.

Support Her Exploration

As teen girls figure out who they want to be, the choices they make along the way may surprise, confuse, or even appall parents. Everything from clothing styles to lingo to sexual orientation can be huge battle-starters. The less familiar a daughter's expressions of personal identity, the harder they may be for a mother to accept.

As Anya, sixteen, looks back at middle school, she says, "I was struggling with who I was. I dressed in boys' clothes." Her horrified mother chalked this phase up to Anya being "troubled." But things eventually changed, as they often do. Anya says, "My older sister told me I'd never get asked out if I dressed in boys' clothes. So I spent a whole year trying to play football in heels and a miniskirt. It was an odd year." At this point, Anya has become the mainstream teen her mother always wanted, but their relationship has yet to recover from these early interactions.

Carly, seventeen, also describes wearing attire that runs counter to her mother's tastes. In her case, she was striving to stake a claim as unique among her peers: "Clothes are a big part of who I am, how I portray myself. I dress weird. Baggy clothes, thirty chains, and black eye shadow—that's my look. I like it when people say, 'OMG, what is she wearing?' This differentiates me from everyone else in school."

It is tricky to give girls leeway to explore different expressions of themselves while also considering propriety and safety. As Mary Kate tells me, "Do I really care about a second piercing? It's not a tattoo. It's not permanent. But I'm old-fashioned and my daughter is still sixteen. So I choose my battles. I tell her, 'Put a shirt on over that crop top.' The blue streak in her hair is fine for summer, but we'll cut it off when school resumes. That's our values."

Your daughter's exploration of her sexuality is a big part of the process of forming an identity. Teens these days are more open about what they think about their own and others' sexual choices. Many more girls are coming out in middle school, expressing confusion about their sexual orientation or gender identity. Others are determined to support friends who are dealing with these issues.

What if, after finally passing her driver's test, your daughter informs you she is opting for the nonbinary gender X—rather than female—on her license? Or she declares that she is bisexual, lesbian, asexual, or pansexual? Or identifies as transgender and is contemplating transitioning? How might you respond when your child asks to be identified by "they" and "them" instead of "she" and "her"? Or insists on being called by a name other than the one you lovingly and thoughtfully gave her at birth?

Teens who announce that they are not heterosexual, or that their gender identities may be different from the ones they were assigned at birth, can elicit rather bewildering and overwhelming feelings in parents. Your first impulse may be to dismiss your teen's feelings, second-guess their motivations, or wait for them to "come to their senses."

Graciella finds justifications for her sixteen-year-old's same-sex relationships: "In middle school, she was bisexual and had an intimate relationship with her girlfriend for a year. When they broke up, she found another girlfriend online. I wonder if she's just protecting herself from getting involved with boys. My older sister is a lesbian. My daughter takes on other people's identities. She wanted to be like my sister, so who knows? Maybe she came out because of my sister."

Mothers with strict conservative or religious backgrounds may struggle most. Rosetta, a first-generation American, could not accept her fourteen-year-old daughter, Layla, having romantic feelings for another girl. After reading affectionate text messages between Layla and her best friend, Rosetta became furious that her daughter was "compromising her reputation" and "choosing to defy our values." She blamed Layla's friend for "preying on my daughter's impressionable nature and putting ideas in her head."

In parent counseling, I explained that Layla feared angering and disappointing them. The reason she shared this information with her mother and father was because she thought being open and honest would allow them to stay close. Still, Layla's parents' value system could not accommodate their only child thinking of herself as a lesbian. Rosetta was determined to end Layla's friendship "to get my daughter back on track."

Estelle, a single mother, was far more accepting and supportive of her thirteen-year-old's journey. Ron, who was assigned female at birth and named Rhonda, had been saying since he was ten that he felt like a boy in a girl's body. In seventh grade, he decided to bind his breasts, stop wearing dresses and other clothing worn by girls, and ask his teachers to call him Ron. When he asked her mother for hormone therapy and surgery, Estelle felt so out of her element that she sought out specialists for guidance.

Because this is a stage of tremendous exploration, teens' professed sexual orientations are not carved in stone. Dee was twelve when she first identified as lesbian. In therapy, she described a powerful attraction to girls while feeling nothing when she kissed boys. In eighth grade, a close friendship with another girl blossomed into romance and sexual experimentation. Fast-forward ten years. Now in her mid-twenties, Dee has had two long-term, serious relationships with boyfriends.

Parents can't consult a crystal ball to know how daughters' sexuality will turn out. They also don't have any say. Girls are who they are. Whether attraction to same-sex friends is a transient phase or the beginning of a lifelong sexual orientation, LGBTQ teens and tweens need family acceptance to counteract the rejection, bullying, and hate they often encounter.

Melinda tells me that during middle school, "I was questioning, 'Do I like girls, or do I like boys?' I was kind of forcing myself to like boys because I know how the world can be with the LGBTQ community. I was scared about what would happen if I was a part of that community. But I am part of it, so . . ." When I ask if her fears of mistreatment were realized, Melinda replies, "This year someone called me a dyke in the hallway. I still don't know whether it was a joke. Another person told me I'm going to hell because I like girls. That definitely wasn't a joke."

Teens identifying as LGBTQ experience vastly higher rates of depression, attempted suicide, unprotected sex, abuse of illegal substances, and other risks to long-term health and well-being. The National Institutes of Health's ABCD study, which followed nine- and ten-year-olds for a decade, found that compared with heterosexual children, nonheterosexual children were three times likelier to have mood disorders and almost five times likelier to have suicidal thoughts.

According to the Avon Longitudinal Study of Parents and Children, young people who are nonheterosexual or unsure of sexual orientations are four times likelier to make attempts to end their lives. This is also true for transgender adults who were exposed to conversion therapy in an effort to change their gender identities to what they were assigned at birth. A survey in *JAMA Psychiatry* also found more psychological distress and more lifetime suicide attempts, especially when conversion treatments occurred before age ten.

The heightened vulnerability to mental health risks reflected in these data should give parents pause. If your daughter confides her own or her friend's sexual journey, listen nonjudgmentally to what she says in that moment. More important, give much thought to how you respond. Most likely, she has worked up the courage to have this conversation and is anxious about your reaction. It is likely she will never forget the first words that come out of your mouth. So if she tells you she is a member of the LGBTQ community, take care not to speak in a way your teen could interpret as dismissive, disgusted, or rejecting:

> **Daughter:** Mom, I've been thinking that I'm into girls.

NOT

> **Mom:** No you're not! A lot of girls develop crushes on friends at your age.

OR

> **Mom:** You're too young to know who you are right now.

OR

> **Mom:** Stop saying that! You've been taught how wrong that is!

INSTEAD, TRY

Mom: You think you might be bi?

OR

Mom: How long have you been thinking that?

OR

Mom: Have you had any experiences with girls? With boys?

OR

Mom: Do you have friends who feel this way? Are you able to talk to them?

Being open-minded and asking gentle questions keeps teens engaged in conversation. Girls whose mothers give them the clear message that it is okay to feel what they feel are less likely to suffer declines in mental health and well-being. At seventeen, Katherine became romantically involved with another woman. Her mother was beside herself. She not only refused to allow Katherine's girlfriend to visit their home, but also she began to track the girls' text message threads. As Katherine increasingly hid "unacceptable" parts of herself from her parents, she began to explore sexual fantasies on risky websites.

According to Quinn, sixteen, the best message to give a daughter who is exploring her sexuality is what her mother told her: "It's fine to experiment during adolescence and see what you like and dislike. But don't feel pressured to make decisions about who you are and who you're attracted to before you're ready. Give it time. When you meet the right person, you'll know—whether it's another woman or a man."

Daughters who feel able to explore and connect with genuine parts of themselves are comfortable in their own skins, more confident, and healthier. Notably, when I ask teens what advice they would give to younger girls, they speak of authenticity. Maeve, seventeen, says, "Be completely honest with yourself and your parents. If you're not honest, it's going to make you feel even worse. Telling yourself that you're fine when you're not fine or telling other people you're fine when you're not isn't good." Grace, eighteen, agrees. "You are who you are," she says, "so you might as well own up to it."

• • •

If you're this far into *Anything But My Phone, Mom!* and feeling like you need a break—from reading or from motherhood in general—fear not. The next chapter discusses not only the dangers of doing too much for daughters, but also how doing *less* actually accomplishes *more* in terms of instilling vital character traits and skills.

CHAPTER SIX

Doing Less to Achieve More

> When my daughter, Amanda, was in high school, her teachers accused her of copying information from the internet into her senior term paper. She was always an excellent student, and was on track to be her class valedictorian. But the school's harsh response to this one little mistake was going to cost her this honor and ruin her chances of getting into a top college. I had no choice but to hire the best lawyer I could find.
>
> —ZINA

No woman wants her daughter to be disappointed or to suffer. As a mother, witnessing this can be so painful that you might want to remove any potential hurdles along her path to success. You may happily dive in to rescue her from any problems—whether academic, social, or emotional—and jump through hoops to protect her from the consequences of her mistakes. In your mind, this may just be what loving mothers do.

In this hypercompetitive world, it is natural to want daughters to have plenty of choices and opportunities. If she is not doing well in school or activities, you may see it as your job to correct any deficits. If she feels lonely, gravitates to friends with questionable values, or is often on the outs with peers, of course you want to do everything possible to make her happier. As one mother put it, "I just want my daughter's life to be better than mine. I don't want her to go through the stuff I did."

When she is hurting, or when you see her doing something you fear will turn out badly, it can be hard to fight the urge to do more than would be sensible. Powerful emotions such as fierce love, empathy, and especially fear can seize the reins from more measured maternal minds. But how involved you get in your teen's or tween's life enormously affects not only her resiliency and well-being, but also how her brain develops, her sense of purpose, the energy she invests in goals, and the intellectual risks she is willing to take.

If your goal is to nurture the skills your daughter needs in her future, such as a love of learning, self-discipline, emotional regulation, resourcefulness, and creativity, you may need to restrain tiger mom tendencies. As I'll explain, psychological research demonstrates that neither clearing obstacles to pave the way for success (snowplow parenting) nor swooping in to fix problems to make teens feel better (helicopter parenting) is constructive.

This chapter guides you instead to find the sweet spot between the extremes of overinvolvement and unhealthy detachment. This delicate balance best prepares your daughter to thrive independently by letting her maturation proceed unimpeded. It requires stepping back and giving her freedom to stumble, fail, and recover. Ironically, by doing less, you will actually achieve more.

Becoming a Consultant

Adolescence requires a gradual shift in the intensity of parenting. When your daughter was a little girl, you gave her rules and expected her to follow them. But as she grows up, you foster greater autonomy. As a warm, nonjudgmental consultant, your daughter knows you are always available to support her. But she does not think you have all the answers—or all the power. As you issue fewer instructions and demands, your teen knows you respect her input and welcome—no, *encourage*—her ability to make decisions and solve problems independently.

An ideal level of involvement deepens the mother-daughter bond throughout the teen years, minimizing power struggles that result in defiance or rebelliousness. In contrast, doing more than what is in teens' best interest frequently backfires. Overinvolvement drains treasured reserves of cooperation, goodwill, and closeness between mothers and daughters.

As Jacki describes, "Whenever I try to fix Mary Anne's problems by offering options one, two, and three, she reacts by rejecting all of my suggestions, telling me, 'You always make things worse!' and stomping out of the room.'" Jacki admits that in that instant, her patience evaporates. She hears herself yelling, which makes her feel terrible.

Despite her intentions to help, no good ever comes of this. It may seem counterintuitive that giving your daughter hands-on assistance with her homework is actually *un*helpful. But there are myriad reasons why this happens.

Mental health professionals and educators concur that parental overinvolvement harms teens' well-being. Rachel Simmons, author of *Enough As She Is*, writes about how to manage parental anxiety and avoid snowplow parenting to prepare young people for failure. In the *New York Times* article "The Relentlessness of Modern Parenting," clinicians similarly blame an overinvolved parenting style for young people's poor coping resources, intolerance of setbacks, and soaring mental health issues.

Research consistently backs up these claims. In one study, students who rated mothers as helicopter mothers were more likely to report symptoms of anxiety, depression, and poor life satisfaction. Another study demonstrated that college students' perceptions of mothers as helicopter parents are associated with significantly lower life satisfaction in young women compared with men.

Surveys of college students found that young adults who had been "excessively monitored" (defined as being raised by parents who were inappropriately involved and controlling for their age) were more likely to burn out and to have a harder time transitioning to the real world.

Overly monitored students want to perform well not so much because they are personally invested, but rather to please parents. As noted in Chapter Three, it is intrinsic motivation that fuels the initiative and perseverance needed for success. Only when permitted to struggle can teens become confident about their ability to cope with pressure, manage tough problems, and make independent decisions.

Shielding young people from mistakes and failures prevents them from toning self-regulation muscles, which stunts character growth, problem-solving, and resiliency.

In my experience, teens who struggle most in college have coasted through high school, barely breaking a sweat as they charm teachers or are propped up by excessive scaffolding. Lacking opportunities to practice problem-solving and develop resiliency, they are unprepared to be resourceful when needs arise. College-age students in this position may get poorer grades, burn out, become anxious and/or depressed, and sometimes drop out.

As I tell parents, I worry far less about teens with significant learning challenges. Lifelong academic struggles taught them to work harder than other students. They were constantly forced to figure out compensatory strategies to get around weaknesses. These teens not only survived setbacks and failures, but also emerged stronger and more determined. Arriving on campus with a robust work ethic and proven study skills, these students rally in tough times.

To give your daughter the chance to develop psychological resources and life skills, gradually retract safety nets. View problems as opportunities for her to experience and bounce back from disappointments. When she struggles, she finds solutions. When she suffers interpersonal hurts or disappointments, she learns to navigate the ups and downs that define adolescent socialization.

It is only by backing off and letting your teen face hardships that you reassure her, "I know you can figure this out" and "I believe in you." Only when you refrain from jumping in to ease her plight does your daughter develop a sense of being in charge of her life, which in turn endows her with conscientiousness and confidence. Beyond her comfort zone lies the fertile place where seeds of resiliency are planted.

The Urge to Do More

Avoiding overparenting may seem simple, even a no-brainer. Yet it takes extraordinary self-discipline to sit back when your daughter struggles. You may be drawn in because you think raising a hapless teen is an indictment of your mothering skills. Some totally honest mothers admit that having mediocre students—and, especially, slackers—is embarrassing.

Especially when academic pressures and the stakes for college rise, even the most mindful of mothers can morph from supportive consultant into nonstop nag. Despite resolving to keep a steady head, you, too, may find yourself stuck in Micromanager Mode. Think about if apprehensions about your daughter's future are silencing your better angels. When parents are overinvolved, some teens get the unfortunate messages that (a) their own academic efforts are inadequate, and (b) using any available advantage or shortcut is necessary and acceptable.

With this mindset, some parents try to get girls the accommodation of extended time to boost SAT or ACT scores. Interestingly, just when the Educational Testing Service stopped informing colleges that applicants took tests with accommodations, requests soared—200 percent from 2010 to 2017 alone. It strains credulity that in seven years 200 percent more students were classified with disabilities under the Federal Rehabilitation Act of 1973.

In some affluent communities, schools are giving test accommodations to as many as one-quarter to one-third of students. Like many psychologists, I get calls every year from parents looking for extensive neuropsychological testing in the hope of finding and documenting a disability that will give teens a leg up in the college application process.

But extended time to complete tests hardly guarantees improvement. Often, in fact, putting girls through extensive and expensive neuropsychological test batteries to qualify them for this accommodation backfires. Although families often believe students with attention deficits need extended time for test-taking, for example, many teens' scores worsen because they get bored and tune out over the extra hours. Girls whose college acceptances are based on scores with unwarranted accommodations may not perform well if later required to work within standard time constraints. Finally, this strategy teaches teens to game the system.

For the same reasons that unjustified test accommodations can be detrimental, it is equally unwise to medicate teens whose assessments do not support a diagnosis of neurologically based ADHD. Psychostimulant medication may help her to focus, but if your daughter lacks self-discipline, she would be better served by working on the self-regulatory skills she needs to succeed. Using drugs to raise her grades also could give her tacit permission to use pills to solve other problems.

Besides, medication is rarely the quick fix parents hope for. Psychostimulants don't remedy underlying learning difficulties in reading, math, executive functions, or study skills. Moreover, pharmacological treatments can cause unpleasant side effects that further disrupt achievement. When teens feel sleepy or foggy, for example, they become more distractible and think less clearly. Girls can also develop new distressing symptoms such as anger outbursts, insomnia, or weight changes.

Cheating and Other Shortcuts

During speaking events, I sometimes ask parents this question: If you knew your teen could get into an Ivy League college by cheating, would you be okay with that? Typically, after a slight pause, a chorus of nervous chuckles from the audience tells me all I need to know.

As always, examples of what *not* to do can be most instructive. A seventeen-year-old girl who was sick during midterms was allowed to take a makeup exam. When she mentioned in therapy her plans to ask friends for the essay topic beforehand, I mused aloud about how her parents might feel about that. "Well," she said, laughing, "my mom was the one who suggested it."

An eighteen-year-old college first-year with dyslexia and mild attention problems came to see me during her first vacation. Faced with a heavier reading load, she found that the strategies that had worked for her during high school were no longer doing the trick. She wanted to try medication, so I suggested consulting her pediatrician before returning to college. Beryl responded, "That's okay. My mother said just to get some pills from my friends at school. Everybody's got some."

The common justification that "everyone else cheats" is becoming ever more accurate. Professor Donald McCabe at Rutgers University, who for decades has tracked the prevalence of cheating, most recently documented that among 24,000 students at 70 high schools, 95 percent of students do so in some way. Unfortunately, Dr. McCabe finds cheating becomes a habit that continues after graduation, showing up as dishonesty in the workplace and lack of integrity in business practices. Teens fare better when urged to adopt integrity over deception and authenticity over false selves.

First, Do No Harm

Parents who scheme daughters into elite schools for which they lack qualifications do them no favors. As I was doing research before writing this book, the Varsity Blues cheating scandal came to light. Since then parents have served jail time for rigging admission tests, posing applicants as star athletes, and paying bribes to get lackluster students into highly competitive universities.

Although the media have focused on the parents, testing officials, and coaches involved, I have been most concerned about the young adults whose parents committed crimes on their behalf. Forced to wonder why parents resorted to such actions, girls might reach disheartening conclusions that (a) the college they attend is critical, which is not only untrue, but also likely to send teens' achievement anxiety into the stratosphere; (b) parents must not think they are accomplished enough to get into a desirable college on their own, a belief that would eviscerate most girls' self-worth; and (c) to attend the schools parents consider adequate, teens need to be like the more accomplished applicants (e.g., elite athletes) they pretended to be.

If you are panicking about your daughter's road to success, talk yourself down from the ledge. Remind yourself of your goals in raising her, practice self-care, and reach out to people whose knowledge and sensible views will reassure you. As you know, your teen is apt to pick up on your apprehensions. Trying to hide them may be worse. A just-published study in *The Journal of Family Psychology* found that parents who suppressed feelings of stress not only were less warm and engaged in interactions, but also transmitted that stress to young teens.

If you're still tempted to pitch in (read as: become overzealous), think about this. If you don't practice letting go now, you may find yourself following in the footsteps of parents who continue to micromanage after daughters are in college and beyond. Speaking with college deans and admissions officers, I hear about parents who get involved in choosing first-year roommates, intervene in friendship and romantic conflicts, contact professors to discuss grades, and call college advisers to overrule students' chosen majors. *Forbes* documents that prospective employers report parents are submitting résumés on behalf of college graduates (31%), contacting them to implore them to hire sons or daughters (26%), and calling them to negotiate adult children's salaries. These days, young adults are not only bringing parents to job interviews, but also asking human resources personnel to send offers home. Take a moment to recall when you got your first job; can you imagine your parents doing that?

Resolve to avoid this level of overparenting. Your teen's growing sense of herself as a mature, capable, and independent young woman depends on it. By doing only as much as is truly necessary, you're giving your daughter the opportunity to develop the following ten essential skills.

1. Stress Management

Preparing teens to manage stress is a key parenting task. Here are the basic facts. Mild, short-term stress can be helpful. Knowing a class presentation or midterm grade is important might prompt your daughter to start studying earlier and try harder. When your teen is taking a test, stress-induced increased blood flow to the brain can keep her alert and thinking sharply.

But more severe, longer-term stress is indisputably detrimental. The longer it lasts, the more likely your teen is to become overwhelmed, exhausted, and unmotivated. Stressed girls often develop difficulties sleeping and other poor habits that impede coping and learning. The potential health risks are scary. Inflammation and weakened immune systems increase susceptibility to depression, heart disease, diabetes, some types of cancer, irritable bowel syndrome, and other gastrointestinal ailments.

Unless you are so detached from your teen that you can't recognize her stress level, you can help protect her from its most harmful effects. Researchers who studied emotions, physical health symptoms, and levels of cortisol, the primary stress hormone that activates fight-or-flight reactions in response to threats, found that teens and tweens aged nine to seventeen reported more negative emotions on stressful days. This is not surprising. But even when experiencing unusually low stress, young people with less warm parents reported more negative emotions and had higher measured cortisol levels.

How you parent your daughter powerfully affects her neurobiology. The Center on the Developing Child at Harvard University confirms that without the "buffering" of safe, stable, and nurturing relationships, stress is especially toxic.

Overinvolvement with stressed teens takes many forms. In the evening, when girls become tired and assignments have yet to be completed, parents may feel compelled to stay up later than usual to help. This could entail coaching daughters through their homework—or actually doing it for them. Mothers may email teachers to excuse girls' late or missing assignments. Although the intent is to relieve daughters' distress, in the long run this approach only reinforces avoidance and triggers helplessness.

Being appropriately involved encourages your teen to find ways to cope effectively with pressures—now as well as in the future. Consider these strategies:

- Ask how stressed she feels—and where pressures are coming from.
- Can she lighten her schedule and/or workload, even temporarily?
- Suggest making a to-do list, prioritizing items, and crossing them off as she completes them.
- Because her health and well-being are more important than her grades, insist on her eating nutritiously and getting enough sleep.
- Ask her to commit to going to bed fifteen minutes earlier every few days, gradually adding an hour or more extra sleep each week.
- Explore potential resources, such as her school guidance counselor, tutor, teacher, mentor, family member, or coach.
- Discuss stress-reducing outlets such as sports, walking, working out, dancing, martial arts, and running. Explain that physical exercise produces the protein BDNF (brain-derived neurotrophic factor), which is thought to enhance human adaptiveness and improve mood. (Please note: be mindful about encouraging competitive sports, which these days sometimes exacerbate rather than relieve girls' stress.)

- Brainstorm a list of activities that she finds most soothing, such as listening to music, cooking or baking, petting the dog, praying, taking a bath, meditating, writing creatively, knitting, catnapping, scrapbooking, or journaling. Post this where she has easy access to stress-reducing ideas.

- Encourage her to socialize. This may seem counterintuitive, especially during crunch times when she may already feel unable to accomplish all that she has to do. But connection to peers has been proven to support girls in stressful situations by lowering cortisol (and can also increase BDNF levels).

- Inspire her to smile and laugh daily, which promotes happiness as effectively as a good night's sleep. Aim for in-person humor, but funny YouTube videos work, too. Smiling stimulates the brain's reward center even more than chocolate. Yes, you read that right.

2. Emotional Regulation

The goal here is helping your daughter learn to tap her inner resources to manage distressing feelings and situations. Detached parents might dismiss teens' misery, wait for it to subside, or ignore age-inappropriate emotional meltdowns. On the other hand, those who get too involved jump in whenever daughters are uncomfortable or things don't go their way. When parents overreact, they don't model for girls how to maintain emotional control. Either extreme approach impedes teens from developing tolerance for discomfiting emotions and confidence in handling them.

Doing less to achieve more—taking the middle road—is the best way to help girls become aware of how they feel, label emotions accurately, and channel them constructively. Raquel has found that not reacting to her thirteen-year-old's surliness, intolerance, and impatience avoids reinforcing negative behaviors. "When she does cross the line into disrespect, which is intolerable," Raquel continues, "I tell her that until she can control herself, I'm not engaging with her."

When teens can take a moment and get themselves together, mothers can commiserate with predicaments while gently encouraging mobilizing all resources at their disposal. The following is a list of ways that mothers can help their daughters manage their emotions without becoming overinvolved.

DON'T RESCUE

During middle school and high school, mothers who get distraught SOS texts or calls from girls who want to come home are often in a quandary. It may be flattering that your daughter confides in you and gratifying to help her. But you know that she must learn to analyze and solve her own problems, even when she's distressed. That pesky voice in your head may remind you that swooping in to make her feel better doesn't encourage inner strengths. And yet, it may feel unmaternal, even cruel, to leave her there steeping in misery.

Doing less is not the same as abandoning your daughter. It may include asking for information, listening carefully, empathizing, and encouraging her to problem-solve. Ask what she has come up with so far. If she is too worked up to generate ideas, you can offer a menu of possibilities. Which option does she prefer? Which faculty member can help? Remind her of when she managed similar situations well—without coming home. By staying at school, she will become acquainted with inner strengths she didn't know she had.

> **Daughter:** Mom, I'm having the worst day ever. You've got to come pick me up right now.

NOT

> **Mom:** Can't do that. I'm out for lunch right now. Besides, your job is to go to school.

OR

> **Mom:** Sure, honey! I'm throwing a coat over my PJs and rushing right over.

INSTEAD, TRY

> **Mom:** You sound really upset. I'm sorry you're having a hard day. Who can you talk to at school right now about what's going on?
>
> **Daughter:** I don't want to. I just want to come home. Please don't make me stay here!
>
> **Mom:** Honey, I know you feel bad, but remember that your guidance counselor and the psychologist are there

to help when students are upset. Who do you prefer speaking to? I know you can work through this.

OR

> **Mom:** I'm so sorry you're upset and I'll be happy to hear all about it as soon as you get home from school. But for now, what could you do to make yourself feel better so you can stick it out for the next couple of classes?

BROADEN HER EMOTIONAL VOCABULARY

When teens and tweens are highly emotional, worked up, or in tears, mothers are understandably upset and perhaps at a loss about how to respond. An overly detached approach minimizes girls' feelings. At best, this comes across as dismissive; at worst, as denying teens' right to their own emotions. Scarlet, seventeen, says, "I was in my bed, crying my eyes out after a painful breakup, and my mother comes in and starts yelling at me. 'What do you have to be crying about?' she said. 'You have such a better life than I did!' It made me feel so much worse."

Conversely, doing too much might make women overly empathize with daughters, lose appropriate emotional distance, and therefore cease to be helpful to them. Overwhelming feelings spur unhealthy actions such as berating the friends who upset daughters, demanding girls respond in specific ways, and directly confronting other parents.

Along with listening and empathizing, a moderately involved approach may entail urging distraught teens to identify and articulate how they feel. The old adage "Name it to tame it" still applies. But by this age, girls must go beyond saying they are sad, mad, or glad. In fact, new research indicates that teens who can label and describe feelings specifically are at less risk for becoming depressed after stressful life events.

The more precisely your daughter can name emotions, the better she will come to know herself and communicate her needs effectively. Expand her emotional glossary to include:

UNCOMFORTABLE EMOTIONS

Frustrated	Anxious	Puzzled
Insulted	Worried	Upset
Contempt	Distrustful	Annoyed
Afraid	Hopeless	Furious
Jealous	Shocked	Self-critical
Superior	Irritated	Surprised
Offended	Resentful	Bored
Confused	Despondent	Hurt
Dissatisfied	Agitated	Desperate
Rejected	Disgusted	Disbelieving

Doubtful	Slighted	Disappointed
Impatient	Suspicious	Depleted
Terrified	Skeptical	Indecisive
Helpless	Horrified	Smug
Distressed	Lonely	Guilty

LET HER BE BORED

Teens complain of boredom when it is hard for them to be alone. Without structure or stimulation, some girls are flooded with unwanted thoughts and intrusive, distressing feelings. Detached mothers are usually less attuned to girls' inner states. Overinvolved parents may preempt daughters' complaints of boredom as well as the risks of "idle hands" by enrolling them in after-school activities—especially those seen as advantageous for later success.

When you support your teen having unscheduled free time, you acknowledge her need to tolerate quiet space. Rather than fearing boredom, think of it as a mental state that promotes vital self-reflection and encourages the development of self-awareness, creativity, problem-solving skills, and other inner resources. Figuring out how to spend alone time in meaningful and satisfying ways may lead your daughter to discover restorative activities that become lifetime pleasures. To raise emotionally capable daughters, downtime is not wasteful, but sacred.

Middle school art teachers, who are in the business of inspiring students' imaginations, use strategies to encourage quiet contemplation followed by creativity. After listening to inspirational passages, practicing yoga, and performing mindfulness exercises, students are asked to mindfully focus on their surroundings. What can they hear in the hallways and outside? Can they hear birds? If they pretend to be at a beach, what do students see when they look around? What can they hear and smell and feel?

At home, suggest that your daughter come up with a list of things she can do when bored. Post it on her bulletin board. Maybe she can compose music, daydream, practice her cello, or do stretches. Or she could write poetry, write in her blog, sketch designs, write a letter, or journal. Many of these activities offer additional psychological benefits of recognizing and managing emotions, reducing anxiety, and lengthening attention span.

ENCOURAGE RECHARGING

In therapy, I often suggest that teens take twenty to thirty minutes to do nothing after school before starting in on homework. This advice flies in the face of what they're usually told. Girls protest, "But if I'm on my bed staring at the ceiling, thinking about what happened during the day, my mom gets mad and says I'm not being productive."

Research on self-regulation suggests another approach. It turns out that self-control is a limited resource. Throughout the school day, teens are continuously depleting their reserves when they try to pay attention, follow class rules, and inhibit unhelpful remarks. If you'd like your daughter to replenish her supply of self-control so she can delay gratification, resist temptations, and do a good job on her homework, she needs a break when she gets home.

3. Effective Problem-Solving

Parenting extremes are usually ineffective in fostering skills. Problem-solving is no exception. Rushing in to rescue your daughter from problems is as ill-advised as telling her to buck up and reap what she sowed. Whether she is struggling with friendships, academic concepts, social media, or extracurricular activities, being appropriately involved supports her in learning to reason, generate ideas, anticipate consequences, and select optimal solutions.

Miriam, sixteen, tells me about "a huge dilemma I can't figure out what to do about. I promised to organize an event for my volunteer club at school, but there's no way I can now. First, my best friend who was supposed to help me flaked, and my teacher just assigned a twenty-five-page research paper that's due around the same time." Take a moment to imagine if your daughter came to you with this problem. How might you respond?

> **Daughter:** Mom, I'm superstressed. There's no way I can organize that clothes drive and I promised. If I don't do it, everyone's going to be so mad at me and they'll never trust me again. What am I going to do (breaking down in tears)?

NOT

Mom: I told you that you were biting off more than you could chew! Why don't you ever listen to me? I know what I'm talking about!

OR

Mom: Listen, this is what you have to do. Right this minute, I want you to go email the teacher who's supervising that club. Here's what you should write . . .

Rather than *telling* your daughter what to do or admonishing her for the problem, inspire her to reason and problem-solve by *asking* her what she thinks she ought to do. Listen attentively and respectfully as she brainstorms possible solutions, refraining from shooting down ideas you consider flawed. Then ask her to imagine the consequences of each plan.

INSTEAD, TRY

Daughter: Mom, I'm superstressed. There's no way I can organize that clothes drive and I promised. If I don't do it, everyone's going to be so mad at me and they'll never trust me again. What am I going to do (breaking down in tears)?

Mom: Okay, I can understand why you're stressed. Let's try to figure this out. What have you thought of so far?

OR

> **Mom:** Let's think about your options. It can help to brainstorm. Just toss out any solutions you can think of, even if they seem silly. No judgment!

OR

> **Mom:** Who is the best person at school to help you deal with this situation?

OR

> **Mom:** Didn't something like this happen when you were vice president of your freshman class? It took a while, but you did a great job figuring that out. Can any of the strategies you used back then help in this situation?

Michaela turned her fifteen-year-old's problem into a teachable moment. Tatiana told her mother she was in a bind and didn't know what to do. She had gotten a 93 on her chem test, but it should have been an 83. Tatiana wanted the 93 because she studied hard and thought she knew the material, but felt bad about getting the better grade because it was a mistake. Michaela tells me that before responding, "I realized that far more important than this grade on a single high school test was what Tatiana learned from this, so I asked what she thought she should do."

By not giving Tatiana advice or imposing her own values, Michaela put the onus on her daughter to find a solution. In the end, Tatiana realized she would feel too guilty if she kept quiet about her teacher's mistake. She went to school early, told him what had happened, and mustered the nerve to ask if she could do anything to show him that she knew more chemistry than her 83 suggested. He told her to review her test answers and if she could prove she knew more, she could keep the 93.

This situation taught Tatiana many vital lessons. First, she learned that resolving this dilemma forced her to think about her personal code of conduct. Second, she learned that violating her standards would have made her uncomfortable. Third, she realized that getting the 93 wouldn't have been gratifying unless she felt that she had earned it.

4. Self-Control and Discipline

Self-disciplined girls are better able to manage behavior, maintain relationships, and accomplish personal goals. To practice and master this skill, they need both guidance and age-appropriate opportunities. With mostly hands-off or anything-goes parenting, teens get carte blanche to do as they please. They lack guardrails that constrain risky decisions and possible self-harm. These girls aren't compelled to make themselves do what they would prefer to avoid.

Overprotected daughters are restricted from less supervised situations that test their judgment and hone their self-control. Mary tells me, "I'm old school and strict. It's hard to instill values when other kids are doing so much more. We're not lenient about letting Lyn go downtown after school and have sleepovers. Who's to say the girls won't leave and go meet some boys? I don't think a fifteen-year-old is capable of making good choices when there's peer pressure."

The desire to keep girls safe is understandable. But it is also important to think about how Lyn will learn to make good choices if she doesn't have a chance to experience typical high school social situations. Andrea tells me, "The other day I asked my daughter if she ever tasted beer. She says, 'Mom! But I'm seventeen.' I said to her, 'I don't want you to go off to college and drink six of them to find out what it's all about.'"

An overly controlling parenting style also heightens the chance of girls defying rules and rebelling to take back control. Jojo, who identifies with this teen scenario, warns, "I always had the strictest parents. I felt they were unnecessarily strict. I was never allowed to sleep out. It didn't matter if there was a birthday party. I had to leave at eleven, when everyone else stayed the night. I found ways around all of it. They didn't have a big reason to be strict, but they saw me as an at-risk kid. I grew into that reputation. It was a self-fulfilling prophecy."

Once again, the best approach is thoughtfully providing—at every moment—only as much structure as your daughter needs. That way, she gradually internalizes external limits to become self-regulated. When she was a toddler, you didn't hand her a whole box of animal crackers just before dinner. You probably gave her a few—at snack time. As she developed more self-restraint, you probably loosened the reins a bit. After mistakes, you tightened them. This is how your daughter gradually learned self-control.

The process is no different now. Intentional parenting guides you to assess whether your teen is capable of handling each situation. To earn privileges, she has to demonstrate needed skills. It is not that forgetting to do laundry, failing to keep an eye on a younger sibling, or leaving her aromatherapy candle lit are causes for putting her in solitary confinement. But these lapses suggest she needs to work on becoming more aware of her surroundings and cognizant of her responsibilities.

The thought of girls socializing with peers who choose to vape, get high, or have risky sexual experiences may make mothers nervous. But it is possible to honor your family values while also allowing your teen to be out in the world, where her maturation can unfold. Women who walk this fine line say, "We talk with our children about when our values are different from other families, to reinforce the values we want them to learn," and "We have many, many conversations. I ask her, 'How are you preparing to make good choices?'"

Daughter: Mom, my friend Kevin is having some kids over Friday night. Is it okay if I go?

NOT

Mom: No, I'm not comfortable because I don't know Kevin or his parents.

Daughter: That's so unfair. They're very nice people. I'm sixteen, so of course you don't know a lot of my friends' parents. I'm never going to have a social life! All of my friends are going! I'll be stuck home all alone with nothing to do. This is so depressing!

OR

Mom: Absolutely not! You're not old enough to go to a party where there are boys and there's probably going to be drinking. What are you thinking? You know your father and I would never let you do such a thing!

Daughter: You're treating me like a baby! It's ridiculous! You just want me to stay home and never have any fun. You're so mean!

INSTEAD, TRY

Mom: Tell me more about it.

Daughter: Well, Kevin's mom said he could have five kids over, so it'll be his two best friends and three of us girls. We're going to watch the new horror movie. His parents will be there.

OR

Mom: Let's talk about what this is going to be like. Do you expect there'll be drinking?

Daughter: I don't think so. Maybe. I don't really know. It doesn't matter, anyway. Everyone drinks. It's no big deal.

Mom: Have you tried drinking?

Daughter: Once or twice. I had a sip at parties.

Mom: What was it like?

Daughter: I didn't like the taste at all.

Mom: It's important that we have an understanding so I can be comfortable with you going to parties. What would you do if everyone was getting drunk, like if they were playing a drinking game and asked you to join?

Daughter: I'd just say I didn't want to.

Mom: It can be hard to be the only one saying no. What do you think you would say?

Daughter: That I'm allergic.

Mom: That could work. Or you can always blame it on us. You can say we're superstrict and if we so much as get a whiff of alcohol on you that you won't be allowed out until you're eighteen. Or you can say you have an early soccer practice and your coach will flip out if you're tired.

Daughter: Yeah, that sounds good.

Mom: What if things get out of hand or people are doing things that make you uneasy?

Daughter: Like what?

Mom: Drinking reduces inhibitions, so people sometimes do things they wouldn't do when sober.

> What if one of your guy friends came on to you or started touching you and you weren't into it?
>
> **Daughter:** I can handle myself, Mom!
>
> **Mom:** I hope so. It's my job to make sure of that, which is why I'm asking you these questions. Remember, if you're uncomfortable, just text the code word we agreed on and Dad or I will find an urgent reason to come get you, no questions asked, and definitely no punishment.

Before girls have the know-how and strength to do what is right, sometimes they have to find out how it feels to do the wrong thing, to disappoint themselves as well as others. That is why you're giving your daughter the chance to test her skills in increasingly challenging situations, while at the same time offering her a ready parachute if she needs to exit fast.

Treat incidents of poor self-restraint as learning experiences. If your teen had never hiked before, you wouldn't expect her to climb Mount Kilimanjaro on her first attempt. Matter-of-factly explain where you think her judgment faltered, and ask how she will do better next time. Eventually, your daughter will use self-discipline to avoid becoming distracted from her studies, sending the nude photo her crush begged her for, and trying the latest designer drug.

A seventeen-year-old I interviewed for this book offered parents this advice: "Give teens freedom. Let them learn about the world, learn there's a different view. Or as soon as they have independence, they won't be able to handle it. They won't know what to do with it."

5. Responsibility and Accountability

By giving your daughter as much responsibility as she can handle, you are also teaching her the fundamental skills of being responsible and accountable. Anticipate her rising to the occasion, taking charge of her life, and feeling pride in her accomplishments. If she falls short, hold her accountable. Don't make excuses or give her outs. If she violates school or home rules, she learns the consequences. If friends or classmates get mad, she learns what happens if she fails to honor teen social codes.

Coach her to anticipate and live with her choices, but refrain from following your teen around and sweeping up her messes. If she waits until you're at work to ask you to edit her language arts paper or until you're half asleep to tell you she needs printer paper, don't spring into action to save the day. How else will she learn to anticipate her needs and plan accordingly?

Roslyn describes her fifteen-year-old's moment of reckoning: "Elena had her field hockey banquet the other night, but she wouldn't go because she didn't have the right clothes. I refused to go on an emergency run to the mall the night before because she was just there two weeks ago, and when I asked if she needed anything, Elena insisted she didn't." Many mothers would rationalize that it would be a shame for teens to miss sports banquets after working so hard all season, and besides, the mall wasn't that far away.

But Roslyn stood firm. "I usually cave," she admitted, "but this time I didn't take her to the mall after getting home after a long day at work because I had warned her that we weren't coming back, and that this would be the consequence if she didn't think through whether she would need a dress." Roslyn also made clear to Elena, "I can't jump every time you want me to. I can't drop everything every time you ask me to do something."

It wasn't until later that Elena realized she could have gone to the banquet without a new dress. When she heard that her teammates had a good time, she may also have learned that sharing occasions with friends matters more than what she wears.

6. Failing Successfully

Overly involved parents often twist themselves into pretzels to prevent daughters from stumbling and making mistakes. But the truth is, if you want your daughter to become confident and resilient, you hope that sometime during her school years she bombs spectacularly. In fact, you might consider it a hugely important part of your job to teach her to fail successfully.

Your teen has to be able to cope with the inevitable flop and occasional fiasco. To prepare, she must find out what real disappointment feels like. That happens when she doesn't get a coveted role in a theater program or a position on an elite sports team, is passed over for an internship she desperately wants, gets rejected by a romantic partner, or is wait-listed by her early decision (ED) college.

Zelda, mother of Morgan, fifteen, says it concerns her that her husband is so protective of his only daughter. "He is determined to keep anything and everything that could possibly go wrong from going wrong. Her father wants to stop Morgan before she makes mistakes. But then she won't have opportunities. I say, 'You'll find out that's not the best way.' I want her to learn from her mistakes. I want her to screw up so she can grow."

Your teen benefits from knowing that despite feeling stung or embarrassed by letdowns and failures, she can pick herself up, do what needs to be done, and survive. She might even find the silver linings in such situations. Equally crucial, she needs to know that you and her other parent also will be fine if she messes up. This reassurance, which relieves her trepidation about future missteps, is a gift.

Your daughter especially needs your perspective. Because teens today are teetering on an achievement tightrope, fearing the tiniest stumble could topple them into an abyss of failure, they look to parents for confirmation of what is and is not important. You are the reality check and voice of reason that helps your daughter to recover from imperfect performances, social humiliations, and disastrous final exams.

Intentional parenting in these situations requires checking your own anxiety at the door. When you remain nonjudgmental about her setbacks, your daughter will learn to do the same. She needs to hear that you don't expect perfection, but rather that her path to success may be bumpy and full of detours. No matter how hard she tries, problems will arise. You will always love her, support her, and respect her for being brave enough to ask for help.

When she makes mistakes, you'll then have to walk the walk. Rather than shame her, assure her that this is part of growing up. She can't always be the best and won't always win. But so what? All she can do is be herself, be the best she can. Use failures as opportunities for problem-solving and self-advocacy.

"I don't micromanage," Evie, mother of four, tells me. "Last year, the last day of school, I got an email that one of my daughters had failed her sophomore math final, and the teacher suggested she might be more comfortable going down a level. I had no idea this was happening; she had never gotten lower than a B in her life. But I didn't call the school. I didn't argue about the grade. She had to figure out what to do."

Have the courage to tell your teen or tween about your own missteps and epic failures, times when you thought the world would end, but somehow it didn't. Since she wasn't around when you were a gawky, awkward, or naïve teen, she will appreciate anecdotes that prove you were not always as capable and confident as you are now. These stories boost your daughter's hopes for her own progress.

7. Getting Along with Authority Figures

If you don't intend to rescue daughters who are freaking out about difficult college professors, internship directors, or job supervisors, practice doing less in response to her clashes with authority figures now. Your student thinks her social studies teacher graded her project unfairly? She thinks her guidance counselor is weird? She's convinced her vice principal has it out for her?

Before you call the school to complain or to request changes, remember that these situations are ideal opportunities for her to practice handling authority figures she doesn't relish. Someday, your young adult daughter will likely have work colleagues, managers, or directors who are not her cup of tea. Now is a good time for her to figure out how to get along with people she finds difficult and make challenging relationships more tolerable.

Start by asking for your teen's perspective on what is going on. What are adults telling her? Can she reflect on what she might be contributing to the tension? Using you as a sounding board can give your daughter greater clarity and insight, which may elicit possible solutions. What can—and can't—she control? How can she make positive changes?

Sometimes the lesson is that your daughter has limited choices. She won't always be able to avoid authority figures she dislikes. To get ahead in her career, she may have to endure supervisors she neither respects nor enjoys working with. Over time, your teen may realize that keeping an open mind helps her to learn from all sorts of people, regardless of her feelings about them. Changing her own attitude and/or behavior can make the difference.

8. Self-Advocacy

If problem situations do warrant action, providing only as much scaffolding as she needs helps your daughter to self-advocate. Does she know what she hopes to accomplish? Has she planned what she is going to say? Would she feel more confident if she wrote out a script and practices it with you? Coach your teen to craft the clear, succinct, and constructive messages listeners are most receptive to hearing.

With achievement, maintaining your role as a supportive coach won't always be easy. Other parents may implore you to get overly involved, but in this case bucking the tide is in your daughter's best interest. Staying in your own lane empowers her with the building blocks of self-advocacy.

Roberta, mother of Yolanda, fourteen, describes a situation with a new math teacher at her daughter's school. "All the moms were up in arms. I tend not to get involved in these things because unless a teacher is abusive, kids need to learn how to deal with lousy teachers. But the moms were relentless that we had to be a united front in confronting the teacher. So I asked Yolanda what she thought and she said she would be mortified, that she is old enough to handle that kind of thing on her own. She spoke to the teacher directly, which is how we're raising her."

Teens and tweens often hesitate to speak up if teachers forget to provide the classroom accommodations to which their Individualized Education Programs (IEPs) or 504 Plans entitle them. Sanya, mother of a sixteen-year-old, treats this as a teaching opportunity: "Myah is supposed to get extra time on tests, but when teachers forget, she wants me to take care of it. If I do it for her, I'm not teaching her an important skill. So I ask her to email her teacher herself and cc me. That way, the teacher knows a parent is silently supporting a teen to self-advocate."

Explain to your daughter that she is her own best advocate. Only she can accurately explain situations to her teacher. As Sanya told Myah, "Your request will be more valid with your teacher knowing it's coming from you rather than a helicopter parent. Your words are most powerful. But your teacher might take you even more seriously knowing that I'm fully behind you."

Being assertive with parents, teachers, and coaches teaches girls to confidently express themselves with other adults, including therapists. Usually, mothers are the messengers for teens who want to end their therapy. But Darla told me that Debi, fourteen, "wanted me to call you and I said absolutely not. She needed to talk to you." When Debi brought this up at our next meeting, we were able to discuss the pros and cons of her taking a break from our work. I suggested she take time to decide. Soon after, her mother emailed, "Debi told me today she is continuing 'for now and into the foreseeable future.'"

9. Life Skills

Of course, you know that teens need basic life skills to thrive once they leave home. And yet, there is a trend for parents to do too much so kids don't have to get their hands dirty—literally and metaphorically. Teachers who work with elementary- and middle-school-age students tell me that, as a result, they are increasingly having to correct deficits.

Madeline works with her youngest students so they can use art materials. She explains, "Kids are being raised holding tablets, not crayons. They're not coloring. I have to begin by teaching them how to press hard and press lightly. If their hands aren't strong enough to hold crayons, they have to learn to stand up and put body weight into it to get color. Basic stuff."

Similarly, Madeline continues, "Now kids can't cut with scissors, either. Parents don't want them to cut themselves. Except for tummy time, they're on their backs so much they're not developing hand muscles. Kids' fine motor skills usually develop through picking up Cheerios and digging in dirt. But everything is on the computer now; they just have to push buttons, so their hands aren't as strong and they tire quickly."

Fast-forward to the young adult years where overparenting extremes similarly hold back "kids" from developing life skills. A colleague says, "My sister-in-law makes my niece breakfast every morning. She's living at home while she goes to a community college. But she's nineteen! Once in a while, it's nice. But every day? She wakes her daughter up every morning, does her laundry. At that age, kids are capable of doing those things. It makes them feel good about themselves to be competent. They need practical skills for their whole lives."

Give your daughter chores around the house and expect her to do them—especially before having fun. Even if she already knows how to separate loads of laundry, she benefits from learning to manage all the tasks on her plate. Don't fall for excuses, as I did. Sadly, my teens totally bamboozled me by convincing me that loading the dishwasher was impossible if I wanted them to finish their homework and get to sleep. Now I'd say, "Ten minutes won't make a big difference. The sooner you do it, the sooner you can start your work."

Essie knows what her daughter needs to grow up. "But her father tries to do it for her. He wants to be helpful," she says. "It's easier to do her laundry because you're sick of looking at the pile. But then I say to myself, 'You can't do that. Then she's not learning and she needs to know how to do it.' I tell my daughter, 'Do your laundry, because I'm not coming with you to college. If you want to put it off until ten p.m., that's on you.'"

Rather than asking girls to load up on extra courses or enrichment work, consider real-life experiences. Far more than from homework, teens learn from shadowing mentors, doing internships in fields that interest them, working at summer jobs that give them responsibilities, and volunteering.

When girls are reluctant to practice adult skills, mothers may have to nudge them in that direction. Note: nudge, not judge—and no nagging, either. Judith wisely set up expectations and then supported her daughter in putting ideas into action. "She's got to get herself a summer job. She works at the Y, but not forty hours, and is saving for college. So I told her she needs to think and figure things out. I reminded her once to make that phone call. Over the weekend we'll have a conversation."

10. Resiliency

Collectively, the nine skills just described create resiliency. The capacity to cope with stress, know herself well and manage her feelings, solve problems, marshal self-control, act responsibly, be accountable, set reasonable goals and expectations, get along with authority figures, self-advocate, and develop life skills will serve your daughter well now and forever.

Bonus for Mothers

Relieved from pressures to do more, you can sit back and watch your teen's unfolding maturation. In return for not micromanaging her, you will enjoy a more peaceful and satisfying mother-daughter relationship. Equally important, you will reap personal rewards. Overinvolvement doesn't just harm teens; it hurts mothers, too.

Research shows that women who base their self-worth on kids' accomplishments often lose sleep, make themselves sick with worry, feel miserable, and experience less joy and personal satisfaction. Overfocusing on teens also means mothers have less time and emotional energy for spouses and partners. With teens occupying more parental bandwidth and tensions heightening over how to raise them, this is often a time when intimate relationships can wither without extra attention and TLC.

Plus, mothers who are overinvolved in teens' lives have less time for their own. Hobbies and stress-reducing activities go by the wayside. There is less engagement with friends, family, and community, which are rich sources of support. Unless you practice self-care and maintain a healthy, balanced life, it is hard to model these priorities for your teen.

OVERINVOLVEMENT CHECKLIST

Do you:

- ☐ Get more disappointed than your daughter when she doesn't get a plum role in a play?
- ☐ Know the SAT or ACT scores of her friends?
- ☐ Freak out when she isn't chosen for an elite team?
- ☐ Lose sleep over whether she'll be asked to the prom?
- ☐ Consider calling the parents of a friend who was mean to her?
- ☐ Scope out the competition before state orchestra or chorus auditions?
- ☐ Calculate the test grades she needs to get an A for the year?
- ☐ See a paper on the floor and race it up to school in case she needs it?
- ☐ Offer to pay her $250 to take advanced math?
- ☐ Rewrite papers you don't think are A-worthy?
- ☐ Call school administrators to protest disciplinary actions?

- ☐ Get a great idea for your teen's college essay, write it up, and stick it under her door?
- ☐ Insist she takes Latin to build her vocabulary, rather than French, which she prefers?
- ☐ Require her to read classics such as *Anna Karenina* in her free time?
- ☐ Quiz your daughter's friends about their GPAs and where they're applying ED?
- ☐ Call in a favor when your teen is pulled over for a traffic violation so she can avoid going to court and sullying her record?
- ☐ Stand outside her door when you hear her fighting with a friend, just in case she gets upset or wants your help?
- ☐ Text your middle school student while she is on a field trip to see if she is having a good time or misses you?
- ☐ While she is in the shower, ask her good friend if she's still talking to the boy she's been interested in?
- ☐ Check her cellphone to confirm that she's standing up to the girl who's been sending her nasty messages?

If these behaviors resonate with you, overstepping the bounds of age-appropriate involvement could be holding your daughter back from developing fundamental inner resources and life skills. Consider doing less to achieve more.

DOS AND DON'TS OF INVOLVEMENT

Overinvolvement	Appropriate Involvement
I'm emailing your teacher on Monday.	How could you handle that with your teacher?
Did you do your homework?	(Silence) **OR** As soon as you finish up what you have to do, we can get those sneakers you need.
Why don't you work on your project now?	How is your project going?
Black holes would be an impressive topic for your research!	What topic seems most intriguing?
You need private voice coaching to get really good.	I know you're really enjoying singing. Do you think you'd enjoy taking some voice lessons?
I'll make a diorama for you; it'll add so much to your project!	Do you need any supplies for your project?
You should break up with him now; he's not good enough for you.	How did you feel when he said that?
I'll write a note to excuse you.	How can you avoid your teacher taking points off in the future?

I'll override your guidance counselor so you can take AP Spanish.	How would you feel about a more challenging Spanish class?
You're going in early for extra help today!	What could clear up your confusion?
I don't like that girl.	What do you like about Cameron?
I'll get you switched out of that chem class.	How can you get along better with Mrs. King?
Here's what you should text back to him.	How do you plan to respond?

• • •

Now that you're doing less to achieve more, your words will have even more impact on your daughter. Communicating effectively is key. The better you can hone your words and express them clearly and respectfully, the more receptive your teen will be to hearing—and thus internalizing—your messages. When you're hit with unexpected questions or provocative comments, knowing how to respond in a measured and thoughtful manner will defuse potentially combustible conversations and keep you on track. The next chapter offers all sorts of tips for productive discussions with daughters.

CHAPTER SEVEN

Fruitful Conversations 2.0

It's important from the start to explicitly state you want girls to come to you. Don't assume they know. It has to be repeated. Say, "Look, I know there's going to be pressure, and I know you're going to feel this way or that way. I want you to know that you can come to me." And actions have to reflect words. If your kid tells you something that happened and you lash out, obviously they're going to withdraw. You can't be judgmental or angry or horrified.

—KITTY, 17

My daughter has become a full-on teenager. She does the push/pull thing kids seem to do at age three or four when they want to be more independent, but then run back to their parents to make sure the tie is still there. So if she hasn't filled me in, I don't ask her. I tell her I'm happy to listen, but will leave it up to her. I've found that reminding her I'm here to listen—about anything—has become more effective than asking her directly.

—RUTH, MOTHER OF ANNA, 14

If my mom picks me up from school and I've had a bad day, she tells me I'm bringing bad vibes into the car because I'm not talking. It happens every single day because I don't feel like having a full-on conversation as soon as I get out of school. I don't like getting screamed at, either.

—IZZIE, 15

Communicating with teens is a timeless challenge, whether you're discussing lunch plans or a serious issue. Around puberty, talking suddenly gets trickier. As girls prioritize peers and seek independence from parents, it may be harder to corral them into conversations. When you do, your daughter's adolescent brain uses its newfound powers of higher-level reasoning to scrutinize your thinking, decisions, and actions. Even seemingly benign chats can turn unfriendly.

But being in the know helps you to stay close to your teen and most effectively guide her. Mutually respectful, nonjudgmental, give-and-take conversations are essential. That is why, for parents of digital natives, communication issues are as *timely* as they are *timeless*. With face-to-face interactions becoming a dying art, staying in the loop is harder. As teens and tweens socialize primarily via silent text messages and social media apps, you are privy to fewer peer conversations. Not to mention, nowadays before contacting your daughter you have to decide which among many modes of communication would be best.

This chapter describes listening and speaking skills that promote fruitful conversations. After reviewing the ABCs of good communication, this chapter provides tips on how to initiate difficult discussions as well as to respond when teens push your buttons. Teen girls' perspectives on what usually halts mother-daughter dialogue in its tracks will help you to avoid derailing conversations.

These tools create a fertile foundation of goodwill, mutual respect, and understanding in your relationship with your teen. From this bed of positivity, meaningful conversations can blossom, the fruits of which can be reaped when important topics and difficult decisions are discussed.

The Special Mother-Daughter Bond

Communication within all intimate relationships is challenging. But between women and teen girls, interactions can reach a whole new level of fraught. This is because mother-daughter bonds are uniquely and exquisitely intense. No matter how old women are, relationships with mothers as well as daughters often evoke the fiercest reactions—both positive and negative. The power of mothers and daughters to gratify and validate each other is rivaled only by how deeply they can disappoint and wound each other.

As a result, women and girls are often supersensitive to nuances in each other's tone and message. Reading into what is said and not said, it is easy to come to conclusions that are just plain wrong. Many teens assume that mothers, who know them best, already know what they are thinking. So girls don't make an effort to explain themselves. This misguided reticence almost guarantees disappointment. Even the most loving, devoted mother is not a mind reader.

When mothers and daughters disagree, conflict may be perceived as a threat to the relationship. In some women's minds, heated discussions are symbols of failure, proof positive of not getting along. Teens, on their part, may fear repercussions of expressing criticism or negative emotions. This is why many mothers and daughters tiptoe around contentious issues. But actually, this puts relationships at greater risk. It is when unexpressed hurts and disappointments are left to smolder that they can become noxious.

Raina's voice is taut with tension as she tells me about what has been driving a wedge between her and her mother: "My biggest issue is driving with friends. I don't have a license, but my friends do. I tell my mom that I should be able to get rides with them. I have a job, I'm seventeen, and I'm still being treated as a child."

Raina is less frustrated by graduated driving laws than her inability to resolve conflicts with her mother: "It's a stupid rule. But the actual rule is never discussed. What is the radius I can drive to? I'm never given an answer. It's vague and unspoken. We can never have a productive conversation without someone lashing out. My dad gets mad at me for fighting with my mother, I get mad at my mom for saying something illogical, and she gets mad at me for having attitude. I know it's going to happen. It's a predictable pattern."

It is up to mothers to break negative cycles. Marshaling self-control and staying composed prevent the angry outbursts that, like fleeting tropical storms, wash away fragile buds of potentially constructive conversations. As Nanette says, "In a perfect world, everybody would talk things out without everybody screaming. If I start raising my voice, it's a lose-lose situation."

With a spirit of constructiveness, embrace confrontations as chances for you and your teen to better understand each other and mutually solve problems. Tackle conflicts head-on, respectfully and constructively. Really hear each other out. Figure out what you agree on and use that as a starting point for tackling your issues of contention. As if you were solving an intriguing puzzle, bring the same flexibility and creativity to resolving your mother-daughter differences.

Throughout this process, teens learn it is possible to tackle tough topics. One or both of you might get upset, but it won't last forever. You will never stop loving each other. In fact, civilly expressing grievances helps to release tension and clear the air between you, which may make you feel closer. Making changes that satisfy each of your needs allows your relationship to evolve and endure. These skills become an essential template for when your daughter is at odds with friends, future partners, colleagues, roommates, or employers.

How to "Talk"

Connecting in the digital age offers many possibilities, each with its own implications. What are the advantages of texting teens and tweens? When is it best to call, and when is that problematic? Is emailing ever a good idea? When are face-to-face conversations best?

Think about the purpose of contacting your daughter. Do you need a quick answer to a simple question? Are you giving her information? Are you asking her to do something? Are you just checking in to see if she is okay? Next, how urgently must you reach her? Do you want an immediate response, or can it wait? Finally, will she need privacy?

Must your teen be able to read and/or respond to your message without her peers' awareness?

Email

Although girls rarely email except to communicate with teachers, if your daughter uses this modality it offers distinct advantages. Emailing is less intrusive than calling or text messaging. Since there is less expectation of an immediate response, when you convey concerns via email your teen is less likely to feel on the spot. With more time to process and think about your message, she may compose a less defensive, more thoughtful response. If you have a lot to say, email also spares your thumbs a painful workout.

Text Message (or iMessage)

As of now, text messaging is most teens' and tweens' preferred way of communicating. In fact, when your daughter says she's been "talking" to a sibling or friend, there is a good chance they're not actually using their voices. Unless they are using a video platform, "talking" nowadays generally means communicating using semisynchronous written words without seeing or hearing each other. Texting's top ten benefits are as follows:

1. Your daughter will get your message right away, since she probably checks her phone often.
2. You can reasonably expect that she will read and respond to your message more quickly because text

messaging is typically more contemporaneous than email.

3. She's more likely to respond because it's easy to hit "Reply" and respond with emojis.

4. She can communicate with you without her peers' knowledge.

5. To make a quick point, texting is less intrusive than calling; after an argument, for example, sending a text message lets her know you love her.

6. She can't get huffy or walk away, as with in-person conversations, so it's a good way to express concerns.

7. You can add a "btw . . ." or "forgot to tell you . . ." to previous conversations, whether they were conducted digitally or in person.

8. A quick text is the digital version of slipping a note under your daughter's door or in her backpack to let her know you're thinking of her.

9. Text messages double as an in-home intercom system. Tori says, "She'll be in bed and I'll be in bed. Instead of yelling to her and not knowing whether she'll hear me, I'll text. I know she's always got her phone with her and her notifications are turned on, so she gets the message right away and then I'll get a response. It's incredible."

10. Since text messages are usually short, this modality encourages you to focus on your most crucial points and express them briefly.

The downsides of text messaging include the following:

1. If you are trying to make sure your daughter is okay, a text message doesn't provide the richer contextual information of a phone call or video chat, such as tone of voice and facial expression.

2. Unless she uses the "Send Read Receipts" option in her phone's settings, you won't know if your teen read your message (she can claim her phone was on Do Not Disturb mode or didn't have service, her volume was off, or she didn't see your message for some other creative reason). She might also insist that her reply to you didn't send.

3. When one or both of you are joking, angry, or being ironic or sarcastic, there is a greater risk of miscommunication because of lack of nonverbal cues, nuance, and emotional tonality.

4. Emojis can clarify intent, but only if both of you know how to use them appropriately; otherwise, emojis can cause a heap of trouble, some of it cringeworthy.

Telephone Calls

It can be tempting to call your daughter on her cellphone to ask for—or give her—time-sensitive information whenever you feel the need for immediate contact. It is often parents' first instinct to reach for the phone during anxious moments and actual crises. Yet calling is the most potentially provocative, intrusive, and troublesome way to contact girls.

Unlike texting, other forms of messaging, and email, phone calls are public. When your daughter's cellphone is not on silent, the ring of an incoming call will be obvious and possibly distracting to everyone within earshot. If she answers, your teen may have to excuse herself from friends and activities or risk being overheard. Calling her while she is driving also puts her in a fix. Despite endless warnings about the dangers of using a cellphone while driving, she may feel compelled to answer if she sees "Mom" on the caller ID.

Video Chatting

Platforms such as FaceTime, Skype, Viber, Google Hangouts, Zoom, Google Meet, Facebook Messenger, and so forth can be ideal for communicating with your daughter while you're traveling for business or pleasure—if she's game. Certainly, many teens and tweens are well versed with these platforms after months of remote schooling during the pandemic.

Seeing her face and hearing her voice can give you a better read on what she is thinking and feeling. Since these technologies simulate face-to-face interactions, make sure to consider your daughter's ability and willingness to video chat with you at a time and in a place she is comfortable doing so.

Technology "Glitches"

Knowing that you and your daughter can always contact each other by cellphone can provide blissful peace of mind. The problem lies in the word *always*. You can't always rely on digital modalities. Besides true tech glitches, which are ubiquitous and frustrating, teens are pros at finding technological excuses for *avoiding* communication. Perhaps your daughter has offered these reasons for your failure to connect with her:

- I *couldn't* call you, Mom! I had terrible cell service.
- I left my cellphone in my friend's car, so I didn't know you called.
- I left a message on the landline letting you know I'd be staying over at my friend's after the party (aka I didn't call your cell because then I'd actually have to talk to you and ask if I could sleep over and you might've said no).
- My phone died because I didn't have time to charge it.

To Track or Not to Track?

When your teen starts socializing with friends you don't know well, concerns about her safety may rise exponentially. You might even be tempted to use a "family communication and safety" app. These allow you not only to track your teen's location, but also to monitor her driving speed and acceleration, her cellphone's battery level, how much she uses her cellphone while the car is moving, and a whole host of other metrics.

Although technology has its uses, there are disadvantages. For one, location-sharing apps can give you a false sense of security. More determined than ever to demonstrate autonomy, today's girls find ways to circumvent safety mechanisms parents put in place. Even girls who are not particularly tech savvy can thwart parents' efforts to keep track of them by disabling functions. One of the six senior girls in a high school focus group told me, "I came up with ways to get around it. The trick is to turn off the location, which you're not supposed to be able to do." Her friend nonchalantly adds, "Yeah, you just have to glitch out those apps."

Second, when teens resent what they view as parents' intrusive and inappropriate surveillance, technology causes more harm than good. Bella, seventeen, describes, "They put all sorts of trackers on my phone so they could pull up my screen on their screen and tell how much power my phone had. I got a text message from them that said, 'Why are you moving?' I was walking down the street to get food! My dad got a notification on his phone: 'Bella is two yards away from the house.' This was the final straw."

In addition, when girls react negatively to location-tracking apps, safety is *less* assured. Bella tells me, "Finally, I gave them back the phone they got me and bought my own." She would not give her parents the new number. After that, her parents had no way of communicating with her when she wasn't home. During a focus group, girls at a rural high school described further how parents' efforts to control teens can backfire. Cami explains, "When we leave our phones somewhere so our parents don't know where we are and something *does* happen, we don't have our phones when we really need them."

The lesson of these anecdotes is that there is no substitute for honest communication between mothers and daughters. If your goal is encouraging compliance, deterring bad judgment, and avoiding unnecessary power struggles, heart-to-heart conversations are more effective than digital surveillance. If your safety concerns are reasonable and expressed respectfully, with an openness to listening to her ideas, your teen should be willing to discuss them without feeling babied or losing face.

Bountiful Conversations

Face-to-face conversations offer your daughter a multitude of advantages. Unlike interacting through texts, email, and social media messages, speaking in person promotes social intelligence. Your daughter is encouraged to become attuned to subtle but essential nonverbal cues of communications. As she picks up on incongruities between what people say and what they mean, she learns to interpret sarcasm and irony. Importantly, your teen also becomes adept at gauging people's trustworthiness.

Communication 101 Reminders

Before getting into more complex skills, let's review the basics of communication. The following time-tested strategies encourage fruitful conversations.

Be Fully Present

Being in the moment with your daughter facilitates true connection. Give her your full attention. Make appropriate eye contact. Put down the mail. Turn off your cellphone, put it on silent, or turn it upside down so you can't be distracted by notifications. Be curious about what is on her mind and hear what she has to say as if for the first time—rather than thinking you have heard this all before. That way, she knows how much you are invested in speaking with her.

Mind Your Mindset

Make an intention to keep conversations constructive and respectful. Remember that both of you want to get your points across, feel heard, and be understood. Rather than just going through the motions because you fear the conversation is a pointless exercise, set an intention to resolve conflicts as thoroughly and judiciously as possible.

Listen to Understand

Improving listening skills with teens will improve communication in all your relationships. Research demonstrates that listening to *understand* the other person's thoughts and feelings creates stronger interpersonal connections than listening to *respond*. When you listen to understand, you're focusing beyond your daughter's words on the bigger, deeper messages she is trying to convey.

Listening to respond, on the other hand, involves critiquing the other person's message and, while they're still talking, mentally rehearsing how you plan to reply. When your teen is speaking, do you ever think, "That can't be true!" "She needs a reality check!" or "I've got the perfect response to that argument."? If so, you may be among the many people researchers identify who mistakenly believe they are listening to understand when actually they are listening to respond.

Ask Questions

When you ask your daughter to elaborate or give you more information, you communicate that you care about her thoughts and feelings. Big caveat: asking questions is a delicate undertaking. Many teens abhor questions they think are too personal, too probing, too hard to answer, or too likely to betray friends' confidences. Tread carefully.

Empathize

Putting yourself in your daughter's shoes and imagining what she experiences is a powerful way to engage her in conversation. But no teen likes to be told how she "must be feeling." So ask—rather than tell—her. Courteously check out whether your intuitions are correct.

Craft Your Message

Your daughter is more likely to hear your message when you do the following:

- Use "I" statements—rather than "You" statements that sound accusatory.

- Take responsibility for your role—rather than blaming her for all problems.

- Stick to the present—rather than rehashing past arguments or transgressions.

Monitor Your Nonverbal Behavior

To convey warmth and positivity:

- Assume a relaxed posture—rather than towering over her or crossing your arms.

- Adopt a neutral facial expression—rather than frowning or glaring.

- Use a pleasant tone of voice—rather than speaking angrily or sarcastically.

- Use the 50/70 rule for good eye contact—gaze at her 50 percent of the time when speaking and 70 percent when listening—rather than either extreme of glancing elsewhere or staring at her.

Conversational Land Mines

Let's say you're in the middle of a conversation that you think is going well, when all of a sudden it goes off the rails. Your daughter gets upset, clams up, or stomps off, leaving you baffled. What went wrong? Fortunately, teens I speak with are more than willing to talk about what mothers do that stops discussions in their tracks. Here are the top nine.

Not Listening

If your daughter thinks you're more interested in what you have to say than in what she has to say, she'll probably avoid conversations.

> **Daughter:** Mom, I had a good reason for coming in after curfew last night. Let me explain.

NOT

> **Mom:** Stop right there! There's no good reason. I don't want to hear it.

INSTEAD, TRY

> **Mom:** I'm listening.
>
> **Daughter:** I was supposed to get a ride from someone who ended up having some beer, so I had to wait for Natalie to take me home and she had to drop off Jesse first. Then it took even longer because she was driving slowly 'cause of the storm.

Demanding or Threatening

Your teen or tween will be more amenable to doing what you ask if she thinks you respect her autonomy. So it is more effective to encourage rather than to demand that she do something. Threatening consequences often triggers power struggles by prompting girls to dig their heels in even more deeply.

NOT

> **Mom:** I'm telling you to do this and I expect you to do it now!

INSTEAD, TRY

> **Mom:** I know you don't have to do this, but I know you can—and I hope you will.

Being Hypocritical

Teens are hypersensitive to inconsistencies, especially when they are held to different standards than mothers. Expectations about screen use are a good example. If you set limits on the family's use of devices but act as if your own work or social demands give you an automatic pass, she'll resent your hypocrisy and be less likely to comply.

Coming Across Off-Putting

Daughters are dissuaded from talking when mothers are (a) negative (e.g., "She focuses on the one thing that needs improvement. I have all As and one B"—Amber, 11), (b) condescending (e.g., "When I ask why she doesn't want me to do something, she always says, 'Because I said so.' It's so frustrating"—Tanya, 12), or (c) sarcastic ("She acts like she's joking, but she's saying mean stuff"—Anita, 13).

Not Acting Trustworthy

If girls think mothers are poor confidantes, they are less likely to talk. Pearl, thirteen, says, "My mom is gossipy. She'll talk to other moms, so I don't tell her anything." Steph, also thirteen, agrees. "My mom tells my aunts and grandmother everything I say. Then they're like, 'So did you bring up your math grade?' Thanks, Mom!"

Disrespecting Them

Junior and senior high school girls get riled up when talking about this. Sam, sixteen, says, "Don't treat me like I'm an employee. It's not a performance review." Mel, seventeen, tells me, "My parents don't recognize that I have a somewhat developed mind and I'm capable of thinking for myself and I can have opinions that differ from theirs." Message received!

Punishing Them for Being Honest

When your daughter comes to you and voluntarily admits to wrongdoing you're unaware of, appreciate her honesty. She recognizes her behavior needs to change. Allyn, sixteen, says, "Don't punish if they tell you. The fact that they told you means they're acknowledging they needed to." She goes on to make the excellent point, "Better that they'll tell you stuff and be honest. Then you'll also get a chance to discuss it with them."

Using Negative Tones

Telling your daughter that you're annoyed or frustrated is one thing; acting irritated or exasperated is another. As you know, teens respond more to mothers' moods than words. An off-putting tone makes her shy away from talking, much less listening to and heeding what you say. Campbell, seventeen, tells me, "If I'm feeling depressed and she tries to cheer me up and it doesn't work, she'll get upset with me. I don't want to talk to her if she gets frustrated with me."

Needing to Be Right

If you come across as self-righteous or moralistic, your daughter will think you've already made up your mind that she is wrong. Expecting not to be heard, she'll avoid or tune out of conversations. Alternatively, she may get defensive, angry, or resentful. Letting go of rigid, right-or-wrong positions invites openness, receptivity, and empathy, all of which facilitate genuine back-and-forth communications and closer mother-daughter bonds.

Dreaded Discussions

At one time or another, every parent is faced with the need to have a difficult discussion with a teen or tween daughter. Topics vary, but are often complex, sometimes radioactive, and usually dreaded. You may feel compelled to bring up issues around sexuality, substances, school performance (e.g., effort, grades, homework completion), character issues (e.g., lying, defiance, unkindness), or choices of friends and romantic partners.

Other factors can make these discussions even more difficult. What is going on with your daughter may elicit painful memories for you. If, say, you were depressed as a result of being teased or socially marginalized as a teen, it could be more difficult for you to discuss her heartbreak when a friend rejects her or a group excludes her. If someone close to you suffered from lung cancer, learning your tween tried vaping or smoking may send you over the edge.

Like most parents facing difficult discussions, you may agonize over the right words to use. To increase the chance of her buying into your core message, you may mentally rehearse your speech. Crystallizing concerns in your own mind will help you to express them more easily. Thinking clearly facilitates communicating clearly.

To have a fighting chance of getting a satisfying response from your daughter, focus on what you really want to know. These days, for example, it is the rare mother who hasn't asked her teen or tween, "Why are you always on your phone?" This question practically invites denial and defensiveness (e.g., "I'm so not!" "I'm on my phone a lot less than my sister!" "Why are you saying that? You know I've cut down!"). But taking a step back, what are women who ask that question really looking for? How are girls expected to respond? What *can* they say?

A better outcome is possible when mothers clarify concerns. "Why are you always on your phone?" becomes "Why aren't you talking to *me* instead of whoever is on your phone?" or "Is there something going on that I should know about?" or "I'd like you to do your homework now so you're not so stressed later" or "Are you still getting mean messages from that girl who's mad at you?" or "Did that boy get back to you yet?" Asking the question you really want your daughter to answer goes a long way in improving communication.

When Daughters Push Buttons

If you think the most challenging conversations are the ones you plan and obsess about, just wait until your daughter pushes your emotional buttons—a notorious talent of teen and tween girls. She may zero in on your vulnerabilities, poke at your deepest sensitivities, venture into controversial territory, or make statements that hit way too close to home. Daughters are savants at holding up mirrors that magnify mothers' most glaring flaws.

Provocative questions and complaints can come out of nowhere. Prepare to be caught off guard. Your daughter might ask direct, personal questions such as, "Did you ever smoke weed?" or "Did you have sex before you got married?" or "How many people have you slept with?" She may insist you are cruel, hopelessly out of touch, or horribly prejudiced. Her observations (e.g., "You never agree with Dad" or "You always use that voice when you talk to Grandma") may make you flinch or recoil.

Here are some strategies to help you respond most constructively when your daughter pushes your buttons.

Recognize You've Been Triggered

It is crucial to recognize in the moment when your daughter's button-pushing triggers you. Everyone responds differently. Your reaction could be physical, emotional, behavioral, or a combination—and run the gamut from mild to volcanic. You may feel nervous, uncomfortable, or strange. Your face may redden, your heart rate may quicken, your palms may sweat, and you may squirm. You may be as emotionally worked up as if facing a dire threat.

Suddenly, you may hear nothing wise coming out of your mouth. Or nothing might come out at all except, perhaps, "Um . . ." Maybe the words coming out of your mouth sound like someone else's entirely, as if you're channeling a person you least want to emulate.

Take Your Emotional Temperature

Pay attention to your body. If you sense a state of high arousal, calm your central nervous system before responding to your teen. That is because once your brain perceives a threat and activates the fight-or-flight survival mechanism, the release of the stress hormone cortisol essentially sends your sensible frontal lobes on hiatus. Without the ability to empathize with your daughter, inhibit unhelpful responses, and be cognizant of how your behavior affects her, the chance of having a fruitful conversation plummets.

Delay Responding

Resist the urge to respond instantly. Instead, consider this game-changing strategy: First figure out what triggered you and restore your emotional equilibrium. Postpone answering your daughter until you can process your reaction, temper your anger or defensiveness, and reply in a way that both validates her and encourages future conversations.

TRY

- That's a good question. I'll get back to you as soon as I've thought more about it.
- I'd like us to discuss that when I figure out how to explain how I feel.
- Let's talk about that this weekend when we're not rushed.
- This is important. Can we make a plan to discuss it when I'm home from work?

Maintain Emotional Control

Because you are the adult, you are in charge of managing emotions aroused by discussions. Keeping it together is key. Jillian explains this challenge: "I have to figure out how not to go from a cup of lukewarm water to boiling in three seconds flat. My daughter provokes me constantly, and then is aghast that I'm raising my voice. I know it's my job to bring it back to a simmer. If I count to five—or ten—and take a breath before engaging, I know the conversation will go so much better. At least I try." What happens when mothers don't do this? As Ramona, sixteen, tells it, "My mom takes it to an intense level it has no business getting to."

Be Constructive, Not Defensive

When your daughter makes provocative statements or accusations, resist getting defensive. Even if you think what she says is untrue, it is possible something in your words or behavior gave her a hint of that impression. When you calmly ask for more information, listen carefully, and remain open to learning about yourself, you demonstrate your openness to constructive criticism, willingness to acknowledge flaws, and commitment to reciprocity in the mother-daughter relationship.

> **Daughter:** You don't like my best friend just because she's bi! You're so biased against LGBTQ people!

NOT

> **Mom:** What? No, I'm not! That's not true!
>
> **Daughter:** (Walks out, slamming door)

INSTEAD, TRY

> **Mom:** I'm sorry something I said gave you that impression. Please help me to understand how you got this idea.
>
> **Daughter:** You hardly ever ask how she is or invite her to stay for dinner like with my other friends.
>
> **Mom:** I appreciate you pointing this out, and I really want to think more about it.

Mindfully Share Information

If you want your teen to tell you the truth, model being honest with her. Since girls' acutely sensitive antennae pick up on mothers' duplicity, fibbing would be counterproductive. According to a study from Singapore, young adults whose parents lied to them when they were children report more dishonest behavior and adjustment difficulties now that they are grown.

You don't have to disclose anything that doesn't feel right to share. But rather than making something up, tell your tween you're not comfortable talking about the subject, at least not right now. Being truthful doesn't require telling her *everything*, either. Start by determining why she is curious.

TRY

> **Mom:** What makes you ask me about this now?

OR

> **Mom:** Can you help me understand why it's important for you to know that?

OR

> **Mom:** I'm uncomfortable answering that question. But here's what I *can* tell you . . .

Know When to Stop Talking

Teens and tweens easily become overwhelmed when discussing intense topics. If a talk is going nowhere or being torpedoed by escalating emotions, tangential comments, or name-calling, press pause. Admittedly, in the moment, this is easier said than done. Confronting a fresh problem or exasperating issue can seem urgent. You may think, "It's now or never." But that is almost never true.

TRY

> **Mom:** You know, I think we should take a break.

OR

> **Mom:** Let's calm down a bit so we can have a better talk.

OR

> **Mom:** Why don't we get a snack and then we can pick this up where we left off?

If your daughter keeps at you, you'll have to take responsibility for de-escalating the situation. Go somewhere private and quiet, preferably outside. A few breaths of cleansing fresh air should restore mental serenity and physical relaxation.

TRY

> **Mom:** I'm going to take a moment. When I'm calmer, I think more clearly. We'll continue this in a bit.

Equally important, honor your daughter's needs when she says, "I can't talk about this now." Mia, fifteen, talks in therapy about fighting constantly with her mother. Mia's frequent inability to pinpoint what causes her bad moods frustrates Terri. When Terri probes intently for an explanation, Mia says, "I just freak out and start cursing and it's bad. So when my mom knocks on my door and starts in on an interrogation, I ask her if we could just not talk about this right now. I *will* talk about it, but I just need to take a break first."

If you call a time-out whenever your teen starts crying, however, she will learn that tears are her handy get-out-of-tough-discussions card. When you help her to listen and speak calmly, she learns it is possible to communicate effectively and productively even when upset.

Special Conversation Challenges

Managing Meltdowns

Distraught daughters are especially hard to reach. No words may be "right." Seeing your teen or tween sobbing may make you anxious about what is causing such deep distress. Your inability to soothe her or to find a solution can make you feel helpless or angry. It may be hard not to soak up your daughter's pain like a sponge. And yet, it's helpful to be aware that these reactions are counterproductive.

Regina describes such a scene: "My mother walked in while I was having a mental breakdown. I was curled up on my bed, crying my eyes out and shaking. And she just started yelling at me to tell her what was wrong. Of course, I'm not going to want to tell you something if I'm getting yelled at while I'm sobbing hysterically in my bed. That's not the way it's going to come out."

Women can also react unhelpfully to girls expressing pain on blogs, online forums, and social media sites. Denise, seventeen, was in therapy for worsening depression. She awakened one morning to a furious mother. Her brother, away at college, had sent their parents Denise's heart-wrenching post in which she explained why she wanted to die. Instead of focusing on Denise's intense pain, her mother berated her for "compromising her reputation by seeking attention" in a public forum.

When I ask girls like Regina and Denise how mothers can help emotionally distraught daughters, they tell me, "Before you ask them what's wrong, ask them what they need. Not everyone wants to tell you immediately what's wrong." This is especially astute advice.

It is important to accept whatever girls are feeling, however strong their emotions. "I need comfort and emotional support," Maya, sixteen, says. "If I tell her how I'm feeling and I get yelled at, of course I'm not going to want to talk to her anymore." Elsa, seventeen, tells me, "I get that it can be annoying when I'm down about something, but I should be allowed to be upset and feel down. Don't poke me until you get a reaction. It won't be a good one."

When your daughter is in the throes of distress, being there may be all you can do. In fact, sitting quietly with her and listening without judgment may be enough. Depending on her tolerance for physical contact, you may be able to express how much you love and care about her nonverbally by holding her hand, giving her a hug, or gently rubbing her back.

The Chatterbox and the Clam

Women who are reserved and taciturn can have loud, talkative teens—and vice versa. Unless this is acknowledged, major misunderstandings can occur. This happened when Haley took her daughter to practice driving. Chattering nonstop, Gaye, sixteen, headed into the next lane, frightening Haley so much that she took over the wheel. Haley was worried because she assumed Gaye's incessant talking meant her daughter wasn't taking driving seriously.

Gaye felt misunderstood, insulted, and hurt. Attributing her mother's reaction to anger, Gaye decided Haley must think of her as an immature, irresponsible kid. When they got home, decompressed, and spoke honestly about what happened, Gaye explained that she always managed anxiety by talking too much. Haley realized that she had misinterpreted the reason Gaye chattered incessantly. The opposite was true: Gaye took driving *very* seriously.

Lawyers in the Making

It may be wonderful to watch your teen sharpen her persuasive argument skills—except when she uses them to drive home a point or question your reasoning and decision-making. Does she seem more intent on disputing what you say than constructively exchanging ideas? Is she quick to interject and interrupt? Might she be enjoying honing her advocacy skills and expressing her opinions a little too much? You recognize that your daughter is developing powers of persuasion that could serve her well in life—perhaps in a legal, business, or political career—but right now she may be making discussions unnecessarily protracted, complicated, intense, or painful.

Meryl tells me, "Whenever we try to have a conversation, we have a fight instead. I'm always asking Marie, 'Why are you always talking back?' and she's always saying, 'Because you're always yelling at me.' 'But if you wouldn't talk back,' I tell her, 'I wouldn't have to raise my voice.'" Round and round Meryl and Marie go, no closer to resolving their real conflicts.

Differentiate the validity of your daughter's arguments from the way she is making them. Set the ground rules. No matter how reasonable her thinking, she still has to abide by basic communication courtesies. Both of you deserve to say your piece without interruption. Both of you should listen for understanding—that is, hear each other without jumping to conclusions or perfecting follow-up arguments.

Managing Indirect Information

If you overhear your daughter's conversation, or happen to see things while monitoring her text message threads or group chats, how can you talk to her about what you learn? Let's say your sixteen-year-old mentions a friend's risky sexual behavior or your twelve-year-old brings up a classmate's bulimia. What can you do with this information?

If you bring it up immediately, your teen or tween may be embarrassed or defensive, and thus unreceptive to discussing it. Plus, you may have misinterpreted the situation, or at least overlooked subtleties that could change the calculus of your daughter's attitude or involvement. Unless there's urgency, file away your concerns until an opportunity arises to raise the topic more organically. Without revealing what you're privy to, you can generally address issues such as when it's okay to keep secrets and when they should be divulged, how to know if friends may need an intervention in the way of professional or parental help, and so forth.

Last-Ditch Troubleshooting

If at this point you're still having trouble engaging your daughter in constructive conversations or you're wondering why she doesn't open up to you as you would like, consider these ten possibilities.

PART A: FIVE MORE REASONS TEEN GIRLS DON'T TALK TO MOTHERS

1. **It's How She Is Wired.** Maybe it is just not your daughter's nature to share her innermost thoughts and feelings. Does she confide in anyone? Is she more introverted than her friends? She may be naturally quiet and taciturn, a girl of few words. Recognize and don't take it personally if she is tougher to crack than a chestnut. Above all, don't make it your mission to force her to talk. As Janet, sixteen, tells her mother, "Don't poke and prod until I lash out, and then yell at me for lashing out."

2. **Lack of Reflectiveness.** Maybe your daughter does talk to you, but you don't get much info beyond the bare minimum. You want her to delve more deeply into what she really thinks and feels about topics that

matter. Again, don't assume this reflects her feelings about you or your relationship. Your daughter might prefer to stick with what is familiar and comfortable. She may need time to mature before she can reflect on her inner life, much less share her insights with you.

3. **The Timing Isn't Good.** Many mothers catch teens when they first get home from school, yet this is almost universally when they're least receptive to conversation. By that time, girls have had to be "on," to endure the questions of teachers, friends, and coaches, for six or seven hours. They're thoroughly talked out. This is why your daughter might respond to your benign "How was your day?" as if it were a verbal assault. Before initiating conversation, best to let her decompress; give her the solitary time she craves.

The same goes for when your teen has her period, is getting sick, or is recovering from an illness or injury. She also may clam up after a major falling-out with a friend. Although that is precisely when you most want her to speak to you, she may be otherwise inclined. Georgina, fifteen, explains, "When I'm upset, I put my music on and I stay in my room and draw. And my parents know that, but they can't ever give me my space."

When your teen or tween lets down her guard around bedtime, say good night and offer to scratch her back or take her out for breakfast the next morning. Better yet, ask your daughter when would be a good time for you two to "chat." A cheery tone and casual language won't arouse her alarm about having a "talk" (aka being lectured to, reprimanded, or disciplined).

4. **Peer Loyalty.** Like many teens, your daughter's fierce devotion and loyalty to her friends may cause her to avoid conversations she views as betrayals of peer confidence or trust. Plus, she may believe telling you what her friends are really up to—online or in real life—could put you in a difficult position. Showing her how you handle peer-related disclosures can allay these concerns.

5. **Help Rejection.** It's common for girls to be so ambivalent about autonomy that they struggle with how much to rely on parents. Leonora, seventeen, says her twin "tells our parents too much. Like, complaining about friends getting drunk and then asking to go over there. First, she says, 'Let's figure this out,' then she says, 'I don't want to talk about it anymore.' Okay, if she didn't want their help, why did she ask for it?" If you get similarly mixed messages, try asking breezily, "Do you want me just to listen and be a sounding board, or should I give you my two cents?"

PART B: FIVE MORE WAYS MOTHERS DISCOURAGE CONVERSATION

1. **Closed-Mindedness.** Your daughter may avoid conversations because she believes you've already made up your mind. Show her you are open to considering alternative perspectives. Listen to understand, refraining from snap judgments and

absolute decrees. Acknowledge that as she is maturing, social dynamics change, friendships shift, and families evolve. When you balance flexibility with firmness, she will see you as fair and approachable.

2. **Judgment.** Whether your teen bares her soul may depend on the sort of response she expects. With her still-developing sense of self, she is probably exquisitely sensitive to criticism and judgment. As soon as girls sense mothers are angry or upset, they are loath to get into discussions. And no teen welcomes punishment. If you are unsure whether you come across this way, do some self-reflection—or ask your daughter for feedback.

NOT

> **Mom:** You've got to stop vaping! I've told you again and again how unhealthy it is. You're making terrible choices. I'm very disappointed in you. If I see any vaping stuff around, you're going to lose your laptop and phone for a long time.

INSTEAD, TRY

> **Mom:** I know we've talked about smoking before, but I'm bringing it up again because I'm still concerned. You said you were going to quit, but I'm wondering if you've tried and what it's been like for you.

3. **Too Quick to Fix.** Girls make clear that when talking to mothers, they are not usually asking for advice. They just want to get something off their chests. Your daughter wants you to know what happened and/or how she is feeling about it. As hard as it is not to help (see Chapter Six, "Doing Less to Achieve More"), this is one of those times when the wiser course is just to listen or ask for her thoughts. Otherwise, your teen will conclude you have no confidence in her ability to solve her own problems, which will cause her to bristle and harden her defenses.

Gigi, thirteen, explains, "I just tell my mom something so I can vent, but she'll start talking and talking and talking. I don't really want a response. I just want to say it because it's annoying. I don't need advice or help." Lorraine, mother of Leila, fifteen, is working on this: "I'm superbusy, but I realized that there's nobody else who's going to listen to her venting and not try to fix it or do anything. It's not exactly my style. I need to improve, so I'm trying to have more tolerance and just listen to her."

4. **Not Empathic Enough.** Forgetting to imagine how your teen's experiences affect her is a common oversight. Delilah, fourteen, says, "If my mother hasn't done it or hasn't had an issue with it, she can't put herself in my shoes as much as she thinks she can." Clarisse, sixteen, advises mothers, "Be more understanding. Try and listen. Don't just explode.

> Listen to what they have to say and try to take into consideration that high school is way more difficult now than it should be. There are lots of issues. Just try and understand what they're going through. Try."

Martha, who is working on controlling her knee-jerk reactions, says, "I'm learning I have to keep my cool. In that moment, I don't think. Stopping for a second lets me put myself back in her sixteen-year-old head. It's only when I've cooled down that I remember, yep, I used to do that. I want to stop myself from escalating, or that's what she'll remember years from now."

5. **Off-the-Charts Anxiety.** Your daughter's *and* yours, that is. If your teen whiffs nervous energy radiating from you, she may well avoid saying anything that could set you off. Priscilla, fifteen, says, "If a mother wants to see her daughter as young, shy, and not interested in talking to boys, someone who would never try alcohol, her daughter won't tell her the truth. I know how she feels. I know my mother doesn't want to hear that. She doesn't need the worry."

Anxious girls also try not to catapult mothers' apprehensions into the red zone to spare themselves over-the-top reactions. Dina admits, "When my daughter gets anxious, it makes me more anxious, and I end up yelling, which doesn't help the situation at all."

When Discussions Don't Go Well

Did you go through these troubleshooting lists and think to yourself, "Check, check, and check"? You thought through what you wanted to say to your daughter and felt good about how you approached her. You followed all the guidelines for having productive conversations. But your teen or tween didn't react as you had hoped or expected. Maybe she freaked out or left in a huff, perhaps sending daggers or choice words your way in her wake. It's natural to wonder, "Where did I go wrong?"

If scrupulous self-reflection still doesn't pinpoint a cause, maybe there is nothing more you can learn from this one exchange. You can never anticipate every possibility or be totally prepared for discussions with teens. Some things are beyond your control—and your understanding. You may just have to chalk up a disastrous conversation to some unknown Factor X.

At some point, your daughter may be more receptive to hearing truths about herself. A month, a week, or even a day from now, after a maturational spurt or social validation or a particularly gratifying accomplishment, she may surprise you. Suddenly, she may see your "personal attack" (aka discussion) in a totally different light. In fact, your teen may even thank you for your fantastic idea or helpful suggestion. Well, maybe not right away . . .

Meanwhile, it is time to mentally regroup. Rather than dwelling and losing sleep over one awful discussion, remind yourself that it will not be your last chance to raise the topic. If the subject is that important, it probably needs to be addressed repeatedly, anyway, in different ways and on many occasions. You can easily create other opportunities to speak with your daughter.

TRY

- I've been thinking more about what we talked about the other day. . . .
- After reflecting on our conversation, I think I might not have been clear about . . .
- Have you thought any more about what we discussed?
- Do you have any questions about ___?

Although daughters eventually stop pushing mothers' buttons, difficult discussions continue long after high school and even college graduations. If anything, talking with your daughter and trying to weigh in on her young adult decisions—choosing a mate, following a career path, deciding where to live—can get even trickier. Fortunately, you've been building a repertoire of trusted skills to turn to for these and other crucial discussions.

• • •

Next, we'll be applying these guiding principles and strategies to specific parenting situations. Part Three shines a spotlight on the dilemmas you most often confront—possibly on a daily basis—as you raise your teen or tween daughter.

How can you make the best decisions about technology purchases and screen time? What's a good way to handle a socially isolated daughter or one who is making poor friendship choices? Why has your home become a nightly battleground about homework, and what should you do about it? How can you manage the fallout of divorce, including your relationship with your ex, and the introduction of stepparents? Is it possible to enjoy the college process—and even see it as a conduit to bolstering your daughter's sense of self and emotional resiliency?

These and other questions mothers find most pressing will be discussed in the pages ahead. The next chapter gets into the nitty-gritty about the pragmatic choices you make at home that can help your daughter stay healthy, find balance in her life, form good habits, adopt your most important values, and enjoy family togetherness, all while developing the self-help skills she needs for greater independence.

Part Three

Dealing with Daily Dilemmas

CHAPTER EIGHT

Establishing Healthy Habits

Whether she is in middle school, high school, college, or beyond, to thrive academically and in the workforce your daughter needs her emotional and social ducks in a row. This chapter suggests the kinds of structures, expectations, and habits you can establish at home that, according to science, are most likely to help her succeed.

Providing Structure

How you set up your home, the household rules you establish, and your lifestyle support your beliefs and promote your goals in raising your daughter.

Creating a Balanced Life

For teens to thrive, a balanced life is vital. Girls have to devote time not only to schoolwork and extracurricular activities, but also to taking care of themselves physically, socially, emotionally, and spiritually. Exercising and sleeping mitigate stress, keeping it from reaching the toxic level that leads to emotional meltdown, physical symptoms, illness, and burnout. Interacting with friends and family counters the disturbing loneliness of this generation by providing much-needed social stimulation and support. Recreational activities are not just relaxing and enjoyable, but also teach teens essential life skills.

Ensuring that your daughter's life is balanced may require reevaluating priorities. She can't possibly join every appealing club and sports team, no matter how valuable these activities may be for her college application. To free up time, commitments must be thoughtfully chosen. This teaches her an important lifelong lesson about managing her schedule. With all her academic and extracurricular pressures, your teen may need encouragement to prioritize activities that seem less urgent, yet are crucial for her physical and emotional health.

MOVEMENT

Exercise is invaluable. Movement releases feel-good hormones in the brain, relieving anxiety and mild depression. Mothering the daughter you have means if she isn't sporty you are not going to force her to join a team. She can still work out at a gym; hike; dance; ride a bike (mobile or stationary); practice yoga, Pilates, or martial arts; or rock climb (outdoors or at a rock-climbing gym). Many parks offer fitness or ropes courses. Your daughter can also access many different types of online exercise classes, and perhaps even enjoy them with you.

ART AND MUSIC

Art and music are soul-nurturing activities that can engage girls in a state of flow. Whether your daughter creates, plays, or appreciates music, the experience can alter her mood, energizing or soothing her. Anna, seventeen, spent three periods a day in art class, where she played music, surrounded by like-minded friends, getting so absorbed in painting that she "didn't have to think at all" about her painful family situation.

READING

A large study of teens' media use over time confirms what every mother knows: as screen time rises, teen reading declines. At one time, 60 percent of high school seniors read a book or magazine almost every day. Now, only 16 percent do. In the past year, only a third have read a single book for pleasure.

This is unfortunate. And I'm not referring to reading's positive effects on vocabulary, writing skills, and SAT scores. Rather, teens today are largely missing out on one of life's most treasured diversions. For a devoted bookworm, nothing could be better than spending hours curled up with a book—or an e-reader—especially when feeling crummy or forced inside by crummy weather.

Getting caught up in a page-turner is a healthy coping strategy. Focusing on what is compelling or exciting lets teens temporarily block distressing thoughts and avoid painful feelings. Books transport readers to other worlds, real and imaginary, imparting knowledge and giving them a respite from real-life challenges. There are different eras to explore, heroes to applaud, adventures to be had, and characters to befriend. And what better sparks girls' own creativity?

SPENDING TIME IN NATURE

Teens and tweens lament having too little time to go outside, run around, ride bikes, and chill out. But the myriad benefits of being in nature warrant *making* time. A recent article in *Monitor on Psychology* reports that the sights and sounds of nature reduce stress; improve cognitive ability, attention, working memory, and behavior; increase happiness and well-being; and inoculate against mental health disorders.

Girls don't have to conquer the outback or navigate level-four rapids to achieve these benefits. They can simply step outside and sit under a tree or take a walk. The wonders of nature are there to observe: the hope of yellow daffodils peeking out after a frigid winter, the mellow sounds of a gurgling stream, the chirping of hungry baby birds. Being in the natural world promotes mindfulness and provides a deep sense of connection and perspective. Bonus benefit: if your daughter needs fresh ideas or an antidote to writer's block, being outdoors also boosts creativity.

SLEEPING

Experts agree that teens need a minimum of eight to ten hours of sleep every night. When I ask girls in Wellness Day workshops or interviews about this, they laugh. While some tweens follow this guideline, by high school most students fall far short. Although you can't expect your daughter to adhere to an assigned bedtime, there are things you can do to promote sleep.

If she is cheating herself of sleep to grab some much-craved me-time, make sure she satisfies this need earlier in the day so she gets to bed at a reasonable hour. What she does late at night also impacts her sleep. Like most teens and tweens, your daughter is probably on one or more of her devices. To fall asleep more easily, experts suggest not looking at screens for at least an hour before bedtime. That is because the blue light spectrum of smartphone and tablet screens suppresses the release of the body's natural sleep aid, the hormone melatonin, which signals when it is time to snooze. Designate a time each evening when all cellphones must be silenced and plugged in for the night—in the kitchen or another nonbedroom location.

If your daughter is staying up until all hours to do her homework and study for tests, it may be harder to persuade her to go to bed. First, make certain she knows that her health is more important to you than her GPA. Don't assume she already knows this; you may have to tell her explicitly and repeatedly. Second, sharing facts about sleep can dispel teens' most common myths about success.

Many ambitious girls who study until the wee hours to ace tests view sleep as the enemy of achievement. The truth is, sleep is one of the most essential ingredients in learning, mastery, memory, cognition, and performance. To perfect a skill, sleep should be your teen's best friend. When at rest, the brain stabilizes and stores newly acquired information (e.g., facts or concepts) through a process called consolidation. When taking exams, girls retrieve that knowledge from memory storage.

Insufficient rest undermines learning and memory in other ways.

Girls who are tired in class have trouble concentrating and paying attention. If new material isn't processed, it will never be consolidated in memory. Brains of sleepy teens are less capable of recalling information on tests. Sleep deprivation is also a risk factor for mental health symptoms of depressed mood and anxiety, which weaken cognitive performance even in college students. When you discuss these scientifically proven evils of sleep deprivation, they may be a revelation to your daughter.

Setting Expectations and Reinforcing Values

The structures you establish at home also set up expectations. If you prioritize health, for example, you encourage your teen's nutritious eating, sleep hygiene, and physical exercise. If education and achievement are important to you, your evening routine may include dedicated homework time and a specific—perhaps limited—window for screen use. If religious observance is valued, you might allocate times for worship and rituals. If you feel strongly about family closeness, you may carve out sacred time for togetherness.

Creating Consistency and Reducing Uncertainty

Structure facilitates much-needed consistency. As they learn to control impulses, girls need to know that parents will provide guardrails, should they be necessary. It makes teens uneasy to grow up with too many choices and without clear expectations and rules. Guidance reduces uncertainty and insecurity. Constancy is comforting. Your daughter closely watches your reactions to her behavior. When you're reliable, she knows she can count on you.

Jill, fourteen, says, "Usually my mom says I'm grounded, but in a day or so it's fine. Most of the time, she's like, 'Just be nice.' Or she'll just walk away. But this time I'm actually grounded. There's definitely something else going on." Jill was troubled by her mother following through on a consequence—not because she was actually punished, but rather because it was unexpected. The unusual shift in parenting caused her to worry.

Avoiding Singling Out Daughters

Family structure can keep self-conscious teens out of the spotlight. If one of your girls needs to work on her reading or has to be reminded constantly to practice her musical instrument, these activities can be included in routines you establish for the whole family. Your daughter is more likely to meet an expectation if she isn't embarrassed about a shortcoming or doesn't think she is being punished for it. Besides, all family members benefit from healthy, skill-building habits.

Says Margo, "One of my girls is pretty overweight and needs to be healthier, but I'm scared to make her feel even worse about herself than she already does. I don't want this to turn into an eating disorder. So we decided to change things up. Now there is a limit to how often all our kids can snack, and we make more nutritious options available. We also expect them to exercise and hike as a family."

Modeling Desirable Behavior

Structure keeps you honest. If you establish a morning routine to encourage your daughter to get up on time and make the school bus, you also have to avoid procrastinating and tackle your to-do list. If you have to be reminded over and again to take her bra shopping, or if you keep putting off filling out her school permission forms, she will get a mixed message, at best, about punctuality and accountability.

Alice, seventeen, tells me in therapy, "My mom keeps saying she'll make an appointment for me with the gynecologist, but she doesn't. Every time I ask her, she has a different excuse for why she didn't call. But if I don't do something the minute she tells me to, I'm in trouble. What's up with that? It's so unfair." Congruity between what you say and do assures your daughter she can trust you. Your behavior backs up your values and expectations. It's a powerful message.

Preventing Unnecessary Conflict

When rules are fuzzy, parent-teen conflict is apt to germinate. But if you communicate expectations clearly, it is less likely—though admittedly far from impossible—your daughter will push back or beg you to reconsider. Suppose, for instance, your thirteen-year-old's friend invites her to a coed sleepover. If she knows your rules, she may ask to go half-heartedly—if at all. If she does, reminding her "That's not something we're comfortable with now, but we can discuss it when you're in high school" can end the discussion quickly and dispassionately.

Making Consequences Explicit

Teens are better able to stop and think before acting if they know what is likely to happen if they step out of line. This is especially true when consequences of rule infractions are logical and fit the transgression.

Nellie, sixteen, told me in therapy, "I'm not allowed to go to any parties for a month." When I asked why, she matter-of-factly replied, "Oh, I came home after curfew and they found out I was drinking." Forewarned, she neither protested nor considered her parents' decision unfair. Moreover, Nellie understood that she now had to prove to her mother and father she could be more responsible. After some deliberation, she came up with a plan to do just that.

Although your daughter might protest, fair rules and reasonable consequences for violating them provide her a necessary sense of stability in an unpredictable adolescent world.

Family Meals

Modern lifestyles make it difficult, if not impossible, for many families to share meals. Yet it is well worth doing so. The research is in: the more family dinners you have, the greater the chance your daughter will eat nutritiously, enjoy better cardiovascular health, and maintain a healthy weight. Psychologically, she is more likely to be well adjusted and inoculated against depression, anxiety, substance use, behavioral problems, teen pregnancy, and violent or risky behaviors. A *single weekly family dinner* is linked to better sleep and higher self-esteem.

Remarkably, regular family dinners more powerfully predict your daughter's academic achievement than whether she does her homework, gets involved in sports or arts, or develops good language skills. This actually makes sense. Sharing meals gives you regular opportunities to communicate face-to-face, check in to see how girls are doing, model desirable behaviors, provide support, and express gratitude.

The goal is simple: spending enjoyable time together, looking into each other's eyes, having reciprocal conversations, and thereby deepening your connections. Preserving this face time, the fabric of family life, will shape the relationship you have with your daughter for years to come. Here are some recommendations for getting the most out of family meals.

Eat Together as Often as Possible

The more family meals, the better. If it is not possible for some family member(s) to be there, gather with everyone who is available.

Think Out of the Box

If dinners are hard to arrange during weekdays, try weekend lunches or brunches; afternoon teas; family movie nights; pizza or taco nights; picnics during family walks or hikes; or Sunday "linners." Anyone whose schedule prevents eating meals with the family can join for a snack, dessert, or conversation.

Minimize Distractions

Whenever and wherever you eat, keep this time special by banning digital devices—no exceptions (note: this includes parents). When conversations are undisturbed by vibrations and ringtones, the family is better able to be in the moment and reap the maximum benefits of pleasant time together.

Don't Get Fancy

Family meals can be quick. No need to get out the finery for long, elegant dinners. The menu needn't be elaborate, either. In fact, exhausting yourself preparing food defeats the purpose of family meals. Take-out pizza or deli rollups are fine.

Don't Stress Too Much About Nutrition

These days, parents are under enormous pressure to prepare healthy meals. But if this is overemphasized, it can be intimidating. It is also a challenge to honor every family member's diet and taste preferences. Again, being together is the main point, not which foods are served. Fussy eaters can make omelets or grab cereal, sandwiches, or yogurt. Microwaved leftovers or frozen food will do—or whatever makes enjoyable family meals possible in your household. Do whatever works, within reason.

Involve Teens

Enlisting your teen's participation in planning menus or making her favorite dish increases the chance of her attending and enjoying dinner. Many teens these days are learning about food preparation from cooking and baking shows on television and videos on YouTube. Let her take charge as much as possible. She can also take pride in serving as your sous chef. Doing the grocery shopping, setting the table, washing the dishes, and taking out garbage teach her life skills as well as give her the satisfaction of contributing to the family.

Let Teens Invite Guests

Encouraging your daughter to bring home friends can be a great bonus: she is more likely to join the family, you get to know her friends better, and she learns to be a gracious host. Win-win-win.

Keep the Tone Pleasant

By the laws of human nature, teens who enjoy being with parents and siblings are more apt to make time for family meals. Make these gatherings judgment-free zones. Avoid putting girls on the spot by asking about test grades, homework, or college applications. Keep the tone of discussions accepting, positive, and supportive.

To encourage conversation, ask open-ended rather than yes-or-no questions. Seek your daughter's opinions about nonstressful current events or issues of the day. Ask for her input in solving problems you or other family members are facing. Reminisce about family vacations, make plans for the next one, or retell funny anecdotes. Talk about movies you saw together, and vote on which TV shows to watch next.

Family Meal Topics

Chances are, you will never re-create the dinner table experiences of old family sitcoms. Despite your best efforts, in fact, what happens at mealtimes may give you indigestion. Girls may get up on soapboxes to opine at length, competing with siblings for airtime. Teens may argue, provoke, and challenge. Emotions may run high. But don't ditch family meals. These animated, occasionally raucous discussions help your daughter to do the following.

Discover Herself

When she challenges your personal beliefs and family values, your teen is actually reflecting upon and tweaking her own.

Become Authentic

Whereas her MO outside the house may be to say what she thinks people want to hear and refrain from ruffling feathers, at home she can practice expressing genuine, but perhaps controversial, opinions.

Clarify Her Values

Debating with family members lets your daughter audition her best arguments to gauge their persuasiveness. Talking things out with others helps her to resolve her own ambivalence and inner conflicts about what she truly believes.

Become More Informed

Back-and-forth exchanges force her to compose counterarguments, thereby helping her to think of more ammunition to bolster her case. She might at times express positions even more extreme than her own as a tactic to learn why you oppose them. Don't be shocked if she later refutes the very beliefs she previously espoused—or, conversely, adopts the views she dismissed as ridiculous.

Find Her Voice

Dinner table discussions give your daughter her earliest practice sessions for defending her thesis, giving a campaign speech, and making her case in a corporate boardroom. She learns how to get people to listen to her, effectively argue her positions, anticipate challenges, and persuade others to become allies.

Test You

Although this goal may be unconscious, your teen's most provocative and extreme statements may be designed to discover how you will respond. Will you be open and nonjudgmental, or critical, disdainful, and dismissive? Truth be told, some self-aware teens sheepishly admit that they enjoy getting a rise out of Mom.

At the end of the day, when you're worn out and frazzled, the last thing you may want to deal with is a contentious conversation. Hearing your teen expound views and values you don't share—or find offensive—can be intolerable. Your reflex may be to shut her down. But your responses to your daughter's confrontational questions and strong opinions teach her the following.

Normalizing Conflict

People can have civil and constructive conversations even—especially—when viewpoints clash.

Her Right to Her Own Opinions

She is entitled to be understood even when she disagrees with others.

Listening Respectfully

Effective communication skills entail people intently and courteously listening to each other.

Expressing Disagreements Tactfully

It is important to think carefully before expressing strong opinions to avoid attacking others or denigrating their views.

• • •

As you guide your daughter to achieve a healthy balance of sleep, exercise, recreation, family togetherness, and enjoyment of nature, the biggest impediment may be her incessant consumption of media. This is undoubtedly just the tip of the technology management iceberg. The next chapter tackles the multitude of decisions and quandaries you likely face around your teen's or tween's screen time and social media activities.

CHAPTER NINE

Managing Screens and Social Media

Technology is a learning curve. I tell my daughter to pretend that everything she's typing she is saying to me, her grandparents, or her pastor. Would she be upset if it came back to her? If she gets caught, people will learn what she says and feelings will get hurt. If she says she's going to a party, bashing a girl about how much weight she gained, or if she likes someone's outfit can all have consequences.

—ELIZA, MOTHER OF TALLULAH, 14

My parents didn't know I had social media for a long time. I wasn't allowed to have Snapchat or Instagram until ninth grade, but I had it. If my mom knew it, she didn't say anything. I was waiting for her to come to me. Like, "Don't ever send nudes" or "Don't have a public account."

—LEONORA, 17

> You're a bad mom if you're not on top of reading all their texts and looking at all their Insta posts. I had my daughter's passwords and used to scroll through once a week. The things I was seeing—how she spoke to friends, the language she used, the things friends were doing. I was knowing things I wasn't supposed to know, and it was affecting how I parented. I wouldn't encourage my daughter to see certain friends. Or I'd have feelings about her friends. But they're just teenagers. If they talked on the phone, nobody would ever have known what they said. I have no business checking—she's sixteen.
>
> —CHARLENE, MOTHER OF WILHELMINA

Digital natives often have enviable tech skills, but need guidance to use them wisely. Maintaining a healthy tech diet requires plenty of nonscreen activities to balance out devices. Otherwise, excessive media consumption—time spent on social media, video chatting, the internet, texting, entertainment, and video games—harms mental and physical health, learning, well-being, and academic performance.

Research confirms the benefits of moderation. Psychologist Jean M. Twenge's vast body of research led her to conclude, "Happiness and mental health are highest at a half hour to two hours of extracurricular digital media use a day; well-being then steadily decreases, with those who spend the most time online being the worst off. Twice as many heavy users of electronic devices are unhappy, depressed, or distressed as light users."

A three-year study of twelve-to-fifteen-year-olds published in *JAMA Psychiatry* concurs. Teens who spend more than three hours per day on social media are likely to report more mental health and behavioral problems (e.g., anxiety, depression, defiance, and aggression) than those who spend little or no time on social media. In England, a three-year study of teens starting at age thirteen or fourteen also found that frequent social media use reduces both sleep and physical activity.

Many mothers ask how much screen time is too much. A more helpful way to look at this may be: While glued to screens, what are teens and tweens *not* doing? What experiences are they missing out on? In a nutshell, girls are spending less time socializing in person, exercising, pursuing hobbies, and sleeping—that is, they are participating in fewer activities that enhance coping, teach other valuable skills, and promote success.

While interacting with her device, your daughter simply can't practice the face-to-face social-emotional skills she needs to read people and navigate real-world relationships. Online, she also cannot get the same quality of emotional support as from in-person visits with friends and family who smile warmly, nod empathetically as she speaks, and hug her tightly. This became patently obvious to teens suffering during the COVID-19 pandemic. This chapter discusses how you can help your daughter to use technology wisely, in ways that serve her best.

Her First Cellphone

When to get your daughter her first cellphone is a big decision. This purchase will undoubtedly open up a whole new realm for both of you. If you have resisted so far, chances are you've heard something like, "But Mom, everyone in my grade has a phone!" or "I'm the only one of my friends who doesn't text; do you want me to be a loser?"

With your daughter resorting to such emotionally tugging ploys, you may feel intense pressure to cave in and buy that device.

Of course, you want to give her the one thing you know will thrill her. The question is, when does this make sense? When a mother told me recently that she had to leave one of her two jobs early to pick up the new iPhone she had purchased for her daughter's birthday gift, I asked how old her daughter would be. I was surprised to learn the girl was turning five. This woman was rightfully proud to have worked hard to provide her daughter with a special gift. However, this child was in all likelihood too young to benefit from and use safely this powerful device.

By high school, when most teens need cellphones, many are mature enough to manage them well. As for younger girls, it is trickier to gauge when the pluses of having a personal cellphone outweigh the risks. Consider why your daughter might need it. Lifestyle issues matter. If she goes back and forth between her other parent's home and yours, a cellphone might help her clarify the schedule or retrieve homework and other school items from the other parent. If she plays sports, she may need a way to contact the adult who is picking her up after practice to communicate a change in plans, such as her coach keeping her late.

Many tweens who feel left out socially beg for cellphones to connect with friends. Even if the thought gives you hives, your daughter's desire to connect with friends is normal and healthy. Overprotection, in fact, may disadvantage her socially. Girls who are sheltered from online interactions don't master the age-appropriate digital literacy and social lingo they need for peer interactions.

Educational considerations also may prompt you to get her a cellphone or digital device. Many students use laptops and tablets in school. At home, they find resources online. Many visual learners or students with language-based learning challenges view YouTube videos to reinforce lessons they're taught in class. Beyond academics, some sites can inspire creativity. A sixteen-year-old watched cake-decorating videos before starting an online bakery business. A fourteen-year-old scoured Pinterest for design inspiration before making purses she sold on her website.

But just because you decide your daughter needs a cellphone doesn't mean you have to run out and get her the latest, most expensive model on the market. In fact, if she is younger than ten or eleven, a smartphone may not be the best choice. A browser would give her 24/7 access to the internet—a function she probably doesn't need and cannot manage responsibly at that age.

Your best bet may be a device specifically designed for younger children's safety, such as a durable watch that includes parental controls, two-way voice calling, and messaging only for trusted contacts (e.g., parents, grandparents, and babysitter).

Setting guidelines and limits as soon as your daughter gets her first cellphone or device decreases the chance of pushback. Technology rules are then part of your family's structure, not an indication of mistrust. Discuss and draw up a cellphone contract, asking your teen or tween to initial each item. That way, she can't say she never knew about or agreed to certain rules. Post the contract in the kitchen or family room, where it can be reviewed at any time. A cellphone contract should address:

- **Ownership.** Whose phone is it? Is it a gift? Is it a loan?

- **Responsibility.** Who is responsible if the phone is lost, stolen, or broken? If it is your daughter, how will she earn or save up money for repairs or replacements?

- **Passwords.** How will you handle your daughter's passwords? Will you know them? Can they be changed without your permission?

- **Privacy.** What are your expectations? Under what conditions will you monitor your daughter's messages, social media presence, and internet browsing history? It is of crucial importance that you let your daughter know up front if you plan to monitor her activity. If you peek into what she believes is her private online world without having clearly told her that you might do so, you risk her feeling betrayed by what she sees as your snooping.

- **Accounts.** On which social media platforms does your daughter have permission to open accounts? Which are forbidden? What will cause her accounts to be closed?

- **Location.** Can she take her phone to school? Will you instruct her to obey the school's rules about phone use—and reinforce them through your own behavior (i.e., don't message her during school if the school does not allow phone use)? What will you do (or not do) if the teacher or principal confiscates her phone? Specify where in the home is off-limits for phone use. Designate times for unplugging, such as meals, vacations, weekends away, and family discussions. If her phone is allowed in her bedroom, when does she need to turn it off or silence it and put it away for the night? To reinforce these rules, consider banning the use of cellphones as alarm clocks.

- **Etiquette.** When she is in public (restaurants, other people's homes, theaters, stores), under what conditions may she respond to text messages and answer or place a call? If you call her, do you always expect her to answer? Are there exceptions? When should her phone be set on silent or Do Not Disturb?

- **Philosophy.** Teach your daughter that paying more attention to her device than to people around her—called *absent presence*—is a misuse of technology. The American Psychological Association specifies, "Technology facilitates relationships with people far away, but not those sitting next to us."

- **Judgment.** Describe your beliefs about respect for others, honesty, integrity, and transparency when using cellphones. Is your daughter permitted to answer calls from numbers that are not in her contacts? Anticipate that she may be asked for naked selfies ("nudes"). Explain that when that happens, no matter who has requested them, you would like her to discuss the situation with you. Assure her that she will not be in trouble. Your goal is to help her think this situation through before she makes a potentially irrevocable decision.

- **Mistakes.** Like any new skill, anticipate that learning to use a cellphone appropriately will take time. Inevitably, your daughter will make mistakes. She should know that you will calmly discuss with her what went wrong and why, and then brainstorm how she can improve. You may temporarily limit her phone use, but you will give her other chances to practice and demonstrate using better judgment.

Teaching Healthy Social Media Behavior

Trepidation about your daughters' social media presence is understandable. The potential risks are on every mother's worry list. Why is your tween so desperate to have a Snapchat account? Why does she feel like a social pariah without one? To empathize and understand where her urgency is coming from, it may help to know what teens find so appealing. In a nutshell, social media counteracts this age group's hallmark insecurity and loneliness by helping them to feel more included, important, and confident.

According to a Pew Research Center report, teens say social media makes them feel more connected to what is going on in friends' lives (81%), shows their creative side (71%), keeps them in touch with friends' feelings (69%), and gives them support in tough times (68%). To stay on top of what is happening in the world, some teens also get most of their information from social media.

Whenever you decide your daughter is ready to join the ranks of teen media consumers, how can you keep her safe? Just as with other milestones, you'll want to find a balance between overprotecting her, which prevents her from developing management skills, and giving her carte blanche, which doesn't teach her what is and isn't inappropriate online. As usual, an intentional parenting approach is best.

From the beginning, set the groundwork by educating your daughter to make healthy, informed decisions around technology use. You can address the basic principles students are learning in school digital citizenship classes: the dangers associated with social media, identity theft, the consequences of sharing personal information, cultivating a positive digital footprint, managing digital distractions, structuring time, and the risks of using smartphones excessively.

Even as you provide guidelines, know that your daughter's adolescent brain is wired to take risks. At this age, reward centers are maximally susceptible to the pleasure-producing chemicals released by screen time. The goal is excitement. Her ability to make decisions, anticipate consequences, and control impulses is still immature. As a result, your teen may give in to temptations and use little to no filter in her digital communications.

When she reads upsetting messages or sees disturbing posts, emotional arousal may worsen her impulsivity and poor judgment. Without fully developed cause-and-effect reasoning capabilities, girls easily convince themselves it is okay to write online what they wouldn't dream of saying in person. Pesky concerns about getting caught rarely triumph over young girls' firm (mis)perceptions of anonymity and invincibility in cyberspace. In tweens' minds, everything will be fine. Everyone else talks like this. No one will ever find out she sent this.

Trisha, a criminal defense attorney and mother of two teens, knows all too well the misery that this mindset can produce. She represents students whose poor digital decisions result in legal trouble at school. Trisha explains that many teens and families are shocked to learn that schools can discipline students for sending messages or sharing videos that can harm others—even when such incidents occur off-campus. Community law enforcement is also ramping up. Arrests for bullying are increasing. Teens who solicit or forward nudes involving underage students are sometimes being charged with child pornography.

Of course, you'll want to prevent these serious mistakes. Your daughter may be using social media mostly to forward funny dog or cat videos to friends. Still, as she learns to self-regulate her media use, it is important to talk about the choices she is likely to face. Better to anticipate and discuss what-if scenarios than to wait until your teen or tween makes painful or irreversible mistakes. At a minimum, discuss the following topics.

How to Stay Safe

Where appropriate, help your tween create a username that disguises her identity. Advise her never to reveal any personal details online, including her phone number, address, school, age, and birthdate. Many girls have to be taught—and often reminded—not to post photos that inadvertently divulge this information (e.g., through a tag or photo that was taken in front of her school, which shows its name). Alert her to the fact that random people will probably add her on Snapchat or direct message (DM) her, often to ask for nudes. It may be annoying—and she will have to block and/or report them.

Everything Is Public

To counteract teens' false sense of anonymity, emphasize that what your daughter posts on social media is never truly private. Anyone can see what she writes and posts publicly—now (e.g., her teachers, friends' parents, and head of school) and in the future (e.g., internship directors, college admissions officers, and potential employers). And, no matter how unlikely she thinks this is to happen, anything she shares privately can potentially be saved and reshared with others without her knowledge. Although many girls think private chats are indeed private, they painfully learn otherwise when screenshots are taken and forwarded to others without permission.

The new golden rule of the digital age is: if you're not okay with Grandma seeing this, don't send or post it.

Everything Online Is Permanent

Teens have to learn that nothing is temporary online. Even Snaps, designed to disappear, become permanent in cyberspace as soon as someone takes a screenshot of them. If your daughter is at a party where there is underage drinking, photos or videos might be posted online that capture her presence in the midst of this activity. Years from now, anyone performing a simple Google search could make assumptions about her based on these images or videos, affecting her future college and career opportunities.

People Can Get Hurt

As a mother, you may be worried about people mistreating your daughter. For good reason. But she needs to know that you don't want her to hurt anyone else, either. She has to consciously avoid harmful behaviors. Your teen or tween must be told up front that saying something mean or starting rumors counts as using technology inappropriately.

If She Feels Threatened

Bullying is prevalent on social media and in discussion forums. Ask your daughter outright, "Do you experience any of that?" "Have you witnessed anything like that?" This puts potential problems squarely on the table to be discussed. Let her know that she is to come to you at any time if she feels uncomfortable, scared, bullied, or trolled. Assure her that you won't take away social media but will help her to deal with the situation.

False Information Is Out There

Like any savvy media consumer, your daughter must not assume that people with whom she communicates online are who they say they are. A seventeen-year-old girl from a different state, for example, may be a fifty-five-year-old man who lives on the next street. She must be on the alert for sites that spew misinformation and be cautious about memes that spread rumors, fearmongering, and hatred. If she is unsure, ask her to come to you so that you can figure out together what is what.

Forget Parental Controls

If the parental controls you've set up on your daughter's phone and other devices help you to sleep easier at night, what you read next will be a buzzkill. Relying on technology to limit teens' and tweens' use of technology is a mistake. Digital natives get around so-called protective features as often and as easily as they do tracking devices.

Even career engineers have trouble figuring out how to set well-hidden, within-app parental controls, much less prevent their own teens and tweens from circumventing them. To gain access—and to get around parental limits—teens find clever workarounds such as resetting devices, creating new Apple IDs, downloading special software, disabling Screen Time, changing the device's time settings to trick the system, or deleting and reinstalling apps.

Collaborating with your daughter is the best way to address these issues. This is when the open, trusting mother-daughter relationship and strategies you have consciously developed pay off. The guidelines you establish for her will be based on the judgments she makes day-to-day and communicated with the conversation skills you've been perfecting all along.

An older daughter who balances her work, social life, and sleep may need little input from you to self-limit her screen time. But a younger teen already struggling to stay organized and to manage her to-do list may need more structure. Many parents specify a block of time after finishing homework for screen time. If this goes smoothly, there's no need to do more. But if you're having nightly battles about shutting down devices, your tween may have to demonstrate more responsible behavior to earn her screen time.

Similarly, if your daughter goes on YouTube to learn how to make friendship bracelets, she might not need closer supervision. But if your fifteen-year-old is flirting with an eighteen-year-old from a different school, you may want to take a quick look at her social media accounts and text messages. When concerns run especially high, it might be necessary to create a record of your teen's phone activity on the home computer, at least temporarily.

Whereas your teen might be permitted to text friends whenever she wants, you might treat group chats or group video chats differently. To supervise these breeding grounds for nastiness, bullying, and hurt feelings, you might require that she asks your permission to participate—and that she keeps you apprised of the content and tone of the conversations (perhaps even showing them to you). As she and her friends demonstrate better self-control and judgment, you can begin to relax rules so she can manage her digital consumption more independently.

Judgment Calls

Since you can't anticipate every online dilemma, you also can't create individual rules to handle every one of them. Once again, the way to go is to have matter-of-fact discussions about the tricky situations your daughter may someday encounter. You can present her with a circumstance and ask her: What would you do? What are the risks? Would it be worth it?

Crafting Her Online Persona

Ask about your daughter's online goals. Is she interested in connecting with an established group of close friends? Are they accepting and supportive? Or does she hope to expand her social group by making new friends? Does she want to escape her reputation at school? Is she interested in venturing beyond her comfort zone?

What is she trying to portray about herself—and why? Just as previous generations of teens experimented with different looks through clothing, makeup, and accessories, your teen might try on various identities through social media posts. But she needs to be prepared for closer scrutiny online, which can heighten self-consciousness. Lina, seventeen, says, "The first thing people see is what we look like, and they make snap decisions based on appearance. It's hard for us to have a voice and be taken seriously. People don't take the time to get to know us."

Is your daughter okay with letting other people's responses to social media dictate how she feels about herself? How will she react if her posts get few likes, comments, forwards, or reposts, or if her phone blows up with photos of friends having a blast somewhere she wasn't invited?

Only in retrospect, when she is more comfortable in her own skin, may your daughter recognize that social media wasn't all that gratifying.

Naima, seventeen, says, "I used to be a tortured little soul. But now I don't feel like I have to portray a certain image on social media. I don't care what people say about me. I can focus on myself. I started wearing my black eye shadow and lots of necklaces again. If someone doesn't respect me or want to get to know me because of how I dress or how I look or how my head works, then I don't need them."

If your daughter is insecure, she may be more vulnerable to peer judgments. Lynelle was eighteen when she realized, "It's so meaningless and pointless to get validation for where you are and who you're with. Snapchat didn't make me feel good about who I am. It's really hard for girls who are susceptible to peer pressure or peer judgment or both." She pauses for a moment, and then confesses, "I say I don't care about what people think of me, but I do."

Critiquing Peers' Posts

Because every other girl is trying to portray herself in the best possible light, your daughter can't take what she sees online at face value. Just as she carefully curates her social media presence to emphasize the positive, she may easily forget that others also do that. Research demonstrates that teens who use online posts to judge peers' emotions underestimate negative feelings by 17 percent and overestimate joyful emotions by 6 percent. This perceptual bias can convince her that while everyone else her age is always happy, surrounded by cool friends who are having tons of fun, she alone is a miserable social misfit.

As girls get older, they get better at discerning reality. Ona, seventeen, says, "I look at what my friends post now and I think, 'I know you. I know you're not this happy. That picture was taken two months ago and you're posting it now.' It makes me mad. I want to say, 'I know the back-story for this, people!'"

Clarifying Subtler Mores

If you dictate what your daughter says and does online, you are constrained by not being privy to the subtle, near-invisible codes of conduct that teens create for themselves. Ask instead what your daughter considers acceptable online. What constitutes a good post? What makes it bad? What makes a post offensive or elicits negative reactions? When does a sexy photo cross the line? How can your tween tell the difference between a sassy comment and a mean one? When does self-confidence become bragging?

To understand these distinctions, ask your teen for examples. Look at memes together to talk about which are inappropriate and why. What criteria does she use to make these calls? While instructing you, your daughter forms clearer values and boundaries for herself.

Monday Morning Quarterbacking

If—no, *when*—she uses poor judgment, see these incidents as teaching moments, problems to be solved, and opportunities for growth. Although it is easy to be appalled by the coarseness of her language, remember that this is teenspeak, not the words she uses with adults. As for dubious photos, try to be nonjudgmental and curious about what she might have been thinking—or, um, *not* thinking.

You might be tempted to yell, for example, "OMG, what on earth could possibly have made you think it was okay to wear a bikini and pose as if you were shooting a *Sports Illustrated* cover?" Instead, try, "Someone just forwarded me what you posted on Instagram. Let's talk about the pros and cons of this." If your teen becomes defensive rather than acknowledging the risks, you may have to spell out how people take screenshots and forward them. How would she feel about strangers, perhaps adult men, looking at that photo and fantasizing about her?

Dealing with Aggression

In cyberspace, a false sense of anonymity makes it easy for shy, reserved, or passive tweens and teens to turn aggressive. No girl is immune. When you find out your daughter was nasty to friends online, being compassionate will encourage her to learn from mistakes. Rather than lecturing or moralizing, ask what led her to be so harsh and how she might handle the situation better in the future. If your teen doesn't grasp the harm in what she did or express remorse, try asking how she would feel if her friend treated her that way.

When girls respond to cyberbullies, it is hard for them not to become perpetrators themselves. When a boy from another state stalked her online, Ariel, fifteen, followed her parents' advice to stick up for herself. She messaged the boy to forcefully demand that he stop harassing her. The next thing she knew, the boy had reported *her* to the police. If your family gets into this sort of fix, it is best to get expert advice before taking any action. Seek guidance from your local police precinct. Many have community youth officers who specialize in cybercrimes.

Learning from Others' Mistakes

During adolescence, girls may not be able to imagine how technology magnifies blips of misjudgment. The best lessons may come from news reports of teens at the community, state, or national level. Paige, a teacher, has a front row seat to the "regular fallout of Snapchat screenshots in my school. I believe my own kids find it easier to listen to examples of what other students do. It's not just their crazy, neurotic mom talking."

Use the online mistakes of your daughter's friends as teaching moments. Expressing sympathy rather than condemnation, ask your daughter where these teens went wrong. What would she advise them to do differently? After seeing what happens to friends, teens do learn to make different choices. Girls often tell me of consciously avoiding getting into similar trouble as peers who ruined their reputations.

Consequences of Tech Mistakes

How you teach your daughter responsible media use is not unlike teaching her to drive. She has to demonstrate competence and good judgment before you give her more autonomy. Just as teens earn car privileges, they prove they can behave responsibly online before they get more freedom.

After violations of rules or incidents of poor judgment, your first instinct might be to take away your daughter's cellphone. If so, be clear about what you want this to accomplish and understand the risks. Even if her "crime" warrants draconian measures to teach her an indelible lesson, keep in mind that your punishment might have unintended consequences.

Your goal is probably not to make her more self-conscious. Remember that along with communicating with you, teachers, coaches, and tutors, your teen uses her cellphone to do schoolwork. Teens tell me, "Everything is posted on Google Classroom, so if you need to study, you need a phone" and "If you don't have one, you get singled out. You have to go up to the teacher and say, 'I need this.' It's embarrassing and stressful. People ask, 'Why don't they have a phone?'"

You also don't want an excessive separation from her cellphone to harm her mental health. Girls who are isolated from peer interactions that support and sustain them can, over time, become anxious and despondent. So if your daughter freaks out when you confiscate her lifeline to the outside world and screams, "Anything but my PHONE, Mom!" explain what she has to do to re-earn your trust so that her cellphone privileges can be restored.

Recall that the teenage brain is highly sensitive to the experiences that shape it. Your daughter learns by first making—and then correcting—her not-so-fabulous choices. This process is reciprocal. As her prefrontal cortex matures, she develops better self-control. And as she learns to manage her impulses, she strengthens synapses in her prefrontal cortex, which afford her even better judgment. Your vigilance and flexibility during this time go a long way toward nurturing her self-regulatory skills.

Self-Limiting Screen Use

Remarkably, of the 58 percent of teens who take breaks from social media, more than half (65 percent) do so voluntarily. For some, social media is interfering with school or work. Others become overwhelmed and want to avoid burning out; 24 percent are fed up with the conflict and drama; and 20 percent are tired of always keeping up with what is going on. Of the 40 percent of teens who decide to unfollow people on social media, most do it because of drama (78%), posting too much or too often (54%), and bullying—whether victims are others or themselves (52%).

Research can guide your parenting decisions. Teens who self-limit media use feel positive about taking time away. Opting for breaks or leaving social media altogether leads to feeling relieved, having more time to do other things, and experiencing a stronger connection to people around them.

In contrast, 49 percent of teens who are forced to take breaks from social media feel anxious and disconnected. When parents take away devices or they are lost, broken, or stolen, teens experience a fear of missing out (FOMO), feel disconnected to important people in their lives, and want to get back to social media as soon as possible. Loneliness drives this desperation.

If your daughter is open to self-limiting her media consumption, teens find these strategies most effective:

- Using Screen Time and other features to keep track of what they are doing and when (e.g., "I saw on my phone that I was on it for hours on end and thought, 'Oh my god, this is why I'm up until two in the morning doing homework.'")

- Turning on the Do Not Disturb feature, which disables cellphones' distracting notifications, but still allows calls from designated contacts
- Silencing cellphones and placing them facedown to avoid seeing screens lighting up with notifications
- Asking friends to change social media passwords and not to reveal the new ones until exams, championships, or other important events are over
- Deleting time-sucking apps during academic crunch times and reinstalling them later

Getting Over Social Media

When cellphone use is temporarily limited, teens and tweens notice benefits. After a five-day science field trip without their devices, for example, eighth-grade students reported feeling happier. Similarly, a middle school that banned cellphones found that students initially complained, but later reported feeling less stressed, happier, and more focused.

Girls I interviewed agreed that after social media is limited, they realize they are more content without it. Zeze, seventeen, tells me, "Snapchat was the place to be in ninth grade. Then I got my phone taken away and my account was deleted. When I got my phone back, I didn't want to get one again. I realized I felt so much better without it."

Before you get too hopeful your daughter will follow suit, note that teens rarely gain this perspective on social media until they develop more mature self-awareness and insight. Annabelle, eighteen, ultimately bowed out when she realized social media wasn't for her: "I wasn't myself when I had it. I did a lot of self-reflecting and it was a big part of why I was upset all the time. Instagram was the big thing. All my friends were posting every other day. It scared me. I realized this wasn't something I needed. I deleted the app off my phone."

For Flo, seventeen, the decision to opt out was a gradual process: "In the summer, I got my phone back, but I didn't feel that compulsion to post all the time and update everyone about what I was doing and who I'm with." I ask Flo what changed for her. "I don't care about all these other people and what they're doing," she says, "so why should they care about me?"

Model Healthy Habits

The best way to help girls achieve a healthy balance of screen and nonscreen activity is by example. Because teens take cues from parents, if you want your daughter to put down her cellphone, she can't see you constantly checking yours. During face-to-face conversations, all family members should leave phones in another room or put them on silent. Research shows that just having a cellphone on the table between two people—or anywhere in sight—changes (a) what they discuss and (b) how connected they feel to each other.

Compulsive Screen Time and Overuse

When girls who are anxious about friendships constantly check text messages, a vicious cycle of compulsive screen use may be created. Always being on the alert for new messages causes further anxiety. On and on it goes. If your daughter can't self-limit or her screen habits affect her sleep and academic performance, this may suggest problematic or compulsive use. Consider whether she is:

- Declining invitations to be with friends
- Reducing or quitting extracurricular activities
- Not finishing homework
- Getting behind on projects and papers
- Repeatedly checking her cellphone even while engrossed in movies and TV shows
- Getting overly upset when you limit device use during family times
- Acting like only screen time makes her happy
- Becoming moodier or more agitated
- Struggling to cut back on her use
- Lying about how much time she spends on devices
- Overreacting to being cut off from screens or social media accounts

If your teen or tween is exhibiting red flags for problematic screen use, what can you do? First ask if she feels unsafe online. Is anything happening in her social life or on social media that is making her more vigilant? If so, solving the problem directly with the people involved could reduce her frantic screen use.

Orchestrate a gradual weaning from devices rather than insisting your daughter go cold turkey. Schedule media breaks for the whole family. Suggest appealing activities that distract from screens and enable her to be with peers offline—perhaps outside in nature. Ask your daughter to temporarily minimize her time on the most troublesome apps and platforms.

If your concern continues or worsens, consider having her professionally evaluated to determine whether she fits the clinical criteria for screen addiction. New programs are being developed across the country to treat this growing problem.

* * *

Screen use may be a major player in the nightly homework battles occurring in your house. Your tween may insist, despite the science, that she is a multitasking pro who can read assignments while also checking social media and monitoring what her friend is doing on FaceTime. Other controversies may revolve around how and when she does her work, what scaffolding she needs, and how willing she is to accept help. The next chapter gives you the inside scoop on how to handle everyday homework challenges in ways that best prepare her for long-term success—while also creating more peaceful evenings at home.

CHAPTER TEN

Calling Off the Homework Police

> It makes me really dread seeing my mother when I know I will just be pestered about my work. I don't really want suggestions. I know what I need to do, and having her add on just makes me more stressed.
>
> —ALICIA, 15

> I can't be a bystander and just leave my daughter alone and "not interfere." It's part of my job as a mother to help guide and do my best to keep her on track. The exercise of getting into college is a defining moment in her life and she needs help to weather it and succeed. She needs to juggle sports, friends, and sleep to put her schoolwork first. But she's not even open to suggestions as to how to prioritize and get the balance right.
>
> —HANNAH, MOTHER OF FRANNY, 16

> I know that I need to step it up and I am trying to, but I need my mother to listen to me and just be supportive instead of nagging, which makes everything a thousand times worse. I'll go to her when I need help, but she needs to let me come to her.
>
> —FRANKIE, 17

Homework battles are as old as time. Parents often believe that unless they get involved, teens won't start homework, stay focused, resist distractions, and do their best work. If girls have trouble keeping track of tests, due dates for papers, and school materials, mothers may think they must step in to organize and oversee academics. But to girls, these efforts are usually seen as unwelcome and unhelpful. Cue exhausting, nightly skirmishes that disturb and drain the whole family.

Many teens and tweens resort to avoiding work—and parents. Leah, sixteen, says, "Fighting's not worth it; I just leave the house." Others skirt conflict by lying about assignments or grades—despite getting in more trouble. For still other students, clashing with parents serves as a handy distraction from work itself. Sami, seventeen, says, "When I was younger, my mom and I, we'd always fight about my schoolwork. I would spend a lot of time arguing with my parents about homework rather than doing it."

To break these unhelpful patterns, this chapter first debunks common myths about achievement. You'll get the lowdown on why reminding, coaxing, and double-checking don't usually improve—and may actually harm—student performance. Then you will be given a myriad of strategies, blessed by neuroscience research, that effectively boost your teen's motivation, productivity, and accountability. These tools not only empower your daughter to succeed, but also make evenings less stressful for you and the entire family.

Rescuing Struggling Students

When I evaluated Caroline, a high school sophomore, I discovered severe deficits in her ability to decode words and comprehend what she read. It was hard to imagine how these difficulties had allowed her to earn good grades. Then Caroline explained. To ease her stress, her mother had done all her English and history homework, and her grandmother, a former teacher, had tackled all her science and math assignments.

Because Caroline's teachers graded her mother's and grandmother's work rather than hers, they never became aware of her significant weaknesses and needs for remediation. By avoiding homework altogether, Caroline never had to learn compensatory strategies. It wasn't until tenth grade that she and her parents realized that unless something changed, her limited academic skills, lack of self-sufficiency, and compromised resiliency would make it hard for her to manage independent learning in college.

Reminding/Questioning/Nagging

No matter what you call it, teens and tweens rarely take kindly to mothers' efforts to make them better students. In fact, the adage "This favor shall not go unpunished" rings especially true with achievement. Girls who hear parental recommendations as critical conclude that they can never do anything right in their mothers' eyes. Women who try to help ungrateful daughters with schoolwork feel exactly the same way.

Girls sometimes refuse to act in their own best interests simply because they abhor being told what to do. Cassandra, seventeen, tells me, "When my mother keeps harping on my junior research project, it just makes me want to do it less. Even though I know I'm gonna screw myself and get stressed out about the deadline, I can't give her the satisfaction of listening to her." Such defiance epitomizes cutting off one's nose to spite one's face.

Monitoring Online Educational Portals

Digital portals were designed for schools to communicate information to parents about students' attendance, work completion, and grades. Nowadays, you probably don't have to wait until your daughter's report card comes out to know how she is doing academically. Some schools limit parental access to avoid overfocusing on every pop quiz grade, but others impose no restrictions. Based on your parenting philosophy and level of apprehension, you may log on rarely, if ever, or—at the other end of the spectrum—you may feel compelled to check on your teen's daily progress in homework, quizzes, tests, class participation, and projects.

Online portals have revolutionized teens' educational experiences—but not, in my opinion, for the better. Constant parental monitoring adversely affects students' stress levels, motivation, attitudes, behavior, academic performance, and family relationships.

HEIGHTENS STRESS AND TEST-TAKING ANXIETY

Getting minute-by-minute feedback on academic performance, much like viewing stock market ticker tapes, creates a nerve-racking sense of urgency for teens and tweens. Every less-than-stellar score is visible, magnified in importance, fodder for parental analysis and discussion, and possibly an impetus for punishment.

Mae, twelve, explains, "I used to get nervous just when report cards came out, but now my parents go online to check my grades, like, every day." Despite being a self-motivated high achiever, Mae's school's portal makes her think of every exam as a do-or-die experience. And she is only in sixth grade.

DEFEATS THE PURPOSE OF GRADES

Ideally, students think of grades as feedback on their progress. Did they master material as well as they thought? How effective are their work habits? Are they managing time well? Do their study strategies need improvement? But online portals make grades less about student feedback and more about pleasing (or disappointing) parents. Plus, the focus on grades, which are external emblems of achievement, interferes with the intrinsic motivation necessary for girls' success.

INTRUDES UPON STUDENT-TEACHER RELATIONSHIPS

Self-initiated learning requires teens to be accountable to themselves and to their teachers. Yet online portals practically invite eager parents to encroach upon previously sacred student-teacher relationships. Parents who communicate directly with teachers undermine students' sense of ownership, dissuading teens from figuring out how to seek help, ask for clarification, learn from their grades, and self-advocate for extended deadlines or test-taking time.

What Does Promote Success

When it comes to your daughter's success, doing less to achieve more is essential. Allowing her school experience to proceed and unfold organically, unencumbered by external pressures, expectations, and interference, is the greatest gift you can give her. At the same time, you can support her in developing the lifelong love of learning, effective study habits, and strong executive functioning (EF) skills needed to achieve her goals—both present and future.

Appropriate Involvement

The happiest and most successful young people have parents who don't do for them what they are capable of doing for themselves. As a warm, supportive consultant, encourage your teen or tween to take charge of her own learning process. Help only when necessary. Rather than doing the work, teach her the skills to do it herself. Instead of writing her English paper, for example, show her how to outline, edit, and proofread. Ask yourself the following questions.

DOES SHE KNOW WHAT SHE IS SUPPOSED TO DO?

You can ask her just that. Girls who are unclear about instructions have trouble initiating work. If necessary, review directions together and clarify any confusion. Then give her space to do her work.

DOES SHE UNDERSTAND THE MATERIAL?

If your daughter is struggling, homework may highlight her shaky grasp of what she's learning. If you can, reinforce concepts. Also encourage other resourceful strategies. Can she review class notes and relevant textbook chapters? Email her teacher? Arrange for extra help? Study with a classmate?

DOES SHE NEED TO PRACTICE?

Some students need warm-up examples to become more confident before digging into assignments independently. Suggest that your tween do a few problems. Once she gets in a groove and develops an approach, she may be able to finish the work herself.

DOES SHE NEED REASSURANCE?

Less academically secure students may need to check in with parents periodically to ensure they're on the right track.

Providing Structure

Your teen may tell you she was doing homework for the entire five hours she was sequestered in her room. Do you know if she was really hunkering down with her books or dividing her attention between writing a paper, checking social media, and watching Netflix? No. Do you know that your tween really completed all her assignments during her free periods? No. You are not—and can never be—the homework police.

What you can do is provide structure. Set a reasonable time frame for homework. Duke University psychologists and neuroscientists found that homework gives students in middle school a small academic boost, but high school students benefited only if they worked for two hours or less per night. In my experiencc, these days most teens are spending far more time.

Based on research with fifty thousand families, the authors of *The Learning Habit: A Groundbreaking Approach to Homework and Parenting That Helps Our Children Succeed in School and Life* recommend ten minutes of homework per day per grade. This comes to an hour for a sixth-grade student and two hours for a high school senior. Parents set a timer, which goes off at the end of the homework period. If girls finish beforehand, they can read.

This approach is sensible because parents hand over responsibility for homework to students, empowering them to develop lifelong skills. Knowing they'll be unchained from their desks at a specific time, girls are less likely to dread homework and procrastinate in starting it. Not staying up late lets teens get more sleep. Most important, this process encourages girls to muster self-discipline to do work regardless of how they feel, to focus on work for a set period of time without distractions, and then to reward themselves with enjoyable down time.

Encouraging Planning and Time Management

Planning skills help your daughter to run her life more smoothly. Or at least to minimize last-minute crises. When she wakes up, she learns to envision the most pressing items on her daily schedule and remember the materials she needs for them. Your teen can look ahead to the whole week to see what is due, and when. Recording deadlines on her calendar or planner can spare her from stressful time crunches and penalties for late assignments.

Once she sets a goal, encourage your tween to work backward to determine what she must do to achieve it. How long will each step take her? To eliminate guesswork, she can estimate how much time is needed for each math problem—and then time herself to check her accuracy. With practice, she'll perfect her predictions and plan her time accordingly.

Praising Effort, Not Ability

Many parents wonder how to instill drive in daughters who are indifferent to achievement. But you can't implant motivation. If you try, it's unlikely you'll succeed in doing anything but cause ill feelings. Offering money or other rewards for good performance, for example, interferes with and can extinguish intrinsic drive, clear thinking, and creativity. Indeed, research shows that what works better to produce favorable academic and emotional outcomes is limiting parental interference and supporting students' autonomy.

Besides modeling a strong work ethic, providing structure, and selectively praising her effort, promote your daughter's success by adopting what psychologist Carol Dweck calls a growth mindset. Such students achieve more because they believe hard work and strategic problem-solving can help them to learn new skills, improve, and succeed. Recognize when she courageously takes intellectual risks and goes beyond her comfort zone to try new, difficult challenges. Applaud her for persevering and overcoming obstacles.

Resist the temptation to tell your teen how smart and talented she is.

Although it may seem counterintuitive, this sort of praise only reinforces an unhealthy fixed mindset, which makes students less motivated to put forth effort and persevere because they think of their talents as simply innate. If a goal is hard, therefore, they believe it to be out of reach.

A study of Dutch tweens ages nine to thirteen published in *Monitor on Psychology* illustrated the powerful effects of a growth mindset on performance. Halfway through taking standardized math tests, students who used encouraging self-talk focused on effort (e.g., "I will do my very best"), consistent with a growth mindset, improved their performance on the second half of the tests. Students who made statements focused on ability (e.g., "I've always been good at math"), consistent with a fixed mindset, and those who made no self-statements experienced no change in performance.

Being Okay with Imperfect Work

Since your daughter was first assigned homework, you may have gotten into the habit of checking it over to correct errors. Now that she is older, it may be difficult to imagine taking a hands-off approach. How can you let her turn in work that may be mediocre or contain mistakes? Yet a focus on mastery requires doing just that. The goal of homework is not the grade itself (the end result), but rather the process of practicing and getting better at learning.

Through this lens, the aim of writing assignments is not to get an A, but to encourage teens to expand their self-awareness, more fully express their creativity, and further develop written expression skills. To support this growth, ask your daughter about her ideas, clarify what she is trying to convey, and suggest edits. Resist, however, taking a red Sharpie to her paper or, worse, rewriting it yourself.

If your daughter is content to hand in error-ridden work, this in itself is a potential learning experience. She will find out how it feels when her teacher calls her out on this or when friends who worked harder feel good about the feedback they get. Over time, these are the moments that can make girls stronger students by compelling them to come up with better ideas, work harder to express them, and improve their study skills.

Parlaying Her Strengths

Even accomplished adults have strengths and weaknesses. Yet middle school and high school students are unreasonably expected to excel at everything. Point out how your daughter can harness her assets. Remind her of when she persevered, met her goal, and felt great about herself. She can apply that same positive attitude and determination over and over.

Let's say she ran successfully for student government with an organized campaign, a persuasive platform, and winning posters. How can she parlay those skills into getting a summer internship or job? Or perhaps she trained diligently for a cello recital or dance competition. How can she apply similar methodology to prepare for an admissions exam?

Supporting Emotional Regulation

As you know, managing feelings is crucial for optimal learning and performance. Intrusive thoughts and upsetting feelings hijack motivation, concentration, and productivity. An inability to stop distressing preoccupations that loop endlessly in their minds makes teens feel utterly helpless.

When your daughter panics because she is sitting in front of her books frozen, utterly unable to do anything, it may be hard not to jump in and do work for her. But take a step back. Remember that for her to persist and prevail, she must learn to cope with and work through discomfort. Acknowledge your daughter's feelings, help her label them, and empathize with what she's going through. Then ask what she can do to regain her emotional equilibrium.

Right now, what will make her feel better? How can she solve the problem? Will writing in her journal help? Would she feel calmer after going on a short run or taking the dog for a walk? It is a myth that absolute quiet and a lack of distractions are required to work. Teen girls, like all students, need an ideal amount of stimulation to thrive. Can she pick out background music that will soothe or motivate her? Is it better for her to sit in the kitchen or family room?

Girls who suffer from chronic anxiety or depression usually function better in mildly distracting environments. Instead of focusing inwardly and getting wrapped up in what is happening in their own heads, some teens benefit from stimulation that helps shift their attention to the external world, where constructive work can take place. Allowing teens to work with ambient noise, a study buddy, or in busy areas of the home can actually reduce the disruption of inner emotional turbulence.

Encouraging Personal Study Styles

When it comes to study habits, there are few one-size-fits-all prescriptions. As just discussed, to get the right amount of stimulation, some teens need to be shuttered in their bedrooms, while others have to sit at the kitchen counter. Your daughter may fare better starting with her hardest task and getting it out of the way before she tires—or warming up with easier assignments to gain momentum and confidence for more difficult assignments.

This is why it is better to ask her—rather than to dictate—which study approaches she prefers, and why. Honor her preferences even if they are counterintuitive or different from yours. While respecting your daughter's authority on study strategies that work best for her, you can share the following helpful findings from neuroscience about optimizing her functioning.

GETTING THE RIGHT KIND OF SLEEP

Getting enough sleep to consolidate memories is a start.

The most effective bedtime routine allows for full nights of sleep and also going to bed and waking up at the same times every day. But if your teen has to deviate from that schedule, different sleep patterns may promote specific kinds of learning and performance.

The deep, restorative stage of sleep, known as Stage 3 or slow-wave sleep (SWS), occurs more in the first half of the night and is thought to contribute to memory, insightful thinking, and creativity. Many researchers believe that this kind of sleep processes and consolidates "declarative" information such as facts, figures, and vocabulary words. If your teen is trying to learn French conjugations or a bunch of historical dates, she might prioritize getting to bed at a reasonable hour to ensure maximum SWS. If she thinks she needs more study time, waking up early to do additional review in the morning is best because this cycle of sleep diminishes throughout the night.

However, when preparing for recitals, performances, auditions, or tryouts, the opposite strategy works better. That is because over the course of the night, increasing periods of REM sleep, which are thought to consolidate procedural or motor memories, occur. This is what your skater, dancer, or violinist needs to perform at her best. If she stays up later to practice, the ideal would be waking up at her normal time to allow for more cycles of REM sleep.

STRENGTHENING HER MEMORY

Because memory pathways strengthen with repetition, if your daughter has lots to learn she should avoid cramming. She should study instead during multiple, well-spaced sessions, which helps her to process information and to minimize interference with material she memorized just before and after. Studying in different rooms and at various times also boosts memory by increasing neural connections in the brain.

So does actively organizing and clustering concepts within material. Encourage your teen to use mnemonic devices and to associate new facts and terms with what she already knows. Other effective memory hacks include making important information into a rhyme or song and creating visual study aids, such as flash cards, illustrations, and diagrams. Repeatedly reviewing material and testing herself works well, too. But the best way to learn, it is said, is to teach. If your daughter can explain concepts well enough that her friends or siblings understand, she has probably mastered the material.

OPTIMIZING HER BRAINPOWER

No matter what girls claim, brains are not designed to do two tasks at once—at least not well. Multitasking undermines efficiency. While checking social media or glancing at a video, for example, your teen can't do even mindless assignments as quickly and accurately as if she ignored screens.

If she doesn't believe you, facts about loss of productivity may convince her. Trying to focus on two tasks at once requires your daughter to shift her attention, which slows her down, causes her to make more mistakes, and drains her brain's energy faster. Assignments can take 25 percent longer to finish.

Remarkably, dividing attention drastically reduces a person's brainpower from the level of a Harvard MBA to that of an eight-year-old child. Just being aware of incoming messages causes stress hormones to spike and can reduce IQ by five to ten points. This is equal to the cognitive impairment caused by pulling an all-nighter or being legally intoxicated. One study found that after incoming email, messages, or phone calls interrupted Microsoft employees from their work, it took an average of fifteen minutes for them to return to the tasks they were doing.

Imagine how much harder it is for your teen, whose self-regulation is still developing, to let go of emotionally gripping text messages and resume her math problem sets. Ask her to do an experiment. If she puts her cellphone in another room and focuses only on her work, is she faster? More productive? Less stressed?

De-emphasizing Failure

Because teens today fear making even small mistakes, it is crucial to normalize—and even to encourage—failure. Otherwise, fears of intellectual risks prevent girls from trying unless success is certain. This is why students in middle school and high school are always delighted to hear reassuring stories about epic failures that turned into fabulous, life-altering inventions.

Just as you didn't critique her earliest drawings or clay "sculptures," restrain yourself from appraising your daughter's work now—yes, even though the stakes are higher. When you barely mention her mistakes, she gets the message they aren't all that important. By not communicating alarm or stepping in to correct them, you give her freedom to develop vital resiliency.

If your daughter acknowledges she made an error, take your cues from the teacher handbook. Matter-of-factly ask your tween, "What is the first thing you have to do with this type of problem?" If she's wrong, say, "Not quite" to prompt her to think more. If she can't figure out the answer, a casual "I bet if you think about it, you'll come up with it" encourages her to grow, which is the point of assignments.

Troubleshooting

Learning is a complex process affected by cognitive, emotional, social, and behavioral factors. If your daughter is not thriving in school, of course you'll want to identify what is going wrong so you can help her. To determine what may be undermining her academic success, ask yourself the following questions.

Could There Be an Underlying Learning Issue?

Don't assume that if your daughter's school hasn't identified a learning challenge that she doesn't have one. Students can compensate—until they can't and hit a wall. Do you see her struggling to decode words, spell, comprehend what she reads, calculate numbers quickly, or express her thoughts—verbally or on paper? Do you suspect she has trouble understanding written or oral language, memorizing information, or staying focused? If so, you can determine her strengths and weaknesses by requesting a comprehensive psychoeducational assessment from a school psychologist or private practitioner in the community.

Testing will pinpoint what your daughter needs to thrive in school. Perhaps she would benefit from extra help, a specific subject tutor, or working with a learning coach. If she has deficits that prevent her from accessing her education, schools are obligated by law to provide Individualized Education Programs (IEPs) or 504 Plans consisting of remediation, modifications to the curriculum, and/or accommodations in the classroom.

Are Emotional Issues Interfering with Her Learning or Performance?

Is your teen or tween depressed or anxious, lethargic, unable to concentrate, or panicky when she takes tests? Is her perfectionism slowing her down or immobilizing her? Does social discomfort make her hesitant to go to school? Feedback from teachers about her classroom behavior may provide insight. A school psychologist could also observe her in class. If you see signs of emotional instability at home, an assessment by a mental health clinician can provide further clarity as well as educational and treatment recommendations.

Is This a Performance/Output Problem?

Does your daughter learn material quickly, but struggle with homework completion? Does she do better on tests and quizzes than on projects and other assignments? Is she messy, disorganized, scatterbrained, and always losing materials? Is it hard for her to judge how long it will take her to do her work? Is she constantly running late? Does she procrastinate in getting started on tasks? Does she have trouble shifting from one problem or assignment to another? Does she often have to reread? Is she easily frustrated or overwhelmed by the difficulty or complexity of her work? Does she skip items or neglect to correct mistakes?

If this describes your daughter, weak EF may be preventing her from demonstrating her knowledge. One or more skills, such as planning, initiation, inhibition, time management, emotional regulation, working memory, cognitive flexibility, or self-monitoring, may be getting in her way. This problem frustrates parents, teachers, and students alike—and often results in afflicted girls being seen as unengaged or underachieving.

In my experience, parents are most tempted to intervene with bright daughters who have EF weaknesses. Tremendous amounts of scaffolding ensure that girls keep up with the workload, but don't teach them to function independently. Although EF usually improves by the twenties, when the frontal lobes fully develop, it is probably wise for teens to work with learning coaches or EF tutors to learn these skills sooner. But parents have to mindfully withdraw help as soon as students demonstrate competence. That way, teens have incentive to practice and apply these skills. Effectiveness in school and work depends on it.

• • •

As discussed earlier, your daughter's academic success also depends on the degree to which she feels socially accepted and included in her peer group. Girls who feel isolated, lonely, or rejected not only dislike school, but also may be at a real disadvantage in the classroom. The next chapter delves into a topic that often sits at the top of both mothers' and daughters' priority lists—teens' and tweens' social lives.

CHAPTER ELEVEN

Fostering Healthy Friendships

Middle school was social hell. In sixth grade, I got bullied. In seventh grade, I had a boyfriend who dumped me over text and then was mean to me, and then in eighth grade I had a bad fight with someone who was my friend and we're not friends anymore because of it. In high school, I had a girlfriend who cheated on me.

—JAYLEEN, 17

My fifteen-year-old is in the thick of it. One of her good friends since preschool—they've had bumps along the way—is going off in a different direction. One of this girl's other friends, who my daughter isn't friends with, gave her a surprise sixteenth birthday party and invited four other good friends, all except my daughter. It's a small school, which makes this especially painful.

—SUNNY, MOTHER OF WILLOW

I had a hard time in middle school. It was the worst three years of my life. What a social hierarchy! The popular girls were wearing push-up bras to school. They ruled everything. I was one of the nerds. I hated it and didn't have a proper set of friends. I just focused on the popular girls and was super unhappy.

—ANGELINA, 16

My daughter is a people pleaser who wants to be friends with everybody. When she entered sixth grade she didn't want to be part of a clique. It worked well; she made lots of friends. But then she didn't feel a part of any group and started to feel like she wasn't connected. In seventh grade, she settled down with a gossipy group of girls. Hailey got caught up sometimes. But often she'd say it didn't feel good. She felt on the outside. Her confidence was shaken for the first time. She wasn't as bubbly or outgoing. Teachers saw that in class. I just hope it comes back.

—FAITH, MOTHER OF HAILEY, 14

Concerns about peer friendships have plagued mothers for generations. Of course, you want your daughter to enjoy satisfying relationships. During the teen years, interactions with friends give her feedback that contributes to her identity and self-worth. Social experiences perfect her abilities to read people, navigate shifting group dynamics, and weather the ups and downs of friendships. She becomes more adept at resolving interpersonal conflicts, advocating for herself, and addressing unhealthy relationships. All these skills contribute to lifelong social competence, confidence, and resiliency.

But gone are the days when all mothers had to do to encourage social development was let girls out in the backyard to play games with whatever neighbors happened to be around. As one teacher I interviewed joked, "What are playdates? Our parents handed us a stick and said, 'Go play!' They didn't orchestrate our social lives." Now your daughter is too old for you to arrange her playdates—or to choose her friends.

If your daughter socializes mostly via apps, how can you guide her in finding and feeling comfortable with her tribe? How can you help her to bounce back from typical adolescent slights and humiliations? What should you do if you read text conversations or posts on social media that raise red flags? What can you do if her romantic choices alarm you?

The pages ahead will guide you to apply many of the parenting strategies previously described to your daughter's social life. When you mother the daughter you have, foster fruitful conversations, do less to achieve more, and help her to learn from experiences and mistakes, you nurture your teen's personal growth, capacity to form healthy bonds, and overall interpersonal competency.

What to Expect in Middle School

This transition ushers in marked change for both your daughter and you. As girls grow more invested in friendships, social stress becomes more rampant. It is a time of learning about themselves and others, trying out new friendships, and figuring out how to get along. Social media is adding further intensity and potential trip wires to this developmental process.

With puberty, friendships abruptly shift and branch out. Psychologists at UCLA found that two-thirds of students at twenty-six middle schools gained and lost friends during the first year alone. Watching your tween distance herself from longtime nursery school or elementary school pals may disappoint you, especially if your families are friendly. If your daughter starts gravitating to different sorts of friends, you may be mystified about why they appeal to her.

Just because these changes are normal doesn't mean they are painless. At a time when girls can't count on the stability of their own minds, bodies, or emotions, going through social upheaval can be tough. Middle school friendships notoriously yo-yo. At warp speed, tweens go from inseparable clones to mortal enemies—or frenemies—and sometimes back again. This is what middle school girls tell me most often causes friendship problems:

- I'm always the one making social plans; nobody invites me anywhere
- If I sit at another lunch table, I'm afraid my friends will talk about me
- Getting caught in the middle
- An acquaintance keeps asking me to join our social group
- Friends always teasing me

- My best friend said something really mean
- Not getting as many likes as other people on social media
- No one is being mean, but they never include me
- My friend hanging out more with someone else
- Deciding what to do together
- Keeping secrets
- Trying to make up after fights
- Being the third or fourth wheel
- When friends take out their stress on you
- Worrying that my friend will get mad at me
- Having to do stuff to get my friend to like me
- Trying to spend time with all my friends
- Someone ignoring me on social media
- Being friends with two people who hate each other
- My best friend telling other people my secret
- Friends who snap from all their stress
- Trying to fix a friendship that's been broken
- When people say stuff about you that's not true

When social turmoil causes your daughter to feel adrift or bereft, you both may hurt. But now she may be less inclined to fill you in on the specifics of what is going on. A previously talkative girl may answer questions in vague monosyllables and eschew any offered advice.

Or, as Lola's mother found, you may find yourself struggle to guide your daughter in how to handle teen drama that seems to have a life of its own. During seventh grade, Lola's best friend, Sara, grew closer to Justine, who Lola knew less well. Lola told Sara how sad she was because they were not as close and asked if the two of them could hang out sometime. Soon Lola learned that Sara had given Justine a different version of that conversation. Sara said Lola was jealous of Justine and Sara's friendship and so eager to have Sara to herself, she had bad-mouthed Justine. Now, both Sara and Justine were angry at Lola and not speaking to her.

What to Expect in High School

The good news is that while girls still search for their "people" throughout high school, social volatility and emotional turbulence decline. As Celine says, "My seventeen-year-old is on the tail end of backbiting, gossip, and friend-today-not-tomorrow stuff. They're maturing and getting more comfortable with who they are."

Older teens more often accept peers' flaws in favor of authenticity, trust, respect, and shared pasts in relationships. They have the courage to speak up when peers are unkind. Aliya, seventeen, says, "Laila has no friends. She talks about money and herself. Our friend group is so not that. But we've been friends since seventh grade. We've gone through so much together. So when other kids talk trash about her and don't take time to know the deeper side of her, I'm like, 'No, that's my best friend.'"

Because the fear of ruffling feathers has eased, by the midteens your daughter may be more candid with friends who upset her—for better or for worse. Carmen, sixteen, explains, "When my friend asks, 'Are we good?' now I can be like, 'Not really. I distanced myself from you because of x, y, and z.'"

Girls in high school say they struggle socially mostly because of:

- Feeling left out after seeing social media posts of friends having fun without them
- Not being sought after or invited to parties
- Competition over grades and college choices
- Friends not paying attention to them while dating
- Learning to accept friends' boundaries
- Friends having different comfort levels with self-disclosure
- Feeling not understood or supported
- Friends going through hard times or having serious/worrisome problems
- Friends having different values or interests
- Issues with sexual orientation or gender identification

- Not knowing why friends or social groups suddenly and inexplicably drop them
- People posting negative comments or unflattering photos online

When She's Excluded, Mistreated, or Rejected

After fighting or falling out with friends, girls react in a myriad of ways. Oftentimes teens and tweens reflexively blame the people who angered or hurt them. But to become socially competent and resilient, honest self-examination is required. Difficult moments can teach your daughter something important about herself, such as how she behaves as a friend and what she might have contributed to a relationship's troubles or eventual demise.

Being blindsided by peers suddenly excluding or rejecting them devastates girls. Not getting explanations for why this happened—if there actually are any—only worsens the pain. To figure out what she may have done wrong, your teen may spend countless hours mentally reviewing conversations and interactions, looking for imperceptible clues. This is rarely a satisfying exercise. Unfortunately, it is usually the case that fear and uncertainty plague girls who are unceremoniously dropped.

Sometimes teens realize that old, trusted friends were not in fact true friends. Your daughter may feel betrayed not only by peers' disloyalty, but also by her own failure to detect such fickleness. How could she have been so "stupid"? If she makes new friends, how will she know whom to trust? This state of mind is like a bullhorn for critical voices in teens' heads. As they greatly magnify perceived flaws, girls imagine shortcomings mothers find absurd. As your daughter's self-esteem plummets, you may hear her proclaim that she's an "ugly loser destined to be alone"—or worse.

To protect against loneliness, some girls invest all their social resources in just one best friend, a steadfast ally who always has her back and is available to get together. While reassuring in the short term, this strategy is precarious; a minor shift in relationship dynamics can set off seismic aftershocks. Usually, one girl branches out, makes new friends, or gravitates to another group. This is most often normal and healthy; the road to self-discovery and social competency is paved with experience. But girls who place all their social eggs in one basket may get their hearts broken.

Other tweens struggle in groups that tolerate but don't truly accept or include them. As Tia, fourteen, put it, "I'm nobody's number one choice." In unhealthier group cultures, teens and tweens desperate to fit in may become targets of cattiness, backstabbing, or scapegoating. It is heartrending for mothers to see daughters tolerate slights, social drama, and disrespect.

What if your daughter goes back to the old clique that dumped her? Even worse, what if she starts ingratiating herself by imitating behaviors she used to condemn, such as gossiping, excluding, manipulating, or being nasty on social media? Or she stoops to out-of-character relational aggression when trying to protect her social status from a girl she thinks is a threat? These behaviors may utterly baffle you.

Neurobiology can explain. For survival, humans have an innate need to belong to social groups. Being rebuffed or rejected elicits intense reactions. Brain scans show that these emotional experiences generate heightened activity in the same areas where *physical* pain is experienced. Imagine how devastating social disappointments are for tweens and teens, whose well-being depends on peer acceptance, and you can appreciate why your teen may contort herself into a pretzel to maintain even the most tenuous and unsatisfying—or even painful—social ties.

At her most insecure, your daughter may fear that making new friends or being alone would be worse than putting up with mistreatment. Jade, seventeen, has been there. She was so socially isolated during adolescence that "I started talking to stoners. I skateboarded, so I got super into it. But I never meshed with them. Everything I was saying wasn't true. I was saying what they wanted to hear. They'd tell me to meet them somewhere. I'd be waiting for them, but they went somewhere else. It happened the whole year."

Remind yourself that after struggle, there is often growth. But only in retrospect is it obvious to girls that social disappointments and upheavals become opportunities. Mothers know this. So often I hear about a teen or tween who "decided she needed a different group of friends. She's much happier now. She found her way back to the girls who made her feel bad about herself, but she also branched out and ended up being in a better situation." Discussions with women and girls support the truism "As one door closes, another opens."

When She Needs Reassurance

Sometimes girls are clear about what they *don't* want from mothers but can't express what they *are* looking for. Most often, it is reassurance. In difficult social moments, tweens and teens need validation that what they are thinking and feeling is normal and okay. When she feels like a social misfit, your daughter most needs proof that you love her and think the world of her, no matter what may be going on in gym class or the cafeteria. Here are some ways you can give her that message.

Physical Comfort and Affection

Unless your daughter recoils at touch, physical comfort may be more immediate and powerful than verbal assurances. Before saying a single word, you might rub her back, give her a hug, or hold her hand. A fifth grader told her mother, "When I'm upset, I just need you to give me a big hug and say, 'Yeah, that really sucks. It's awful.'" Not starting conversations right away also gives your tween or teen time to get ready to talk about her distress.

Normalize Experiences

Remind your teen that all friendships go through ups and downs. In lasting relationships, close friends inevitably disappoint, irritate, or mess up occasionally. No one is perfect. If your daughter is receptive, tell her about similar social heartaches her sister, cousin, and you endured at her age. These stories are irrefutable evidence she is not alone and should not be ashamed. Like all the women she knows, she, too, will survive.

Quality Tops Quantity

Tweens often gauge self-worth by how many friends they have. They may not recognize yet that the quality of relationships matters more. Research bears this out. Teens who had many, but more superficial, school friends became more anxious as young adults. Plus, contrary to what most girls think, being popular doesn't alleviate loneliness. A social status that is achieved by grasping power at the expense of others is inherently unstable and therefore difficult to maintain. Deep down, the most popular girls are just as, if not more, insecure than everyone else.

Reassure your daughter that she does not need hundreds of friends, either on social media or in real life. A few will suffice, so long as they are loyal, trustworthy, and supportive. Both you and your daughter may be heartened by this research finding: at least one strong, healthy friendship predicts both good school performance and psychological well-being (e.g., higher self-esteem and less anxiety).

Focus on the Positive

Teen girls often dwell on one social slight or disappointment, which in that moment looms larger and more pressing than all the positives in their lives. While empathizing with her distress, refocusing your daughter's attention on her most recent social triumphs and pleasures lets her appreciate the bigger (and brighter) picture. Pepper tells me, "I try to remind my fifteen-year-old of good times with people and other options, girls she had good experiences with who may not go to her school. I say, 'I understand that happened with Jasmine, but you've been talking about Sophie. Why don't you try to get together with her?'"

Provide Hope

Tell your daughter that although she is going through a rough time now, it will not last forever. Things will get better. This is not a platitude. Social situations will change because *teens* will change. She just needs to be patient while she and her peers mature. If she tries to make changes in her friendships, remind her that turning things around takes time. But for now, what she *can* control is how she acts in socially challenging situations.

Studies of high school students demonstrate the value of social hope. Ninth graders were asked to read a short brain science article about how personality can change. Then they read anecdotes seniors had written about eventually learning to shrug off and move on from peer conflicts. Finally, the group was asked to write encouraging advice to younger students.

After stressful tasks, the intervention group had 10 percent lower levels of cortisol than the control group, indicating that students who read inspiring information coped better. At the end of the school year, these ninth graders were 40 percent less likely to be depressed and earned slightly better grades than control students.

Fostering Social Competency and Resiliency: What You Can Do

Besides offering reassurance, here are other practical ways you can help.

Step Back

You may want to protect your daughter from the pain of social exclusion, rejection, and mistreatment, but she needs to experience them to learn how to bounce back. In fact, according to a meta-analysis of seventy studies involving more than two hundred thousand kids, overprotection can actually *increase* her risk of being bullied.

Years ago, I saw an eleven-year-old whose parents were so afraid of negative peer influence that they forbid Olga from staying after school, listening to popular music, and participating in field trips unless her mother chaperoned. Olga's isolation allayed her parents' anxiety, but also prevented her from learning to talk with classmates and make friends. Her social isolation and naïveté set her apart so much that she became a target of peer ridicule.

Teachers, who are less emotionally invested than mothers, often are more clear-eyed about the benefit of allowing students to resolve social issues for themselves. Lucinda explains, "Two girls are arguing, it doesn't matter about what, and I take them into the hallway. All I care about is that they work it out before coming back in the classroom." She gives her tweens these guidelines: "There are certain words you can use, certain things you can do to make someone feel better. You can take ownership of what you did, but no one is perfect. Maybe you don't know why you did something. You don't have to analyze it, just make it right."

Empathize, Don't Criticize

When she is hurting, she needs empathy above all. It can be hard not to criticize her for acting in ways that are against your values or contributed to her predicament. But if you lead with judgment, you'll probably put off your daughter before you can help. To drum up compassion—and humility—recall a time when you made foolish social choices as a teen.

Similarly, rather than dismissing her larger-than-life reactions, remember how it felt when peers put you in your place by rolling their eyes, exchanging knowing looks, or subtly not making eye contact with you. Think about painful public embarrassments and imagine far worse digital humiliations. In this context, your distraught teen or tween looks less like a drama queen.

Ask, Don't Tell

When daughters are suffering, the urge to offer solutions may be overwhelming. But this is an ideal time for her to ponder the situation for herself. Brainstorm ideas with her or act as her sounding board. That is how she learns what is in her heart, what she values in friends, when she overreacts, when she should speak up, when it is time to forgive, and when relationships are no longer worth keeping.

> **Daughter:** I'm going up to Pam and Tracie tomorrow and telling them how I feel.

NOT

> **Mom:** No, just ignore those girls! Don't sit with them at lunch tomorrow. When you leave them alone, they'll realize they miss you and they'll come back.

> **Daughter:** But, Mom, I don't want to ignore them. I want to make things better.

Mom: You'll only make things worse if they think you need them. Be strong!

INSTEAD, TRY

Mom: What do you want to say to them?

Daughter: I don't know. This situation doesn't feel like it's finished. I hate loose ends. And I don't want to be the victim.

Mom: But what if the girls aren't nice to you?

Daughter: I still feel like I need to explain my position, whether or not they like it. Will you talk to me about what I could say to them tomorrow?

Mom: Absolutely, we can discuss various options and, if you'd like, we can role-play.

Honor Her Autonomy

Forget giving unsolicited advice. But what about when you respond to your daughter's request for help? Does she take you up on your suggestions? The answer is probably "sometimes." Although you might feel good about your wise idea, she might reject it out of hand—along with all your other recommendations. A day or two later, she might come around. Meanwhile, rather than feeling slighted and making this about you, let her know you're okay with her choices.

TRY

> **Mom:** Okay, I've given you three options. Let me know if any of them work for you.

OR

> **Mom:** Okay, now that you know what you *don't* want to do, I have faith that you'll be able to come up with a better idea.

When Makayla confided in her mother that her friend Naomi was ghosting her on social media, Liza learned the value of this approach. Naomi was furious because friends who were home for a college break had invited Makayla, but not her, to a party. Makayla agreed with her mother that Naomi's anger was unreasonable. But while Liza thought Naomi's pattern of behavior warranted a strong reaction, Makayla chose not to "make a big deal about it."

Makayla simply texted Naomi, "I know you're upset, but you know I had nothing to do with you not being invited. I know you'll get over this and our friendship will be okay. So let me know when you stop being mad at me." A day or so later, Naomi did just that. Liza realized after the fact why it was better for Makayla to rely on her own judgment. Her daughter was far better able to appreciate the nuances of her friendship with Naomi than she was.

When empowered to figure out the approach that feels most natural, girls come up with good ideas. A fourteen-year-old told her mother, "There's a girl who's sitting by herself in the cafeteria every day, so I invited her to sit with us." A twelve-year-old realized, "I'm so sick of being stuck between two friends, so I told them I wanted to be friends with both of them and they should work it out themselves." With her group crumbling, a fifteen-year-old turned to a friend she'd known since first grade and said, "Denise, I'm having a hard time. Is it okay if I sit at your lunch table tomorrow?"

There also may be times that your daughter asks for help one moment and then, the very next moment, rejects your attempt to come to her aid. One reason for this seemingly contradictory behavior is the push/pull dynamic of teens yearning for autonomy. She may resent you precisely because she has to depend on you.

Another explanation is that, as many parents experience, you may try your teen's or tween's patience by failing to immediately grasp the nuances of the situation, thinking too long, or giving her too detailed an answer. You may hear, "Stop! This is taking too much time. I just need a simple answer," or "That's not at all helpful! Never mind!" And if she follows your advice and things don't go well, you know who she'll blame.

When you face these reactions, it can help to remember where her frustration is coming from and not take it personally. Remind yourself that even if she doesn't say it, she benefits from—and probably secretly appreciates—your willingness to help. As always, try to give her only as much help as she wants and truly needs so she will figure out dilemmas on her own.

Promote the Big Picture

To make sense of social situations and solve problems well, girls have to rely on accurate information. But emotions can cloud perceptions. When upset, your daughter sees the world through the prism of her own idiosyncrasies, preoccupations, and insecurities. Facts are likely to be distorted. Parents of a thirteen-year-old I tested, for example, astutely described Margaret as "a master perceiver but poor interpreter who misreads others' intentions and motivations."

Your teen, too, may be overly sensitive to peers' benign comments and behavior. Help her to keep an open mind, imagine others' perspectives, and refine her social inferences. Without excusing a friend's hurtful behavior (which she'll hear as you taking the other girl's side), you can wonder if your daughter considered alternate explanations. Is she sure her sources of information are reliable? Has she spoken to the girl who upset her to get her perspective? Don't get discouraged if you hear, "You just don't understand!" Matter-of-factly tell her that that's exactly why you're talking to her about the situation.

Empower Her to Self-Advocate

Girls who are brought up to be kind, thoughtful, or selfless are sometimes unsure when it is okay to focus on their own needs. This hesitation can hold them back from taking necessary action. To avoid feeling selfish, teens may need mothers' blessings to self-advocate. After two close friends excluded her from a school project, Yolanda, fourteen, told her mother, "You always said I had to include everybody on the playground. Sometimes I just wanted to go out there and play. I still feel responsible for everyone's happiness and inclusion. But no one is worried about mine."

Counsel your daughter that she does, in fact, have personal agency; speaking up for herself is a normal and healthy way to get her needs met and maintain relationships. Just as she can't be expected to read her friends' minds, she can't count on girls knowing what she is thinking and feeling. If she's upset, she may want to communicate that to friends—and expect them to do the same.

Practice Confrontations

Teach your daughter to respect others as she stands up for herself. Using the strategies described in Chapter Seven, "Fruitful Conversations 2.0," remind her that how she speaks affects whether people listen to her. Coach her to maintain comfortable eye contact, a friendly but confident posture, and a neutral tone of voice while conveying a straightforward, clear message. All she has to say is "I'm wondering why you didn't invite me over Saturday. Did I do something?" If your teen or tween thinks it would be helpful, she can practice what she plans to say with you.

Anticipate Consequences

As your daughter considers solutions to social dilemmas, ask her about the probable outcomes of each option. Cause-and-effect thinking helps her understand how her behavior affects others. Instead of giving your daughter specific solutions, you can ask, "If you say that, how are you hoping your friend will react?" "What if she doesn't do that?" "How would you feel if she is not open to hearing what you have to say?" or "What might happen if the girls don't believe you? Or they still stay mad and don't forgive you?"

Celebrate Courage

In therapy and workshops, girls talk about pretending disagreements never happened ("so I don't make things worse"), automatically apologizing ("so maybe my friend will, too"), ignoring people who upset them, and sneakily seeking revenge. These approaches neither resolve conflicts nor make teens and tweens feel good about themselves.

When your daughter calls out a friend, whether she gets the response she wants is often beside the point. Notice and applaud the strength it took for her to act. She may have prepared herself to be disappointed—or been fearful of causing a social disaster. Yet despite all that, she decided it was worth the risk to honor her inner voice telling her this was important to do. Regardless of the outcome, your teen should take pride in how she handled herself. Plus, the skills she is practicing now will probably produce even more satisfying results in the future.

Let Her Stumble

Even for adults, misjudgments and gaffes often become memorable social lessons. Still, it kills mothers to see daughters learning the hard way. Kristina tells me, "I begged her not to date the guy who just broke up with her best friend, but she kept saying it would be fine. I could give her advice, but I couldn't make her do what I thought was the right thing." Kristina stepped back, let her daughter make her choice, and "held my breath for what I knew would happen."

When the consequences she predicted came to pass, Kristina comforted and supported her distraught teen. She tells me, "Months after ignoring my advice, my sixteen-year-old said, 'Mom, you were so right. I can't believe I didn't listen to you.'" That is all you can do for your own daughter. And if you're lucky, you might just hear a mea culpa like Kristina did.

Hold Her Accountable

Girls sometimes deal with conflict by appearing to sweep it under the rug. They act as if everything is fine, but then, without owning their hostility, resort to underhanded or subtly aggressive tactics. When hurt by an alpha girl, for example, tweens might try to seek allies by soliciting other classmates' sympathy. Getting peers involved and creating drama might be satisfying in the moment, but hardly resolves problems constructively.

When Nan picked up her daughter and her teammates from a soccer game, the girls disparaged the goalie's performance and the outfit she wore to school that day. Nan tells me, "I wouldn't say anything in front of Lianne's friends, but as soon as we got home, we had a talk about how to treat people. I had to remind her, 'How would you like it if a group of friends bad-mouthed how you played or made fun of your clothes?' These girls have to be taught that this isn't the right way to act."

Rather than making excuses or minimizing your daughter's "crime," expect her to be accountable. How she treats people matters. If she is spiteful or cruel, she needs to fess up and apologize for her behavior. If a friend catches her using a flimsy excuse to decline a sleepover invitation, she should own up to having previous plans. Unless she takes responsibility for her errors, even unintended ones, she won't feel good about herself—and other people may not, either.

Help Her to Let Go

Moving on from painful experiences is key to your daughter's mental health and well-being. Holding a grudge, refusing to forgive, staying bitter, or being vengeful eat away at her. Maintaining high levels of stress hormones is toxic to her mind and body. Teach your teen not to let anyone else's bad or hurtful decisions take her to a place of despair or unkindness. She can get through negative social experiences in ways that strengthen rather than diminish her.

What NOT to Do

Micromanage

Trying to orchestrate your daughter's relationships will most likely fail. Mothers who set up teens or tweens with potential friends are usually subjected to cringeworthy encounters. Matchmaking is difficult, if not impossible; with social nuances nearly invisible and difficult to detect, you cannot predict whether girls will click. Also, your daughter is apt to resent your interference—as well as its subtext: you think you know best what she needs socially.

By middle school, stepping back is mandatory. As a psychologist working in a parochial school told me, "I tell parents of fifth-grade girls, 'This is probably the last year to try to affect your daughter's social life. Next year, you're not going to be able to nudge her.'"

Confront Other Parents

When peers wrong your daughter, it can be tempting to seek justice from their parents. Although exceptions occur, this course of action is usually regretted. More often than not, other parents will hear you as being accusatory and become defensive or vindictive in response. As an example, after speaking to a longtime friend whose teen was bullying her daughter in text messages, Mo was shaken by the backlash.

She tells me, "It blew up in my face. The other mom denied that her daughter was writing texts like that. I suggested she might want to read them. She said, 'I don't have time to read my daughter's texts. Some of us can't be Mother of the Year, like you.'" Ouch.

There are times when mothers make a pact to share this kind of information with each other, which can work out well. But no matter how gentle and tactful you are, this all could go south if the other mom decides to shoot the messenger. This approach has such a high failure rate, in fact, that I have to recommend avoiding it.

Get Even

Watching daughters suffer is so torturous that some women fantasize about giving the perpetrators their comeuppance. Obviously, thinking this is one thing; doing it is crossing a massive line. More to the point, remind yourself that this is not about the teens or tweens who make your daughter's school years difficult. Your focus should be on helping her to master skills so she can more capably navigate socially, both now and throughout her life.

Should Friendships End?

Teen girls have to evaluate when to invest in saving friendships and when it is not worth the effort. This is rarely an easy decision. When might your daughter ignore friends' trivial slights and oversights? When is it best to distance herself from offensive girls? When should she confront peers who wrong her? When is it in her best interest to forgive and move on? At what point should she end relationships? Talking through these quandaries with her qualifies as a difficult discussion that will call upon your best communication skills.

Rather than grilling her about a particular incident or making a snap judgment, ask what she looks for in friends. You might hear words such as accepting, nonjudgmental, supportive, genuine, caring, respectful, inclusive, trustworthy, understanding, and encouraging. Also question your daughter about her limits. What is intolerable to her in friendships, and what are absolute deal-breakers? If her friend were in this situation, what advice would your teen offer? Clarifying her own standards helps your daughter to use them to guide her decisions.

Be prepared for the possibility your daughter may draw different conclusions than you do. Her choices may well puzzle or frustrate you. But only she knows how serious problems are with friends, if issues are worth addressing, whether conflicts are likely to blow over, and whether relationships are solid enough to withstand temporary turbulence. Most of all, only she can predict the cost of ending friendships.

Some girls choose to let friendships die a slow, quiet death. A painful, public rupture, with mutual friends in an uproar and feeling compelled to take sides, can seem worse. If your teen imagines this sort of scenario, you might ease her mind by pointing out that decisions don't have to be black and white. Instead of abruptly ending friendships, a cooling-off period or break may be a better approach. During that time, your daughter can devote herself to hobbies and other friends. After seeing how things go, she can reassess her position.

If your daughter opts out of an unhealthy friendship, her feelings may run from relief to grief. She may need to mourn this loss along with whatever social opportunities and security the friendship provided. Or she may behave as if nothing of import happened and immediately gravitate to a different friend or new group. Whatever her reaction, the experience will provide grist for the mill of her social learning.

Dating

Along with friendships, dating is another ubiquitous maternal worry. You might find the whole prospect as overwhelming as Marilyn does; she told me, "I just don't know how to handle teenage dating. What's acceptable and what's not? My daughter is a young fifteen and has a crush on an eighteen-year-old senior. I don't even know how to grasp the whole thing."

When seen as part of an essential learning process, your teen's dating life may seem less daunting. From her first infatuation through more serious, longer-term liaisons, each experience teaches her how to choose partners, develop gratifying relationships, and extricate herself when they become unhealthy or no longer meet her needs. Learning all this may well require your daughter to kiss a bunch of frogs before finding her prince or princess.

Wherever she is on the continuum of dating and sexual exploration, you hope she makes wise decisions. Now is when you most want her to believe in herself and to remember her own value. You hope that with romantic partners, she can call upon the skills you have been encouraging, such as knowing and articulating her feelings, empathizing, dealing with conflict, and asking for what she needs. Okay, great, you may be thinking, but what *else* can I do?

Just as with other rites of passage, there are few hard and fast rules for dating. You're aiming for that razor-thin place that keeps her safe while also encouraging age-appropriate, skill-building experiences. With that mindset, saying yes or no to each of your daughter's requests is less important than discussing the reasoning behind your decisions.

Start well before there is an actual romantic partner on the scene—or even on the horizon. Hypotheticals are easier for teens and tweens to talk about because (a) without specific love interests, they're less defensive and (b) in the abstract, emotions are unlikely to run as high. What does she think about her best friend or cousin dating? What is most important to her in a romantic partner? In her mind, what makes a relationship good? What would make it bad? Does she feel ready to date? In my experience, girls are pretty honest about this.

When it comes to guidelines, your values and your daughter's readiness for dating should be the primary considerations. Have her experiences thus far prepared her for this next step? What strengths and weaknesses does she bring to dating? Is she comfortable flirting and talking in person, or just over social media? In emotionally charged situations, can she keep a cool head and hold her own? Does she know her limits? Can she state them clearly?

If your daughter is determined to date, proceed in baby steps. As she develops more skills and confidence, you'll both get more comfortable. Start by suggesting that she invite over her crush. Specify when and where she is welcome to entertain, such as the family room, den, or game room; if doors must remain open; and whether parents and/or siblings must be home.

You can observe how your teen acts around this person. Is she grounded and in charge of herself? Does she behave differently than usual? How does her crush interact with you and her siblings? Are the teens relaxed, or do you pick up tensions? How is your daughter treated?

You and her other parent can demonstrate respecting her by not making jokes at her expense, "just teasing," or using childhood nicknames she prefers to shed.

Sometimes parents need to step in to make dating expectations crystal clear. Meg told me that her sixteen-year-old's "boyfriends would drive up and text for her to come out. I stopped that right away," she told me. "Are you kidding me? The nerve! It's a lack of common courtesy. Any boy that you're going out with has to come to the door. And he would come, I would take his phone, put his number in my contacts right away, and put my number in his contacts. In case of anything—because you never know."

Heed your gut instinct. If, for example, you are sensing that your teen shouldn't date someone older, trust that. A gap of even two grades creates a potentially problematic imbalance of power. Surveys indicate that the older teens' romantic partners are, the more likely they are to experience dating violence and engage in risky sexual behaviors.

From the time she was a little girl, you may have imagined the kind of person your daughter would date. Don't panic if the person she finds appealing now doesn't pass muster in your book. This is a process of discovery that may take time. She has to learn which personal qualities and habits are a turnoff in a romantic partner. Your daughter has to figure out if she is wildly attracted to people for the wrong reasons. She has to experience a crush who is perfect on paper—cute, smart, funny, athletic, musical, or creative—but actually isn't at all right for her.

Maybe your daughter becomes aware that she never gets to talk about herself or choose the video or activity. Or she realizes the relationship is one-way. Or her partner's jokes cross the line into subtle put-downs. Just as with friends, feeling manipulated, coerced, or demeaned raises red flags. Your teen may need perspective to notice that the person she is dating makes her feel bad about herself and chips away at her self-esteem.

It is crucial to make sure your daughter knows what is and is not acceptable in romantic relationships. According to a 2011 National Longitudinal Study of Adolescent Health, 30 percent of young people 12 to 21 in heterosexual relationships and 20 percent in same-sex relationships suffered psychological abuse inflicted by their partner in the past 18 months.

Knowing how prevalent this is, you can keep an eye out for signs and provide a reality check, if necessary. Tory, sixteen, told me that the boyfriend she met on Snapchat made her duck down in the car when he picked her up "so nobody would see us together. I was supposed to look down and not make eye contact with him. I didn't think it was normal, but I never had a guy into me and I wanted acceptance."

Digital dating abuse is even more common. Among other troubling behaviors, a third of teens report that a current or former partner checked up on them multiple times a day, using the internet or a cellphone to ask where they were, who they were with, or what they were doing. Teens use cellphones to keep tabs on partners' whereabouts and message histories. A fifteen-year-old explained, "He made me keep my Read Receipts on so he could see if I read his messages and was ignoring him." Other romantic interests intimidate or pressure girls to send sexually inappropriate digital pictures—the stuff of parental nightmares.

According to the Youth Risk Behavior Survey, 26 percent of women who were victims of physical violence, contact sexual violence, and/or stalking by an intimate partner at some time in their lives first had these experiences before age eighteen. Make it a point to talk with your daughter repeatedly about the role of consent. Keep in mind that young women who have been sexually assaulted may avoid those words, most often to unconsciously deny or minimize what happened—or to prevent parents from becoming aware of it.

More commonly, girls describe partners as inattentive; persuading them to do unwanted sexual acts ("I was no, no, no until he would talk me into it, and I'd be like, fine"); or failing to respond to requests to stop ("If I said, 'Hey, can you stop? It hurts! Or slow down,' he'd make it worse. So I'd stop saying stuff").

Girls cling to romantic relationships for the same reasons they tolerate friends who mistreat them. For many, getting attention is a big draw. Others hope things will improve. Still others dread painful breakups—or their backlash. But many other girls in this culture grow up not feeling entitled to stand up for their rights. Along with your support, your daughter's self-respect allows her to make clear she won't tolerate mistreatment. She has to be able to say: "That was hurtful. It's not okay to insult me or call me names" or "I expect to be treated well" or "This is my body, and I get to decide."

Young women who cannot assert themselves or are repeatedly victimized in unhealthy relationships need to understand the root of these problems and make changes before they can move on. Tory, who was so grateful for male attention and validation that she dutifully ducked down in her boyfriend's car, realized, "It was like, whatever they wanted was fine. I've been like a puppy following them. I don't speak up. I don't assert myself. I can't be myself." Facing this truth led her to psychotherapy to work on respecting herself and more confidently expressing her needs in romantic relationships.

As you step back and support your daughter's dating experiences, check in with yourself periodically. Is there something you're overlooking? Are you making more of an issue than necessary? Are you maintaining appropriate boundaries? It is easy to get caught up. If your teen is in the thralls of first love, her excitement may be contagious. You may get overly attached to a partner you adore. As Olive realized, "I was pushing too much. I was making her boyfriend's favorite foods, including him for dinner, and inviting him on family vacations—sometimes without consulting her."

When your daughter's romance ends, manage your own reactions so you can be fully emotionally available for her. Regardless of whether you are thrilled the person is out of her life or just as sad as your teen, she needs space to discover her own feelings. Even if they were dating for a minute, she might be shattered. She may mourn the loss of not just her partner, but also her fantasies about what was possible in the future. If she was dumped, public embarrassment may intensify the sting of rejection. More than anything, the security she forfeits along with the relationship may explain why a breakup is such a big deal.

What If She's Not Popular?

Many parents imagine adolescence as a whirlwind of get-togethers, parties, and sleepovers. When daughters are homebodies or rarely socialize with peers, it is easy to assume they are isolated and unhappy. But this is often untrue. In fact, being "unpopular" may be a good thing. Your daughter may deliberately opt out of the teen social scene because she is uneasy at loud, unsupervised parties or with the experimentation that may occur there. If so, her prudent decision-making should delight you. Your teen or tween may have more fun hanging out in her room, with a friend or two, or with her family. If she prefers solitary activities, she has a leg up for creative endeavors.

If on the other hand your teen admits to feeling lonely or wishing she had more friends, these strategies can encourage more peer interactions:

- **Family Get-Togethers.** There is less pressure on girls to act as hosts when parents make plans with other families who have teens. Family friends who go to different schools offer her a chance to escape her social status or reputation and start afresh.

- **Summer Camp.** For many teens and tweens, summer camp is a much-anticipated safe haven where friendships nurtured year after year can be counted upon, no matter what is going on in school. Camp friendships are described as uniquely close and special.

- **Specialized Sports Training.** Attending a weeklong training program to improve her basketball or soccer skills can broaden your daughter's social sphere by introducing her to girls with similar passions, yet who may be less competitive than her usual teammates.

- **Community Service.** Teens who participate in service organizations meet new people of all ages. The collaboration of group projects helps students create quicker and more lasting bonds. Knowing they are making a difference can inspire girls' social confidence.

- **Volunteer Work.** For the same reasons, many teens enjoy working with children in day care or summer camp, or helping with animals at shelters, zoos, and parks.

- **Technology.** Isolated girls can form connections with communities of peers through online video games and social media groups formed around shared interests (art, politics, journalism, etc.). Joanie, an offbeat seventeen-year-old, isn't lonely because of a girl she "met on Instagram and have been best friends with for three years." Although they have never met face-to-face, Joanie considers this relationship a lifeline. Joanie says, "In school, I'm with a bunch of stuck-up kids I don't get along with."

Sleepovers and Technology

When are girls ready for sleepovers? What rules, limits, and guidelines should be set? What cautions do parents need to take in an age of texting, tweeting, and electronics?

If your daughter is reasonably mature and self-regulated, inviting a friend to sleep over at your house is a good first step. Do the girls choose appropriate activities, follow rules about screens, and get enough sleep so they're not cranky zombies the next day? If your tween can be away from home without getting unbearably homesick, the next step may be allowing her to stay at the home of a friend whose family makes you comfortable.

Sleepover trouble skyrockets when the number of girls involved rises above two. Even three friends can be unstable. As the evening progresses and tweens get tired, self-regulation ebbs. Girls get ill-tempered and less kind. That is why, until you are convinced your daughter and her friends can keep things peaceful, it is best to limit the number of sleepover guests.

Technology adds a whole other set of challenges. One, girls often stare at personal cellphones rather than interacting with each other. Two, in a group, they are more susceptible to making poor choices than they are when alone. Thanks to unfinished brain development, teens and tweens are primed for getting bonus social rewards when they take risks in front of peers. This explains why the mob mentality of girls at sleepovers leads to using technology to mistreat and sometimes bully those not present.

When guests arrive for sleepovers, it is prudent to confiscate all cellphones and return them as girls leave. It is still necessary to stay vigilant and monitor the goings-on. As brain research spells out, groups of girls may need support to avoid getting carried away and losing the good judgment that prevails when they are alone.

Bullying

Bullying, defined as repeated, one-way aggression targeting someone who cannot defend herself because she lacks necessary power, is getting the attention it deserves. According to the National Center for Education Statistics, nearly one-quarter of girls ages twelve to eighteen were bullied in 2017. More than half of teens and tweens report being bullied by someone more popular, and 62 percent by someone who can influence what other students think of them.

Check It Out. Just because your daughter is hurt or teased doesn't mean she is the victim of bullying. Was it a onetime occurrence? Could she have misinterpreted or overreacted to teasing or normal jockeying of power? Ask how often it has happened, whether other students observed it, if school personnel are aware, and how she responded. If you are still unsure whether her experience rises to the level of bullying, run it by an expert trained in these matters, such as a guidance counselor, school psychologist, social worker, or youth officer. You might gather general information about resources and strategies available for dealing with bullying without informing your daughter, but let her know if you plan to notify other adults about the particulars of her situation.

Arm Her with Strategies. Meanwhile, give your daughter coping tools. Suggest she avoid places where she is most likely to see students who harass her. Having a friend with her discourages bullies, who prey on the most vulnerable; there is safety in numbers. Coach your tween or teen to respond to bullying briefly and assertively to project self-confidence.

Call In the Guard. If you believe she is being harmed or is at risk, tell your daughter that this is not okay and you will do everything in your power to keep her safe. You need her school's help. Like many teens, she may be afraid that taking this step will worsen her situation by making bullies angry and vengeful. Assure her that schools are obligated by law to protect all students. Speak to administrators. Find out the district's protocol for bullying. Ask what steps will be taken to help your daughter. (Note that the same student privacy rules that protect your teen will also prevent the school from updating you about specific actions taken with other involved students.) Thank personnel for their efforts, follow up at reasonable intervals (don't expect an immediate turnaround), document responses, and stay in close contact until the situation is resolved.

Witnessing Bullying. Studies show that being a bystander to bullying can be just as stressful as being a victim. Teach your daughter that this is a time to follow her conscience, be courageous, and do what she thinks is right. Her decisions should be based on her values; does she want to tacitly condone or encourage bullies, or be a leader who refuses to take part? She can deter bullies by walking away and depriving them of an audience. If she witnesses peers teasing or making jokes at others' expense, she can refrain from laughing (even nervously), as laughter can look like she approves of or encourages this behavior. Point out that girls who bravely reach out to vulnerable students can significantly change school cultures.

The good news is that as girls mature, bullying dies down. Whereas 25 to 30 percent of girls report being bullied during the three years of middle school, by ninth grade that percentage drops to 19 percent and declines further to 12 percent by senior year.

* * *

Just as your daughter embarks on dating, you and her other parent may find yourselves in a similar position. During her teen years, your decision to separate or divorce will greatly affect her—and likely elicit many opinions. In my experience, the healthiest outcomes for families occur when parents are thoughtful and clear-eyed about the choices they make at this difficult time. The next chapter discusses key considerations for parents who go their separate ways, start dating again, and perhaps remarry.

CHAPTER TWELVE

Parenting After Divorce

Today, there is a 40 to 50 percent probability that women's first marriages will end in divorce. As societal stigmas and religious prohibitions abate, more teens experience parents' marital separations and divorces, which occur every thirty-six seconds in the United States. Girls react in all sorts of ways. Some are heartbroken, scared about how lives might change, or worried about the effects on one or both parents. But just as many teens and tweens are palpably relieved—and even quick to describe the advantages of parents divorcing.

Before her parents announced their split, Eve, who is just twelve, tells me, "I hope my parents get a divorce. They don't get along and aren't right for each other. My brother and I have known that for a long time. I don't know why they don't just do it already." After the separation, Eve confirms, "It's fine. No, actually it's better. Things are much nicer because I can't hear any more fighting and yelling at night."

Camille, sixteen, describes an unexpected silver lining of her parents' divorce: "I'm close to my siblings because of it. We went through it together as preteens and go back and forth together." Dolores, now in her twenties, says, "I learned from an early age to be flexible, to see things from different angles, and to be more accepting. I was forced to adjust, and I think it helped me in my own relationships when I got older."

When parents who are considering divorce seek my advice, I reassure them that teens and tweens are adaptable. But I have to add this caveat: what most determines whether girls thrive is how parents handle the divorce. Are parents thoughtful about making choices that are in teens' best interests? Can they stay attuned and responsive to daughters' emotional needs? Are they self-aware enough to avoid spiteful or selfish behaviors that ultimately harm teens and tweens? This chapter describes the proactive, intentional parenting and strong communication strategies that I believe facilitate the best adjustment throughout the divorce process and beyond.

Maintaining Healthy Boundaries

With divorcing parents locked in emotional survival mode, kids' best interests may be overlooked. Witnessing heated arguments deeply affects girls, often compelling them to choose sides. Adding to the emotional distress, teens may be pressured to keep marital problems a secret. Dakota, thirteen, explains, "My father refused to move out, and it was bad. No one knew what we were going through, so I didn't have anyone to talk to."

For your daughter to feel safe during and after divorce, she must know what to expect, trust her parents to remain in charge, and see adults behaving responsibly. This is no easy task. These suggestions can help.

Good Communication and Healthy Family Boundaries

- ☐ Be as decisive as you can. When parents repeatedly change their minds about when (or whether) to separate, it is much harder for teens to manage soaring hopes and demoralizing letdowns.
- ☐ To avoid mixed or contradictory messages (and to model future coparenting), be together, if possible, when telling girls about marital decisions and divorce plans.
- ☐ Give her truthful information that is appropriate for her age and maturity—that is, enough to answer her questions, but not so much as to overwhelm her. If in doubt, ask her what she would like to know.
- ☐ To avoid your daughter blaming herself and feeling guilty, assure her that neither she nor her problems caused the breakup—adult matters did.
- ☐ Give advance warning if she needs to move out of her home or change schools.
- ☐ Never bad-mouth her other parent.
- ☐ Never ask or expect your daughter to act as a go-between or messenger between the two of you.

- ☐ Never ask or expect her to keep secrets from her other parent(s).
- ☐ Never use financial support as a weapon to punish, spite, coerce, or shame your ex.
- ☐ Make sure your daughter can get emotional support from another adult, such as a school counselor or mental health clinician.
- ☐ If you share legal custody, make the most collaborative decisions humanly possible.
- ☐ Assure your daughter that she will have separate relationships with each of her parents–and make sure this happens.
- ☐ If the divorce process is contentious or if parental antagonism develops (or continues), seeing a professional can help defuse tensions, create new communication methods, and foster healthier coparenting with your ex.

When parents are able to put kids' needs first, everyone benefits. Stacy, mother of four, describes the arrangement she and her husband created: "When we got divorced, we really wanted to make sure we were a bike ride away from each other so the kids would always have a parent nearby. It's really hard to make a plan when parents are miles away. So we live on the same street. Either their father or I am home to meet the kids after school. We work together. I'm getting lots of support from my ex. It's not all on me."

It is hard enough for married parents to agree on rules and expectations for teens and tweens. After a divorce, disagreements about chores, bedtimes, and screen time can become polarizing. Although adjusting to two homes is possible and potentially advantageous in some ways, it helps girls immensely when their parents respect, if not honor, the other household's culture.

Conversely, parents who exploit these differences to gain favor with daughters—or, worse, try to drive wedges between teens and their other parents—may be momentarily gratified but end up ruing having modeled vindictiveness. Teens who feel emotionally manipulated usually become angry, resentful, and far less trusting of adults. Unfortunately, sometimes girls adopt similarly devious means to get what they want, much to their parents' chagrin.

When Parents Start Dating

After being divorced or widowed, 52 percent of women remarry. If you have a new partner, be cautious about introducing your daughter. First reflect on your goal. Has the relationship reached a stage when it makes sense to integrate the person into the family? Will your daughter benefit from having this new person in her life? Is she receptive to the idea? Or could you be basing your decision on a desire to spend more time as a couple?

Many women who face this predicament say, "There's really no good time to introduce new partners." It's true that daughters present different challenges at different ages. But a good rule of thumb is to wait until there's an expectation the relationships will last. Although there's no guarantee, you want to spare girls from more sad or disappointing breakups. A string of losses can sour teens on meeting parents' future partners—and possibly relationships in general.

Like many mothers I speak to, Amanda feels distraught and helpless about how her former husband's dating practices affect her tween: "My ex brings home a succession of girlfriends while he has my daughter. It's like a revolving door over there. At this point, she doesn't get attached because she knows they're probably not going to be around very long."

Even when conditions are right, introducing teens to new romantic interests should be handled delicately. For one, it is hard for a teenage girl, who is learning to manage her own sensuality and burgeoning sexual desires, to contemplate a parent dating, especially someone who is not her other parent. To most, the mere thought of parents having sex—much less seeing evidence of this—is overwhelmingly repulsive. Put yourself in her shoes; did you want to know about your parents' sex lives?

At a time when teens are intensely focused on their own attractiveness and sex appeal, watching parents date can arouse or intensify competitiveness. Your daughter may try to one-up women who draw her father's attention. She may imitate how you look and act when you go out. Some women and teens bond over dating, but this is a slippery slope. Empathizing with your daughter's dating quandaries supports her and may draw you closer, but this can easily slide into sharing inappropriate intimacies. To respect mother-teen boundaries, confide in friends about these topics instead, at least until your daughter is older (if ever).

Before bringing partners into your daughter's life, talk with her honestly. Be direct about your hopes as well as concerns. In return, ask how she feels. Often, teens and tweens worry about being disloyal to the other parent. What if she really likes the person who is making you happier? Reassure her that she never has to choose between her other parent and your new partner, or her other parent's new partner and you. Teach her that love is limitless; it can be given and received in abundance, without ever being depleted.

TRY: I'd like you to meet the person I've been dating so you can get to know each other.

NOT: I love this person so much and I know you will, too!

OR

TRY: Dad seems to really like his new girlfriend. She seems nice, so keep an open mind.

NOT: Why do you want to hang out with some horrible woman who wrecked our family?

OR

TRY: Will you be comfortable if I invite this person I've been seeing to dinner sometime?

NOT: I expect you to be extra nice to this person's kids and treat them like new siblings.

Being a Stepmother

You also might become a stepmother to a spouse's previous children. Thanks to classic fairy tales and pointed media portrayals, this title might conjure up images of pure evil and malice. Like many women, from the outset you may feel compelled to overcome stepmothers' bad rap. But the real challenge is navigating an extraordinarily complex role with stepdaughters, particularly during the teen years. Some of those who've experienced this admit, "If I had to do it again, knowing what it's been like, I don't know that I would." Stepmothering a teen can be exponentially trickier than mothering a daughter you birthed or adopted.

High Stakes—with Little Room for Mistakes

Women trying to connect with teenage stepdaughters encounter many hazards and an exceedingly narrow margin for error. Like boats cautiously tacking through shallow, shoal-infested waters, an absence of authoritative clout stills stepmothers' sails. Responsibility without power breeds a sense of futility—a common theme among stepmothers.

Talia, stepmother to nineteen-year-old Georgina, explains, "As a stepmom, you have to get it right. You feel like you have to be perfect because the consequences are so f-ing miserable. There's so much pressure. You have a loose cannon always aimed at you." Shelley, whose fourteen-year-old stepdaughter is with her every other weekend, says, "If a kid says to her father, 'I hate my mom,' the father says, 'Okay, go wash your hands for dinner.' But if a kid says, 'I hate my stepmom,' you'd better call in the first responders—the reaction's totally different."

The self-doubt of stepmothers is a highly magnified version of what mothers often experience during the teen years. Shelley adds, "I hesitate before sticking my neck way out. Should I show her how to put mascara on? What if she bursts into tears? My husband would be like, 'What happened?' I'm always wondering if something is going to backfire."

What's Your Role?

Knowing that it's impossible to replace a mother, what role will you play with your stepdaughter? Will you see yourself as a close friend, mentor, older sister, confidante, or cool aunt? Someone who offers her the unvarnished truth, the total objectivity that can be provided only by an adult who is not her parent? If you do step in when your stepdaughter needs a sounding board, should you keep her problems confidential, or must you tell her parents?

While the role of stepmother places you in a good position to observe the dynamics of your partner's former family, what do you do with your insights? If you share them, will they be welcomed, tolerated, or resented? Are you better off keeping your observations to yourself? Shelley discovered "my husband's two kids were really good at manipulating him and their mother. Also, his ex-wife was a pro at getting him to do her bidding. I could see all this, but I always felt uncomfortably smack in the middle, with nowhere to go with the information."

Will You Love Each Other?

Just because you love your partner doesn't mean you will automatically love the kids. Despite your intentions to develop a close, gratifying relationship with your stepdaughter, whether this happens is not entirely under your control. It depends on the circumstances, her personality and age when you came into her life, the dynamics of her family, and a whole host of other factors.

Some women describe sensing tense undercurrents or stepdaughters treating them with disdain, indifference, rudeness, or hostility, which make it hard to like, let alone love, them. Shelley describes, "My stepdaughter is indirect with her hostility. She stops talking when I enter a room and avoids being in my presence. When I'm there, she makes little or no eye contact with me, directs her comments to her father, and often mentions memories from before I was in her father's life. It's hard to address these things because I'm probably the only one who's aware of them and it sounds so petty."

Often, stepdaughters' treatment feels unfair. Carol tells me, "When my husband told me his ex-wife said their daughter doesn't feel welcome in our house, I was stunned. We moved in together when she was fourteen, and the first thing I did was take her shopping and let her decorate her new room, including picking out furniture and bedding."

Realize that the reasons your stepdaughter gives you grief may have nothing to do with the reality of who you are. The problem may not be you so much as what you represent:

- The handiest and safest repository for all her dissatisfactions and irritations
- Someone to blame for breaking up her family, which helps her to avoid recognizing painful truths about her biological parents
- The person who is trying to replace her mother—at least in her other parent's heart

- A way to unite with her mother over a common "enemy"
- A means of pleasing or proving her loyalty to her mother by bad-mouthing you and complaining about the time she spends with you
- A reminder of the constant empathy, kindness, and emotional availability she wants, but may not be getting, from her mother
- The best alternative to taking out her feelings on her father, who she still needs
- A way to idealize her relationship with her mother to avoid facing how much her mother's behavior disappoints, confuses, or infuriates her

As a result you may feel as if you are singled out and can't win. Talia, whose stepdaughter is now in college, describes poignant sorrow as a result of a difficult relationship: "There was one time when she gave me a genuine hug and it immediately broke my heart because it was a glimmer of what could have been, but probably would never be. It's been hard. I kept telling myself, 'If I keep trying, it'll get better.' But it never did."

Isolation and Lack of Support

The peculiar position of stepmothers, many tell me, means that "you can't count on the system to support you through making mistakes and correcting them." Being a stepmother can be a lonely business.

Talia explains, "It's hard to know who to confide in. Some women friends don't have this experience, so they can't really understand or help. Others may be seeing the situation from the other perspective." Case in point: although Talia's sister is her best friend, Talia hesitates to share details about her problems as a stepmother.

She explains, "My sister is divorced and her husband remarried. She's the biological mom. When her kids express love for their stepmom, she recoils and feels insecure, and then she's ashamed. I need her support, but I'm aware she relates to what I say and it gets all tangled up emotionally. We each represent the other side—the biological mother and the stepmother. When she tries to talk to me about her situation with her daughter's stepmother, she asks, 'Is this triggering you?' And when I try to discuss my situation, I feel like I can't tell her about how my husband's ex-wife uses the kids to get her own needs met."

Never Say Never

Although your stepdaughter's initial behavior toward you may disappoint or sting, it is important to stay open to the possibility of creating a more gratifying relationship with her. An authentic connection with a stepdaughter can't be rushed. It has to evolve organically, at its own pace, when she is receptive. Over time, she may well recognize and be grateful for your steadiness, empathy, acceptance, and absence of a personal agenda. Time is on your side.

Kim, seventeen, tells me that in the four years since I last saw her, she has grown "really close" to her stepmother, Delaney. This was a long time in coming. When Delaney joined the family, the court had just forbidden Kim's drug-addicted, neglectful biological mother from having any contact with her. Delaney bore the brunt of Kim's confusion and distress.

It took years, but once Kim was able to work through her feelings about her biological mother's limitations in therapy, she could appreciate Delaney's steadfast concern and opened her heart to her. "Now," Kim says, "I don't know what I would do without Delaney."

* * *

Soon enough—perhaps too soon—you'll be thinking about college. The thought may be enough to make you want to turn back the clock. These days, the search and application process has been getting a lot of bad press. Chances are, you've had your own trepidations and may be seeing your daughter start to get worked up about standardized tests, where she wants to go to school, and where her older friends are and aren't getting accepted.

Fear not. Although much about the college process is beyond your family's control, there is much you can do to enjoy this part of your mother-daughter journey. Yes, you read that right. The next chapter will tell you more.

CHAPTER THIRTEEN

Savoring the College Process

> There's so much societal pressure for me to go to college because all my friends are going. But I know myself. If I went to a four-year uni off the bat, I'd be more focused on social things rather than on what's important. Moving away from home, with no rules, I think I'd be too wrapped up in that. At an older age, I wouldn't be acting childish.
>
> —MARIAH, 17

If this chapter's title strikes you as paradoxical, you're probably not alone. Many women I speak with fear—and sometimes dread—the college process: girls taking stressful standardized tests, everyone agreeing on a list of schools, having to nudge teens to complete applications by deadlines, overseeing girls writing personal statements, visiting campuses, and awaiting admissions decisions. But in my experience, when teens have become self-aware, authentic, self-regulated, and resilient, this rite of passage becomes smoother—and, yes, even pleasurable.

This is when the hard work of the past few years pays off. Not because of a specific decal on the car, but rather because of the joy of watching college-bound girls plan, set realistic goals, make smart decisions, and, most of all, be wholly themselves. Campus visits offer a rare opportunity to spend one-on-one time with busy teens. The ultimate reward, of course, is seeing daughters choose colleges wisely and thrive as undergraduates.

If you're thinking about this as a stressful ordeal, take a moment now to confront your worst fear. Deep down, what are you worried about? That your daughter will do poorly on her admission tests? That she won't get into her top-choice schools—or any "great" college, however you define that? That she'll be utterly devastated by rejections? If any of these worries resonate with you, thinking about the following points may ease your mind.

One, no college or university, no matter how prestigious, is right for everyone. I have seen a multitude of girls transfer after their first year from the Ivy League schools that admitted them early decision (ED). Your daughter will flourish when an educational institution matches her interests, values, personality, and priorities.

Two, the best fit for her may be her safety school. Too many teens to count have visited me after their first year of college to tell me how grateful they were to have been rejected everywhere but their safety schools, which "turned out to be perfect."

Three, rejections will teach your daughter the essential life skill of how to cope with letdowns and come to terms with events beyond her control. Because she still lives at home, you're best positioned to support her.

Four, and most important, only when she looks back on this disappointment may she realize that her future success was never going to be determined by where she went to college. What mattered was what she did while on campus. Your young adult will likely get out of her undergraduate years what she puts into them.

As this chapter demonstrates, intentional parenting principles are especially applicable and helpful during the college process. Managing your own apprehensions, mothering the daughter you have, and fruitful conversations foster your teen's authenticity and autonomy, guide her to get the most out of campus visits, encourage her to make wise college decisions, and model managing disappointments. Setting her up for success may also entail assessing her readiness for college and exploring alternatives should she need more time.

Promoting Authenticity

From a psychological perspective, the college process can promote maturation. Girls who take the lead in researching schools, thinking about courses of study, pinpointing priorities, and figuring out where they can thrive solidify their personal identities. Authenticity and insight facilitate better decisions, helping girls to land at schools where they succeed.

No question about it, achieving an ideal level of involvement in a daughter's college process requires finesse. Many parents have strong opinions about where teens should apply, the benefits and risks of ED or early action, activities that look good on applications, and the most compelling topics for personal essays. Unfortunately, college counselors and independent educational consultants unanimously regard all this advice as heartfelt, but most likely outdated and inaccurate.

The world of higher education is too different now for parents to skillfully advise their own teens. Let the professionals who are up on colleges' current leadership, mission statements, majors, policies, and admissions strategies guide your teen. Years of experience in this area—and, often, inside knowledge—enable professionals to best judge your daughter's prospects at particular schools. If you respect these individuals, heed their recommendations. If not, get a second opinion.

Soul-searching is crucial at every step. Could this process be eliciting an unexamined, personal need for gratification or an unhealthy investment in a certain outcome? Does your teen really need another community service project or her own website to sell baked goods? If her application to a conservatory or art institute requires her to produce the strongest audition video or portfolio she can deliver, why are you insisting that she have six other extracurricular activities on her résumé?

If your daughter and her college consultant or guidance counselor have spent weeks or months crafting her essay, resist the urge to veto the finished product. You may prefer she write about a topic you've heard impresses college admissions officers. But a great essay comes from a place of self-awareness and authenticity. She needs freedom to express what truly resonates with her and portrays who she is at her core. Whether her final draft is serious or goofy or earnest or whimsical or sardonic or irreverent or self-deprecating, it must reflect *her*.

Advise your daughter not to say what she thinks people want to hear.

Instead, encourage her to write from her heart. As you read over her essay—if she wants you to do so—ask yourself if it captures her essence. If she wishes, help her edit for grammatical and spelling mistakes, but studiously avoid rewriting it. The words must be hers alone.

Hardest of all may be refraining from pulling out all the stops to get your daughter admitted to college. It is one thing to use your resources to help her get information, such as asking a friend who is an alumna to speak with her about the school. It is another thing altogether to use connections, donations, or ethically dubious backchannels to get her into a prestigious and highly selective college.

If your daughter can't get in on her own, trust me, you don't want her there. She'll know she wasn't accepted on her own merits. Along with feeling like a smaller fish in a larger pond, she may well suffer a blow to her self-confidence. Better that she goes to a college that chooses her because they see her as an asset to the undergraduate community. This kind of acceptance letter is a better testament to your daughter's hard work and a validation of her self-worth.

Planning Campus Visits

Websites often provide initial information about colleges (e.g., size, diversity of student population, offered majors, cost, recreational facilities). If you are also able to arrange in-person exploratory, information-seeking visits for your teen, these can be beneficial. Just as your daughter has to try on clothes she buys online to see how they fit, in-person visits allow her to get a feel for a campus's aesthetics and student life.

Campus visits can be a big deal for teens. This may be the first glimpse of life after high school. If the school is high on your daughter's list, she may be eager to assure herself that it is truly right for her—and anxious about getting in. If she dislikes the campus, she may worry about going back to the drawing board. For women, college visits often are a stark reminder of daughters leaving home—and therefore a harbinger of loss. For all these reasons, these can be emotionally loaded experiences for mothers and girls, eliciting a gamut of feelings from self-consciousness to excitement to grief to apprehension.

Prepare your teen to visit schools by suggesting that she come up with a preliminary list of criteria for her ideal college. Arriving for tours or information sessions with questions focuses her attention on what is important while she is on campus. This helps you, too.

With girls on edge, prepare yourself for the possibility of knee-jerk reactions. Driving up to campus, some refuse to get out of the car. Why? Believe it or not, the reasons I've heard include: "The buildings are too tall!" "The kids look weird!" and "I hate this place!" There are also lots of complaints that the tour guide "wasn't funny," "wore ridiculous clothes," "was so not cool," "kept repeating himself," and "talked about boring stuff." Even visiting on a rainy day turns off many a would-be applicant from her future alma mater.

Attempts to dissuade girls of superficial—and highly emotional—snap judgments are usually useless, much to the exasperation of travel-weary parents who favor more thorough and levelheaded decision-making. But in those moments, it is best to consider all this grist for the mill, to be discussed later, after your teen has gathered additional information, lets the dust settle, and is possibly more receptive to reason.

At the end of the visit, you and your daughter may leave campus with far different takeaways. It is okay and even healthy for you to have unique perspectives. Yet I would advise keeping your opinions to yourself until she has a chance to reflect on her impressions. That way, you allow her to fully develop her views without interference. While memories are fresh, each of you can jot down your respective thoughts for later discussion.

To get the most out of campus visits, make this time with your daughter truly special. Treat this as a minivacation with her. Take advantage of out-of-town travel by leaving as much responsibility as you can at home. Explore college communities with fun side trips, adventures, and new cuisines. Perhaps while visiting campuses declare a moratorium on talking about stressful subjects such as admissions tests and applications so you can create happy memories for years to come.

Making College Decisions

The college process facilitates another critical developmental task of later adolescence: separation and individuation from parents. At a time when autonomy is at a premium, teens should take responsibility for as much decision-making as possible. Developing this skill will enable your daughter to figure out later whether and where to go to graduate school, how to choose a gynecologist, whether to buy a condo or home, and where to purchase her first car.

Whereas some teens approach college decisions intellectually, making lists of pros and cons, others follow their gut. The instinctual method by which girls decide "This is it!" or "No way would I ever set foot here" is much harder to explain to parents as well as to themselves.

But my sense is that teens visiting campuses get a visceral feeling for academic challenges and stimulation, the student body, availability of support, and quality of campus life, all of which determine whether they can imagine themselves living in first-year dorms.

If your daughter approaches decisions methodically, she may wish to speak to students or recent graduates who can answer her questions. And yet, one may rave about student life; another may be dissatisfied. Some may view classmates as competitive, others as collaborative. Without a consensus, how does she reconcile divergent opinions?

Your teen learns to process information through the filter of the person it comes from. If a known partier tells her campus social activities are boring, it may be because the college strictly regulates Greek life and has a zero-tolerance policy for illegal substances. If she hears that professors in her intended major are uninspiring, she may chalk it up to a particular student's academic struggles, need for academic support, or one bad experience with an instructor.

This is why, along with tapping into external sources of information, your daughter must cultivate trust in her own observations and reactions. When she walks on campus thinking, "I belong here," or conversely, "Not a chance!," she is tuning in to what her mind, body, and heart are telling her. Would she fit in? Can she picture the students she sees congregating on quads or eating in dining halls as part of her new tribe?

The best decision-making process relies on both imagined and actual experiences. Psychologists know that people who base choices on what they might want or need in the future are often wrong. Also, the information your teen gathers on campus visits is greatly affected by random events—for example, an unseasonably cold, blustery day or bumping into a student from her high school that she doesn't particularly like.

Overnight stays at schools after she is offered admission provide more authentic experiences. Staying with current students and participating in social events gives your daughter an invaluable feel for campus culture.

Of course, as her parent you'll set parameters on nonnegotiables such as financial considerations—including distance from home—and available support services if she has a learning difference or developmental disability. For example, her well-being in college may depend on learning and/or emotional support. Beyond these criteria, your daughter may make vastly different choices. She may gravitate to schools you find totally unacceptable. Her reasoning may mystify and fail to convince you. It may seem, in fact, that she is going out of her way to resist your influence and use the college process to establish herself as her own person.

Like many parents, you may wonder if you should respect your daughter's decision or override it and insist that she attend a college you think is more suitable. Rather than getting into a battle of wills, try being a sounding board. Ask for your daughter's thoughts rather than telling her what she *should* think. Since no school is perfect, what is most important to her? Is she getting accurate information? What can make her most confident about her choice?

Unless you have specific, serious reservations, I have come to believe it is probably best to honor your teen's choice. Here's why. If she goes to a school that she feels lukewarm about, she may always think the grass is greener on the quad of her first-choice college. Your daughter will blame you for any problems or disappointments she suffers.

If it is her own decision, she is more likely to make the best of her experience. Worst-case scenario, she ends up realizing her decision was a mistake, learns more about herself, and, if necessary, transfers to a school that is a better fit for her. More likely, as for many students, she adjusts and grows happier with her current college as time goes on.

Dealing with Rejections

These days, educators think of applying to college as much like buying a lottery ticket. If your daughter isn't rejected by at least one college, maybe she selected wisely, has impeccable credentials, got lucky, or didn't aim high enough. Although rejections are often the stuff of maternal nightmares, in my experience hearing no prepares teens for future disappointments. For sure they'll be rebuffed by romantic partners, graduate school programs, and job recruiters.

Anticipate this possibility at the beginning of the college process. Girls need to be told explicitly that there are so many qualified applicants these days that even the most prestigious colleges can fill incoming classes many times over. Your teen has done everything possible to create her best application. Whether she gets accepted to particular colleges is out of her hands now. At this point, it's a crapshoot, a numbers game beyond her control.

The only thing setting her apart from accepted students may be demographics such as where she grew up or went to high school, her gender, intended major, or random factors such as the mood of the admissions committee member who read her application. In other words, your daughter may never know why she was rejected. But she still needs to come to terms with it and move on.

Give her room to feel—and to express—her thoughts and emotions. Your teen learns that although rejection is painful, it is not life shattering. If ever she needed you to tolerate her venting, it is probably now. Your empathy and acceptance of however she reacts validate her genuine internal experience.

The clear boundaries you've created between your daughter and yourself allow you not to take on her despair. This helps both of you. Without being weighed down by her sadness, you can think clearly and dispassionately enough to be helpful. Conversely, your equanimity about any rejections spares your teen from feeling doubly bad for letting you down along with herself.

Differentiating yourself from your teen allows you to be disappointed *for* her instead of *in* her. When you comment, "Their loss," "I guess it wasn't a good fit after all," or "Another college will be lucky to get you," you powerfully reinforce your unshakable belief in her. The importance of this perspective can't be overstated. You didn't need your daughter to attend a certain college. Moreover, you appreciate what your daughter may not just yet: this is but a minor setback on her journey to the gratifying future that awaits her.

Determining If She's Ready

These days, many students graduate from high school with good enough grades but underdeveloped study and self-help skills. Teens succeed because scaffolding from parents, tutors, and peers props them up. Once they arrive on campus, there is no one to track their assignments, check their grades, edit their papers, remind them to do homework, and quiz them prior to exams.

If your goal has been setting up your daughter for success, your priority hasn't been getting her into college; it has been making sure she can thrive once she gets there. A critical step of the college process, therefore, is assessing her readiness to leave home and be on her own. No matter where she matriculates, only when she has the necessary know-how will she feel competent and confident enough to move forward with her life. Consider how well she is equipped in the following areas.

Managing Her Life

Are you providing so much support that you're afraid your daughter would fall apart without you? Do you worry about her eating, sleeping, and study habits? Does she need constant reminders to fulfill her obligations? Do you have to drag her out of bed in the morning after she repeatedly hits the snooze button? Is lateness a pattern? Are you often running forgotten homework, musical instruments, or sports equipment up to school because she can't keep track of her belongings or remember to bring what she needs?

Taking Care of Herself

Does your daughter maintain a healthy balance of work, play, socializing, and rest? Do you worry that her coping strategies are unhealthy? Does she stay up too late, nap in the afternoon, and sleep in too late on weekends? Are her emotions and energy on an even keel, or do they fluctuate unpredictably? Does she binge on snacks and junk food, avoid eating, or use food to self-soothe? Is she often sick? If she has mental or physical health conditions, does she manage them responsibly, including following her doctors' orders and faithfully taking her medications?

Using Self-Discipline

Does your daughter procrastinate, get distracted by social media, or have trouble self-limiting her screen use? Does she often regret how she acts in social situations? Have there been incidents of defiance, substance abuse, not following rules, school disciplinary infractions, or legal troubles? What does your gut tell you about whether these behaviors are typical adolescent judgment errors or harbingers of bigger problems to come when she's on her own?

Navigating Relationships

How well does your daughter cope with new people and situations? Does she have satisfying friendships, or struggle socially? Is she prone to withdrawing or isolating herself when uncomfortable? Can she successfully resolve conflicts with peers? Is she assertive enough to ask for what she needs and set limits in intimate relationships? Can your teen focus on her own needs and responsibilities when friends go through difficulties? Does she regularly need your help to navigate conflicts with peers and/or adults?

Advocating for Herself

How confident are you that your daughter can assertively express her needs in common college scenarios—for example, if her roommate takes her clothing without permission, uses illicit substances in their dorm room, or awakens her while coming in at 3 A.M. during exam week? How about if her teaching assistant makes inappropriate comments or her professor gives her harsh feedback? Is she receptive to constructive criticism? Willing to follow advice? Does your teen recognize when she needs help? Can she figure out whom to approach for assistance?

Keeping Up Academically

Do you have nagging worries about why your daughter is not that interested in school or motivated to do well academically? Has she always needed help to understand her assignments, start her homework, write papers, and study for tests? Has she relied on tutors in her core high school subjects? Have you observed difficulties with organization, concentration, distractibility, reading comprehension, math, or higher-level reasoning and problem-solving? Does your teen dislike school or see herself as a poor student?

Maintaining Emotional Well-Being

A laser focus on getting into college can cause some parents to overlook the bigger picture of ongoing mental health issues. Does your daughter self-harm? Has she had suicidal thoughts? Has she been hospitalized, or is she in intense outpatient treatment? If so, does her mental health team think she has the inner resources and resiliency to cope with the additional stresses and demands of first-year college life? Would professionals be available in the college community to take over her care? Or is she too emotionally fragile to thrive away from home?

If You're Still Not Sure

In some cases, your daughter may make your decision easier. As college nears, her behavior may suddenly improve or worsen. She may unconsciously sabotage plans to leave home by not turning in work or not passing enough classes to fulfill high school graduation requirements. Or the stress of anticipating independence may worsen her anxiety, depression, or eating disorder to the point that she needs more intense treatment.

Barring these clear game changers, whether to have your daughter delay college is a tough call. As a loving mother who wants only the best for her, you may not think you have the expertise or objectivity to assess how prepared she is. If that's true, seek out recommendations from psychologists, psychiatrists, learning specialists, educational consultants, or executive functioning coaches who can perform thorough assessments that provide the answers you need.

Psychoeducational testing clarifies what makes students tick, including girls' strengths, challenges, and educational needs. Are teens prepared for the academic rigors of college? Do they have sufficient emotional skills, coping resources, and resiliency to flourish on their own? If not, what accommodations or support services will they need to succeed? As you weigh this information, make your daughter's well-being the utmost priority. When she goes to college is not nearly as important as the shape she's in when she's there.

If you still have doubts about how ready she is to leave home, it is better to err on the side of caution. Having to leave college is emotionally as well as financially costly. Failed attempts at independence indelibly shake girls' beliefs in themselves, making starting again that much more difficult. It is always better to build on initial successes. When in doubt, consider suggesting that your daughter defer matriculation by a semester or two.

Gap Years

Taking time off between high school and college offers teens extra time to learn about themselves, take breaks from academics, and have different, growth-inducing experiences. Along with traveling, these are in fact the top three goals of students who opt to defer college. For late bloomers, gap years offer more time for maturation. For parents who regret not holding back immature five-year-olds from kindergarten, this may be another chance for girls to catch up to peers academically, socially, or emotionally. For these same reasons, colleges are asking some accepted students to wait until January or the following fall before matriculating.

Gap years are also a great equalizer for uneven experiences. Students who focused early and intensely on academics, sports, or music may have missed out on formative social experiences. Teens who struggled with learning may not have the wherewithal to mature in other ways. And girls whose inner resources were focused on emotional challenges may need extra time to bolster academic skills.

Many teens push back against taking time off from college. Unless your daughter has friends or relatives in the UK or Australia, where gap years are standard, or in Israel, where a mandatory three-year army stint begins at age eighteen, she might balk at deferring college.

You may hear, "I want to go when my friends go," "Don't worry; when I can choose classes I like, I'll do the work," or "I'll be more motivated when I get to college."

Her reluctance to delay college is understandable. This has been the much-anticipated end point of your daughter's high school experience. For months, the talk has been all about who is going to which college. Students have been showing up at their lockers proudly wearing T-shirts, sweats, and hats emblazoned with the names and logos of the schools they're planning to attend.

Delaying college may feel like an embarrassing failure. Your daughter may not know what to tell friends and relatives. Or, in a great rush to "start the rest of my life," she may not want to begin her career a year later. You also may fear your teen getting off track. Once she takes time off from school, what if she never wants to go back? If she is much older than other first-year students, both of you may worry that she won't fit in and make friends.

You'll be happy to know that research and clinical experience dispel these concerns. Gap years are often transformative. Burnt-out teens who went through the motions in school, detached from the joys of learning, often emerge from time off seeing the world through different eyes. Gratifying activities usually shore up self-confidence, refresh intellectual curiosity, refocus goals, and reboot determination to excel.

Besides, tasting campus life may inspire girls to do well, but probably won't do much to build the strong skills they need to excel. Similarly, despite good intentions, less mature teens can't possibly grow up overnight to meet the higher-level demands of college. Rather than sending your senior off hoping for the best, make sure that once she arrives on campus she'll be able to take care of herself and make the most of her opportunities.

When you present the chance to take a gap year as the gift it truly is, it may help to pique her interest in the appealing activities she could do during this time. That way, she focuses not on what she would be missing, but rather on looking forward to a uniquely gratifying experience. Fortunately, as gap years gain traction, families can choose from a growing number of opportunities and programs.

For students who dislike school, real-world activities can spark both motivation and success. Hands-on or experiential learning promotes passions that can be elusive in the classroom, such as environmental or political activism. Girls who discover new life goals may be more determined to get necessary degrees. After becoming certified as a wilderness first responder during a gap semester, Lydia redoubled her commitment to becoming a physician—despite always struggling in school due to dyslexia. Years later, she emailed to say she was matched with her first-choice residency program in emergency medicine.

Students also can work, travel, study, do community service, or learn extraordinary skills. This is a rare chance for girls to focus on themselves and grow. In all the years of seeing young people in my practice, not one has ever regretted taking a gap year before college. The only students who were sorry were those who decided against taking time off but wished they had.

This is one of those times when you may have to do what you firmly believe is best for your teen. If she is embarrassed to tell her peers, coach her in how to explain her decision: "I'd like to travel before I go to college" or "I decided to defer college to make time for some things I've always wanted to do." When you tell friends or relatives, follow the same advice you give your daughter. A matter-of-fact statement is all that is needed. Remind her that getting through college is not a race. What matters most is her well-being.

Community College

For various reasons, community colleges are becoming more popular. Some high school graduates opt for community college to test their skills and develop confidence in themselves as students. Teens may start out slowly, taking a class or two. Either on their own or with the support of tutors or learning coaches, girls practice study skills, keeping up with work, and not getting overwhelmed. Taking classes while living at home postpones the need to manage independent living at the same time, enabling a sharper focus on the learning process.

Tamara, seventeen, a rising senior who is refreshingly self-aware, figured this out on her own: "I'm not ready to live on my own, as much as I say I am. I'm going the community college route and living at home for the first two years while I continue to learn about myself and feel stronger. I need more time to figure myself out. I'm not in the right headspace to be on my own at eighteen. It's not me yet. You're going to college to grow as an individual, not to please others."

With that mindset and determination, my bet is that after a couple more years' practice using self-discipline, setting priorities, and making good choices, Tamara will be in a far stronger position. When she transfers to a four-year college, more mature insight and improved decisions will enable her to thrive as a residential student. Whatever challenges Tamara faces as she pursues her career goals will be no match for the emotional regulation skills and resiliency she develops in community college.

Conclusion

A Bright Future

When a daughter first leaves home, reactions may swirl within you like a kaleidoscope: pride, worry, sadness, relief, exhilaration, grief, and wonder, to name just a few possibilities. Like many women, you may feel bereft one day, liberated the next. Knowing that motherhood has irrevocably changed for you may feel like a wrenching loss—regardless of whether you have other children living at home.

You can't predict what comes next in your mother-daughter relationship. Will your emerging adult choose to share her post-high-school life with you? Will you feel as close to her—or perhaps even closer? Or do you worry that once she is out of the house you will no longer be at the top of her "Favorites" contact list?

Take heart that your mother-daughter relationship will always be sacred. Regardless of where your daughter lives or the adult life she creates, your mutual love and respect can remain strong. If anything, the intention and thoughtfulness you bring to parenting during her teen years will likely, over time, strengthen the bond you share. As she goes out into the world and learns more about her roommates and colleagues' family lives, she will increasingly recognize how fortunate she is that you are her mother.

Not only have you appreciated the daughter you have, but also you've made it a point to tailor your parenting according to what she has needed. You've been thoughtful. You've been deliberate. You've prioritized her best interest. Being human, you've also said and done things you've regretted. But by taking responsibility for your missteps, you've freed her from excessive guilt, shame, and self-blame. The incomparable gift you've given her—a sense of herself as a young woman who deserves to be heard, understood, and treated well in relationships—will pave the way for well-being and contentment in her future.

That's not to say you won't get panicked calls at 2 A.M. if she gets locked out of her dorm or her first college love interest ends it. You may be the first to know when her wallet is stolen or her roommate is threatening self-harm or she can't get into the website to sign up for classes. Maybe you'll hear when she completely forgets about a scheduled meeting with her adviser or is disciplined for breaking a campus rule. After all, you are still her mother.

But before you let yourself get worked up hearing about these sorts of life challenges, you'll remember that you've raised your daughter to be a capable problem-solver. She may be upset when she tells you what's going on, but after venting to you she'll take a deep breath and do what needs to be done. She expects you not to magically fix everything, but to support her in brainstorming solutions and figuring out best decisions.

As always, you'll do only as much as she needs, which tells her how assured you are in her abilities. At the same time, your daughter knows you will be there for her if necessary. This crucial dual message allows her to gain confidence along with new skills. More and more, you may see her taking surer steps into less familiar territory, willing to venture beyond what's been comfortable. Your daughter's accomplishments over time tell you that she has developed the traits and skills you've been trying to nurture.

You can remind her of her remarkable resiliency. Her adolescence was probably not problem-free. Like any girl this age, she faced and surmounted normal struggles. While growing up, she experienced a once-in-a-century pandemic that disrupted her formative years and took a disproportionate toll on her age group. She not only survived but also may have stepped up—providing emotional support, doing errands or working when family members got sick or lost jobs, and helping younger siblings with remote schooling. Looking back on these invaluable contributions should fill her—and you—with pride.

It might also give you pleasure to think about the bright future that lies ahead for your daughter. This is a wonderful time to be a girl. Now, more than ever, daughters can grow up with a broader sense of what is acceptable—and possible. Rather than seeing themselves in rigid categories, girls can have a range of interests and identities.

Women and teens are making history by breaking barriers. In politics, Kamala Harris is the first woman and first woman of color to be elected vice president. As of January 2021, twelve women are slated to serve in Cabinet positions—the highest number ever. Eight of the twelve are women of color. In addition, just over one-quarter of all members of the 117th US Congress are women, which represents a 50 percent increase from a decade ago. If you count the 100 members of the Senate as well as the 435 voting and 6 nonvoting members of the House of Representatives, 144 of 541—26.6 percent—are women.

National sports, too, are seeing breakthroughs by women. At the time of the 2021 Super Bowl, Sarah Thomas became the first female NFL down judge. Two NFL coaches were women—who earned Super Bowl rings.

Your daughter has role models closer to her age who demonstrate the possibilities that await her. Malala Yousafzai and Greta Thunberg are lighting the way for young women who are committed to education and climate action. While still an undergraduate at age nineteen, Amanda Gorman became this country's first National Youth Poet Laureate. In 2021, she not only performed a poem at the Presidential Inauguration, but also at the Super Bowl, her truth and poise embodying the promise of this generation of girls.

Girls less often feel the need to stifle their voices. They are speaking up and speaking out. People are paying attention.

As she makes her way in the world, may your daughter's inner beauty, self-reliance, buoyancy, and graciousness delight you. May you admire the principles, power, and fortitude that drive her accomplishments. May all her relationships be infused with love and respect. Most of all, may the time you spend together be a never-ending source of joy.

Enjoy every moment.

Let's continue this discussion. I'd love to hear from you and your daughters. Please contact me at:

AnythingButMyPhoneMom.com
RoniCohenSandler.com
Twitter: @DrRoniCS
Facebook: Dr. Roni Cohen-Sandler
Instagram: @DrRoniCS

Acknowledgments

Many people helped to make this book happen. First, I've had the great fortune to work with Nick Mullendore, my literary agent, for over twenty years. Every author should have such a knowledgeable, responsive, and supportive agent who also can be counted upon to tell it like it is. Second, I'm indebted to Gretchen Schmid, my editor at Penguin Life, who shared my vision for *Anything But My Phone, Mom!*—and, through her astute guidance, made it ever so much better.

While the pandemic quarantine gave me plenty of solitary time to finish writing, I would have felt unbearably isolated without the dear friends and colleagues who reached out. Thanks to all of you for the supportive texts, calls, and Zooms that meant so much to me. That we were able to stay so closely connected throughout those long months, despite what was going on around us, sustained me more than you can imagine.

Without question, my family deserves my deepest gratitude. Throughout many decades of marriage, my husband, Jeff, has been the biggest champion of my work. In spreading the word about this project, he discovered innumerable mothers and teen daughters who were eager to be interviewed and tell their stories—then he graciously took over household responsibilities while I was finishing this book. My son, Jason, who continually refines my understanding of technology, expands my professional network, and miraculously fixes my tech glitches, painstakingly proofread my first draft of this manuscript. If I succeed in using gerunds instead of pronouns, my readers have Jason to thank.

My daughter, Laura, has always inspired my focus on mother-daughter relationships, never more so than now, when I have the exquisite joy of seeing what a sweet, wise, patient, and loving mother she is to my first baby granddaughter, Olivia, and bonus granddaughter, Alessandra. I cherish the incredible woman she has become and every moment we share. (The beautiful foreword she wrote for this book says it all.) My son-in-law, Dimitri, who is thoughtful, perceptive, and compassionate beyond measure, is a treasured addition to our family. I also adore and appreciate the love and support of my sister, Brena; niece, Aly; and nephew, Zach.

My heartfelt gratitude goes to all the women and girls I have seen in my practice, met at speaking events, and volunteered to be interviewed for this book. Thank you for entrusting me to tell your stories. (Please note that I have changed all names and identifying information to respect your privacy.) I am confident that the insights, experiences, and wisdom you shared with me have enriched these pages and will tremendously benefit readers who love, raise, and care for adolescent girls.

Notes

Introduction: Mothering Girls in the Digital Age

4 **not only do 95 percent:** Monica Anderson and Jingjing Jiang, "Teens, Social Media & Technology 2018," Pew Research Center, May 31, 2018, https://www.pewresearch.org/internet/2018/05/31/teens-social-media-technology-2018/.

8 **When asked in an interview:** Jennifer Jolly, "In 'Screenagers,' What to Do About Too Much Screen Time," *The New York Times*, March 15, 2016, https://well.blogs.nytimes.com/2016/03/15/in-screenagers-what-to-do-about-too-much-screen-time/.

Chapter One: A Changed Adolescent Landscape

19 **a majority of teens feels:** Jason Plautz, "The Environmental Burden of Generation Z," *The Washington Post*, February 3, 2020, https://www.washingtonpost.com/magazine/2020/02/03/eco-anxiety-is-overwhelming-kids-wheres-line-between-education-alarmism/.

19 **found that Gen Z adults:** *Stress in America 2020: A National Mental Health Crisis*, American Psychological Association, October 2020, https://www.apa.org/news/press/releases/stress/2020/report-october.

19 **troubled by current events:** *Stress in America: Generation Z*, American Psychological Association, October 2018: 3, https://www.apa.org/news/press/releases/stress/2018/stress-gen-z.pdf.

20 **in 2018 alone:** Steven Rich and John Woodrow Cox, "What If Someone Was Shooting?," *The Washington Post*, December 26, 2018, https://www.washingtonpost.com/graphics/2018/local/school-lockdowns-in-america/.

21 **from 2019 to 2020 there was:** R. T. Leeb, R. H. Bitsko, L. Radhakrishnan, P. Martinez, R. Njai, and K. M. Holland, "Mental Health–Related Emergency Department Visits Among Children Aged <18 Years During the COVID-19 Pandemic—United States, January 1–October 17, 2020," *The Morbidity and Mortality Weekly Report* 69 (2020): 1675–80, https://doi.org/10.15585/mmwr.mm6945a3.

22 **The Center for Promise's:** "The State of Young People During COVID-19," America's Promise Alliance, June 11, 2020, https://www.americaspromise.org/resource/state-young-people-during-covid-19.

22 **As far as educational markers:** Melanie Hanson, "Education Attainment Statistics," July 10, 2021, https://educationdata.org/education-attainment-statistics.

23 **A recent *Washington Post*:** Nick Anderson, "Early Applications Surge at Prestigious Colleges. So Does Early Heartache," *The Washington Post*, December 28, 2018, https://www.washingtonpost.com/local/education/early-applications-surge-at-prestigious-colleges-so-does-early-heartache/2018/12/28/12479e66-078c-11e9-a3f0-71c95106d96a_story.html.

26 **eight-to-twelve-year-olds in the US:** Victoria Rideout and Michael B. Robb, *The Common Sense Census: Media Use by Tweens and Teens* (San Francisco: Common Sense Media, 2019), "2019 The Common Sense Census: Media Use by Teens and Tweens," https://www.commonsensemedia.org/sites/default/files/uploads/research/2019-census-8-to-18-full-report-updated.pdf.

34 **Psychological dependency on devices:** Trevor Haynes, "Dopamine, Smartphones, and You: A Battle for Your Time," Harvard University, The Graduate School of Arts and Sciences Blog, May 1, 2018, https://sitn.hms.harvard.edu/flash/2018/dopamine-smartphones-battle-time/.

43 **According to Cigna's:** "Most Americans Are Considered Lonely," U.S. Loneliness Index Report, Cigna, 2018, https://www.cigna.com/assets/docs/newsroom/loneliness-survey-2018-infographic.pdf.

43 **lack of real-life social interactions:** Jean M. Twenge, Brian H. Spitzberg, and W. Keith Campbell, "Less In-Person Social Interaction with Peers Among U.S. Adolescents in the 21st Century and Links to Loneliness," *The Journal of Social and Personal Relationships* 36, no. 6 (March 19, 2019): 1892–1913, https://doi.org/10.1177/0265407519836170.

45 **According to a 2018 Pew Research:** Juliana Menasce Horowitz and Nikki Graf, "Most U.S. Teens See Anxiety and Depression as a Major Problem Among Their Peers," Pew Research Center, February 2019, https://www.pewresearch.org/social-trends/2019/02/20/most-u-s-teens-see-anxiety-and-depression-as-a-major-problem-among-their-peers/.

45 **depression rose by more:** Jean Twenge, Thomas Joiner, Mary Duffy, Bell Cooper, and Sara Binau, "Age, Period, and Cohort Trends in Mood Disorder and Suicide-Related Outcomes in a Nationally Representative Dataset, 2005–2017," *The Journal of Abnormal Psychology*, published online March 14, 2019, https://www.apa.org/pubs/journals/releases/abn-abn0000410.pdf.

45 **In the decade from 2007 to 2017:** Sally C. Curtin and Melonie Heron, "Death Rates Due to Suicide and Homicide Among Persons Aged 10–24: United States 2000–2017," NCHS Data Brief No. 352, October 2019, https://www.cdc.gov/nchs/data/databriefs/db352-h.pdf.

46 ***The Washington Post*'s profile:** Kent Babb, "Driven to the End: Olympic Cyclist Kelly Catlin Could Do It All. Until It All Became Too Much," *The Washington Post*, July 29, 2019, https://www.washingtonpost.com/sports/2019/07/29/kelly-catlin-death-cyclist/.

48 **A 2018 National College Health:** American College Health Association National College Health Assessment 2018, https://www.acha.org/documents/ncha/NCHA-II_Fall_2018_Reference_Group_Executive_Summary.pdf.

Chapter Two: New Challenges at Home

50 **In 2019, about 15.76 million:** "Number of Children Living with a Single Mother or a Single Father in the U.S. from 1970 to 2019," Statista Research Department, January 20, 2021, https://www.statista.com/statistics/252847/number-of-children-living-with-a-single-mother-or-single-father/.

53 **as many as 77 percent:** Kevin Eagan, Ellen Bara Stolzenberg, Hilary B. Zimmerman, Melissa C. Aragon, Hannah Whang Sayson, and Cecilia Rios-Aguilar, *The American Freshman: National Norms Fall 2016* (Los Angeles: Higher Education Research Institute, UCLA, 2017), https://www.heri.ucla.edu/monographs/TheAmericanFreshman2016.pdf.

55 **According to the Pew:** A. W. Geiger and Nikki Graf, "About One-in-Five U.S. Adults Know Someone Who Goes by a Gender-Neutral Pronoun," Pew Research Center, September 5, 2019, https://www.pewresearch.org/fact-tank/2019/09/05/gender-neutral-pronouns/.

58 **Getting fewer than the recommended:** "Chronic Sleep Deprivation Suppresses Immune System," *Science News*, January 27, 2017, https://www.sciencedaily.com/releases/2017/01/170127113010.htm.

58 **Too few zzzzs impairs learning:** "Sleep, Learning, and Memory," Harvard Medical School, December 18, 2007, http://healthysleep.med.harvard.edu/healthy/matters/benefits-of-sleep/learning-memory.

60 **"emotional sanctuaries":** Personal communication, 2018.

60 **68 percent of teens said:** Jean M. Twenge, Sarah M. Coyne, Jason S. Carroll, and W. Bradford Wilcox, "Teens in Quarantine: Mental Health, Screen Time, and Family Connection 2020," Institute for Family Studies, https://ifstudies.org/ifs-admin/resources/final-teenquarantine2020.pdf.

60 **With Gen Z teens more anxious:** Kimberly Leonard, "Are Today's Teens Better Behaved Than Their Parents Were?," *U.S. News & World Report*, September 10, 2015, https://www.usnews.com/news/blogs/data-mine/2015/09/10/todays-teens-use-less-alcohol-tobacco-drugs.

61 **nearly 30 percent of high school:** Mason Butts, "Question of the Day (Update): What Percent of High School Seniors Have a Driver's License?," *Next Gen Personal Finance*, October 21, 2020, https://www.ngpf.org/blog/question-of-the

-day/question-of-the-day-update-what-percent-of-high-school-seniors-have-a-drivers-license2/.

Chapter Three: Flourishing in Her Future

67 **Resiliency, along with grit:** Emily Hanford, "Angela Duckworth and the Research on 'Grit,'" American Public Radio, https://americanradioworks.publicradio.org/features/tomorrows-college/grit/angela-duckworth-grit.html.

68 **According to the UCLA:** Ellen Bara Stolzenberg, "The Mental and Physical Well-Being of Incoming Freshmen: Three Decades of Research," American Council on Education, September 6, 2018, https://www.higheredtoday.org/2018/09/06/mental-physical-well-incoming-freshmen-three-decades-research/.

68 **The American College Health Association's:** "National College Health Assessment Spring 2019 Reference Group Data Report," The American College Health Association, https://www.acha.org/documents/ncha/NCHA-II_SPRING_2019_US_REFERENCE_GROUP_DATA_REPORT.pdf.

69 **A positive mindset about stress:** Kelly McGonigal, "How to Make Stress Your Friend," TEDGlobal 2013, https://www.ted.com/talks/kelly_mcgonigal_how_to_make_stress_your_friend.

70 **Using MRIs to study youth:** Hilary Hurd Anyasaro, "Resilience May Be Neurobiological," Northwestern Medicine News Center, December 17, 2018, https://news.feinberg.northwestern.edu/2018/12/resilience-may-be-neurobiological/.

70 **According to *The American Freshman*:** Ellen Bara Stolzenberg, Kevin Eagan, Edgar Romo, Elaine Jessica Tamargo, Melissa C. Aragon, Madeline Luedke, and Nathaniel Kang, *The American Freshman: National Norms Fall 2018* (Los Angeles: Higher Education Research Institute, UCLA, 2019), https://www.heri.ucla.edu/monographs/TheAmericanFreshman2018.pdf.

72 **It is impossible for them:** "6 Famous Authors Who Once Faced Rejection," Wild Mind for Authors, https://wildmindcreative.com/bookmarketing/6-famous-authors-who-once-faced-rejection.

72 **Girls are utterly shocked:** "23 Incredibly Successful People Who Failed at First," *Business Insider*, https://www.businessinsider.in/science/23-incredibly-successful-people-who-failed-at-first/slidelist/31624813.cms.

74 **This winning trifecta:** Angela Duckworth, *Grit: The Power of Passion and Perseverance* (New York: Scribner, 2016).

76 **higher emotional intelligence:** "Students Do Better When They Can Understand, Manage Emotions," American Psychological Association, December 12, 2019, https://www.apa.org/news/press/releases/2019/12/students-manage-emotions.

79 **A fascinating study demonstrates:** Amy Novotney, "Resilient Kids Learn Better: New Research by Martin E. P. Seligman Shows How a More Positive Curriculum

Pays Off," *American Psychological Association Monitor* 40, no. 9 (October 2009): 32, https://www.apa.org/monitor/2009/10/resilient.html.

80 Overlapping with self-discipline: "Executive Function and Self-Regulation," Harvard University Center on the Developing Child, https://developingchild.harvard.edu/science/key-concepts/executive-function/.

82 "In solitude we learn": Sherry Turkle, "Stop Googling. Let's Talk," *The New York Times*, September 26, 2015, https://www.nytimes.com/2015/09/27/opinion/sunday/stop-googling-lets-talk.html.

84 Articles in business journals: Mark Feffer, "HR's Hard Challenge: When Employees Lack Soft Skills: The Soft Skills Increasingly Needed in Today's Workplace Are the Hardest to Teach and, Increasingly, the Hardest to Find," Society for Human Resource Management, April 2016, https://www.shrm.org/hr-today/news/hr-magazine/0416/pages/hrs-hard-challenge-when-employees-lack-soft-skills.aspx.

84 According to professors: Hakan Ozcelik and Sigal G. Barsade, "No Employee an Island: Workplace Loneliness and Job Performance," *Academy of Management Journal* 61, no. 6 (2018): 2343–66, https://doi.org/10.5465/amj.2015.1066.

86 After the pandemic: "Top Creative & Marketing Jobs in Demand 2021," Career Group Companies, February 17, 2021, https://careergroupcompanies.com/top-jobs-in-demand-2021-creative-careers-provide-new-opportunities/.

86 from 1976 to 2016: Jean M. Twenge and Heejung Park, "The Decline in Adult Activities Among U.S. Adolescents, 1976–2016," *Child Development* 90, no. 2 (March/April 2019): 638–54, https://doi.org/10.1111/cdev.12930.

87 The fact that IQ has: Matt Swayne, "More School, More Challenging Assignments Add Up to Higher IQ Scores," *Penn State News*, March 24, 2015, https://news.psu.edu/story/349747/2015/03/24/research/more-school-more-challenging-assignments-add-higher-iq-scores.

Chapter Four: Parenting with Intention

95 70 percent of parents: *Stress in America 2020: A National Mental Health Crisis*, American Psychological Association, October 2020, https://www.apa.org/news/press/releases/stress/2020/report-october.

110 A *Wall Street Journal* article: Elizabeth Bernstein, "Why Mothers and Daughters Fight So Much," *The Wall Street Journal, Personal Journal*, June 30, 2015, https://www.wsj.com/articles/why-mothers-and-teenage-daughters-fight-1435596179.

Chapter Five: Mothering the Daughter You Have

133 **In his book *Range*:** David Epstein, "You Don't Want a Child Prodigy: What 'Roger' Dads Will Do Better Than Tiger Moms Ever Will," *The New York Times Sunday Review*, May 21, 2019, https://www.nytimes.com/2019/05/24/opinion/sunday/kids-sports-music-choices.html.

137 **The National Institutes of Health's:** Kirstein Weir, "A Deep Dive into Adolescent Development," *Monitor on Psychology* 50, no. 6 (June 2019): 20, https://www.apa.org/monitor/2019/06/adolescent-development.

137 **According to the Avon:** George W. Citroner, "Sexual Minorities More Likely to Self-Harm," *Medscape*, December 21, 2018, https://www.medscape.com/viewarticle/906924.

137 **A survey in *JAMA Psychiatry*:** J. L. Turban, N. Beckwith, S. L. Reisner, and A. S. Keuroghlian, "Association Between Recalled Exposure to Gender Identity Conversion Efforts and Psychological Distress and Suicide Attempts Among Transgender Adults," *JAMA Psychiatry* 77, no. 1 (2020): 68–76, https://doi.org/10.1001/jamapsychiatry.2019.2285.

Chapter Six: Doing Less to Achieve More

144 ***Enough As She Is*:** Rachel Simmons, "How Not to Be a Snowplow Parent," *The New York Times*, March 19, 2019, https://www.nytimes.com/2019/03/19/well/family/college-bribery-snowplow-parenting.html.

144 **In the *New York Times*:** Claire Cain Miller, "The Relentlessness of Modern Parenting," *The New York Times*, December 25, 2018, https://www.nytimes.com/2018/12/25/upshot/the-relentlessness-of-modern-parenting.html.

144 **In one study:** Peipei Hong and Ming Cui, "Helicopter Parenting and College Students' Psychological Maladjustment: The Role of Self-Control and Living Arrangement," *Journal of Child and Family Studies* 29 (2020): 338–47, https://doi.org/10.1007/s10826-019-01541-2.

144 **Another study demonstrated:** Chrystyna D. Kouros, Megan M. Pruitt, Naomi V. Ekas, Romilyn Kiriaki, and Megan Sunderland, "Helicopter Parenting, Autonomy Support, and College Students' Mental Health and Well-Being: The Moderating Role of Sex and Ethnicity," *Journal of Child and Family Studies* 26 (March 2017): 939–49, https://doi.org/10.1007/s10826-016-0614-3.

144 **Surveys of college students:** Cory Stieg, "Kids with 'Helicopter Parents' More Likely to Burn Out, Have a Harder Time Transitioning to 'Real World,'" CNBC Health and Wellness, November 22, 2019, https://www.cnbc.com/2019/11/22/study-kids-who-have-helicopter-parents-experience-burnout-in-school.html.

146 **Interestingly, just when:** Douglas Belkin, Jennifer Levitz, and Melissa Korn, "Many More Students, Especially the Affluent, Get Extra Time to Take the SAT,"

The Wall Street Journal, May 21, 2019, https://www.wsj.com/articles/many-more-students-especially-the-affluent-get-extra-time-to-take-the-sat-11558450347.

146 **In some affluent communities:** Belkin, Levitz, and Korn, "Many More Students."

148 **Professor Donald McCabe:** "Plagiarism: Facts and Stats: Academic Integrity in High School," June 7, 2017, https://www.plagiarism.org/article/plagiarism-facts-and-stats.

149 **A just-published study:** Sara F. Waters, Helena Rose Karnilowicz, Tessa V. West, and Wendy Berry Mendes, "Keep It to Yourself? Parent Emotion Suppression Influences Physiological Linkage and Interaction Behavior," *The Journal of Family Psychology* 34, no. 7 (2020): 784–93, https://doi.org/10.1037/fam0000664.

150 ***Forbes* documents:** Amy Morin, "Parents, Please Don't Attend Your Adult Child's Job Interview," *Forbes*, August 29, 2017, https://www.forbes.com/sites/amymorin/2017/08/29/parents-please-dont-attend-your-adult-childs-job-interview/.

151 **Researchers who studied emotions:** M. A. Lippold, K. D. Davis, S. M. McHale, O. M. Buxton, and D. M. Almeida, "Daily Stressor Reactivity During Adolescence: The Buffering Role of Parental Warmth," *Health Psychology: Official Journal of the Division of Health Psychology, American Psychological Association* 35, no. 9 (2016): 1027–35, https://doi.org/10.1037/hea0000352.

151 **The Center on the Developing Child:** "The Impact of Early Adversity on Children's Development," Harvard University, https://46y5eh11fhgw3ve3ytpwxt9r-wpengine.netdna-ssl.com/wp-content/uploads/2015/05/inbrief-adversity-1.pdf.

152 **Explain that physical exercise:** "Brain Derived Neurotrophic Factor (BDNF) and Exercise," https://exerciseright.com.au/brain-derived-neurotrophic-factor-bdnf-and-exercise/.

153 **But connection to peers:** R. E. Adams, J. B. Santo, and W. M. Bukowski, "The Presence of a Best Friend Buffers the Effects of Negative Experiences," *Developmental Psychology* 47, no. 6 (November 2011): 1786–91, https://doi.org/10.1037/a0025401. Epub 2011 Sep 5. PMID: 21895364.

153 **Smiling stimulates the brain's:** Ron Gutman, "The Untapped Power of Smiling," *Forbes*, March 22, 2011, https://www.forbes.com/sites/ericsavitz/2011/03/22/the-untapped-power-of-smiling/.

159 **Research on self-regulation:** Simon Moesgaard, "8 Scientific Facts About Self-Control," Reflectd, December 30, 2013, https://reflectd.co/2013/12/30/8-facts-about-self-control/.

Chapter Seven: Fruitful Conversations 2.0

203 **The stress hormone cortisol:** "Protect Your Brain from Stress," Harvard Women's Health Watch, February 15, 2021, https://www.health.harvard.edu/mind-and-mood/protect-your-brain-from-stress.

206 **According to a study:** P. Setoh, S. Zhao, R. Santos, G. D. Heyman, and K. Lee, "Parenting by Lying in Childhood Is Associated with Negative Developmental Outcomes in Adulthood," *The Journal of Experimental Child Psychology* 189 (January 2020): 104680, https://doi.org/10.1016/j.jecp.2019.104680. Epub 2019 Sep 26. PMID: 31500808.

Chapter Eight: Establishing Healthy Habits

225 **A large study of teens':** J. M. Twenge, G. N. Martin, and B. H. Spitzberg, "Trends in U.S. Adolescents' Media Use, 1976–2016: The Rise of Digital Media, the Decline of TV, and the (Near) Demise of Print," *Psychology of Popular Media Culture* 8, no. 4 (2019): 329–45, https://doi.org/10.1037/ppm0000203.

226 **A recent article in:** Kirsten Weir, "Nurtured by Nature," *Monitor on Psychology* 51, no. 3 (April/May 2020): 51–55, https://www.apa.org/monitor/2020/04/nurtured-nature.

226 **Bonus benefit:** Candice Gaukel Andrews, "Want a Creativity Boost? Take a Walk in Nature," *Good Nature Travel*, October 16, 2018, https://www.nathab.com/blog/want-a-creativity-boost-take-a-walk-in-nature/.

226 **Experts agree that teens:** "Sleep in Middle and High School Students," Centers for Disease Control and Prevention, CDC Healthy Schools, https://www.cdc.gov/healthyschools/features/students-sleep.htm.

227 **To fall asleep more easily:** Danielle Pacheco, "How Electronics Affect Sleep," Sleep Foundation, November 6, 2020, https://www.sleepfoundation.org/how-sleep-works/how-electronics-affect-sleep.

227 **When at rest, the brain:** "Sleep, Learning, and Memory," Harvard Medical School, December 18, 2007, http://healthysleep.med.harvard.edu/healthy/matters/benefits-of-sleep/learning-memory.

228 **Sleep deprivation is also:** Thea Ramsey, Amy Athey, Jason Ellis, Andrew Tubbs, Robert Turner, William D. S. Killgore, Chloe Warlick, Pamela Alfonso-Miller, and Michael A. Grandner, "Dose-Response Relationship Between Insufficient Sleep and Mental Health Symptoms in Collegiate Student Athletes and Non-Athletes," *Sleep* 42, suppl. 1 (April 2019): A362, https://doi.org/10.1093/sleep/zsz067.899.

Chapter Nine: Managing Screens and Social Media

239 **Psychologist Jean M. Twenge's:** Jean M. Twenge, "Stop Debating Whether Too Much Smartphone Time Can Hurt Teens, and Start Protecting Them," *Time*, March 21, 2019, https://time.com/5555737/smartphone-mental-health-teens/.

239 Teens who spend more: K. E. Riehm, K. A. Feder, K. N. Tormohlen, et al., "Associations Between Time Spent Using Social Media and Internalizing and Externalizing Problems Among US Youth," *JAMA Psychiatry* 76, no. 12 (2019): 1266–73, https://doi.org/10.1001/jamapsychiatry.2019.2325.

240 In England, a three-year: "Social-Media Use 'Disrupting Teen Sleep and Exercise,'" BBC.com, August 14, 2019, https://www.bbc.com/news/health-49330254.

245 teens say social media: Monica Anderson and Jingjing Jiang, "Teens and Their Experiences on Social Media," Pew Research Center, Internet & Technology, November 28, 2018, https://www.pewresearch.org/internet/2018/11/28/teens-and-their-experiences-on-social-media/.

256 As her prefrontal cortex matures: A. Griffin, "Adolescent Neurological Development and Implications for Health and Well-Being," *Healthcare (Basel)* 5, no. 4 (September 2017): 62, https://doi.org/10.3390/healthcare5040062.

257 Remarkably, 65 percent of teens: NORC at the University of Chicago, "Almost 6 in 10 Teens Take a Break from Social Media," *ScienceDaily*, May 3, 2017, www.sciencedaily.com/releases/2017/05/170503092233.htm.

258 Similarly, a middle school: Jenny Brundin, "This Colorado Middle School Banned Phones 7 Years Ago. They Say Students Are Happier, Less Stressed, and More Focused," Colorado Public Radio, November 5, 2019, https://www.cpr.org/2019/11/05/this-colorado-middle-school-banned-phones-seven-years-ago-they-say-students-are-happier-less-stressed-and-more-focused/.

Chapter Ten: Calling Off the Homework Police

269 Duke University psychologists: Harris Cooper, "Homework's Diminishing Returns," *The New York Times*, December 20, 2010, https://www.nytimes.com/roomfordebate/2010/12/12/stress-and-the-high-school-student/homeworks-diminishing-returns.

269 Based on research with: Stephanie Donaldson-Pressman, Rebecca Jackson, and Robert Pressman, *The Learning Habit: A Groundbreaking Approach to Homework and Parenting That Helps Our Children Succeed in School and Life* (New York: Penguin Group, 2014).

270 Besides modeling a strong: Carol Dweck, "Carol Dweck Revisits the 'Growth Mindset,'" *EducationWeek*, September 25, 2015, https://www.edweek.org/leadership/opinion-carol-dweck-revisits-the-growth-mindset/2015/09.

271 A study of Dutch tweens: "'I Will Do My Very Best!' Children Who Engage in Positive Self-Talk About Effort Can Boost Their Math Achievement," Society for Research in Child Development, December 17, 2019, https://medicalxpress.com/news/2019-12-children-engage-positive-self-talk-effort.html.

274 **The deep, restorative stage:** Eric Suni, "Stages of Sleep," Sleep Foundation, August 14, 2020, https://www.sleepfoundation.org/how-sleep-works/stages-of-sleep.

274 **Many researchers believe:** S. Gais and J. Born, "Declarative Memory Consolidation: Mechanisms Acting During Human Sleep," *Learning & Memory* 11, no. 6 (2004): 679–85, https://doi.org/10.1101/lm.80504.

274 **That is because over:** Gais and Born, "Declarative Memory."

276 **Trying to focus on two:** "Multitasking: Switching Costs," American Psychological Association, March 20, 2006, https://www.apa.org/research/action/multitask.

276 **One study found that:** Jeremy Reimer, "Study Says: Leaving the Multitasking to Your Computer," *Ars Technica*, March 27, 2007, March 20, 2006, https://arstechnica.com/uncategorized/2007/03/study-says-leave-the-multitasking-to-your-computer/.

Chapter Eleven: Fostering Healthy Friendships

284 **With puberty, friendships:** L. M. Lessard and J. Juvonen, "Losing and Gaining Friends: Does Friendship Instability Compromise Academic Functioning in Middle School?," *The Journal of School Psychology* 69 (2018): 143–53, https://doi.org/10.1016/j.jsp.2018.05.003.

289 **For survival, humans have:** "Study Illuminates the 'Pain' of Social Rejection," University of Michigan Medical Press, March 28, 2011, https://medicalxpress.com/news/2011-03-illuminates-pain-social.html.

293 **Studies of high school students:** Jan Hoffman, "Teaching Teenagers to Cope with Social Stress," *The New York Times*, September 29, 2016, https://www.nytimes.com/2016/09/30/health/teenagers-stress-coping-skills.html.

293 **In fact, according to:** S. T. Lereya, M. Samara, and D. Wolke, "Parenting Behavior and the Risk of Becoming a Victim and a Bully/Victim: A Meta-Analysis Study," *Child Abuse & Neglect* 37, no. 12 (2013): 1091–1108, https://doi.org/10.1016/j.chiabu.2013.03.001.

303 **Maintaining high levels:** Kari Phang, "Toxic Stress: How the Body's Response Can Harm a Child's Development," Nationwide Children's, July 13, 2007, https://www.nationwidechildrens.org/family-resources-education/700childrens/2017/07/toxic-stress-how-the-bodys-response-can-harm-a-childs-development.

309 **According to a 2011:** "Prevalence of Teen Dating Violence," National Institute of Justice, December 5, 2011, https://nij.ojp.gov/topics/articles/prevalence-teen-dating-violence.

309 **Among other troubling behaviors:** Amanda Lenhart, Monica Anderson, and Aaron Smith, "Chapter 6: Teen Relationship Struggles: From Potentially Innocuous to Annoying to Abusive Digital Behaviors," Pew Research Center, Teens, Technology, and

Romantic Relationships, October 1, 2015, https://www.pewresearch.org/internet/2015/10/01/teen-relationship-struggles/.

310 **According to the Youth Risk:** "Preventing Teen Dating Violence," Centers for Disease Control and Prevention, https://www.cdc.gov/violenceprevention/intimatepartnerviolence/teendatingviolence/fastfact.html.

315 **According to the National Center:** "Bullying," National Center for Education Statistics, https://nces.ed.gov/fastfacts/display.asp?id=719.

317 **Studies show that being:** Sherri Gordon, "6 Ways Bullying Impacts Bystanders: Kids Who Witness Bullying May Be as Affected as Victims," *Very Well Family*, December 1, 2020, https://www.verywellfamily.com/how-witnessing-bullying-impacts-bystanders-460622.

318 **Whereas 25 to 30 percent:** "Bullying," National Center for Education Statistics.

Chapter Twelve: Parenting After Divorce

319 **Today, there is:** "How Common Is Divorce and What Are the Reasons?," https://yourdivorcequestions.org/how-common-is-divorce/.

323 **After being divorced:** Gretchen Livingston, "Chapter 2: The Demographics of Remarriage," Pew Research Center, Social & Demographic Trends, November 14, 2014, https://www.pewresearch.org/social-trends/2014/11/14/chapter-2-the-demographics-of-remarriage/.

Chapter Thirteen: Savoring the College Process

347 **Along with traveling:** Abby Alcala, "QoD: Can You Name ONE of the Top 3 Reasons Students Take a Gap Year After Graduating from High School?," *Next Gen Personal Finance*, November 3, 2019, https://www.ngpf.org/blog/question-of-the-day/question-of-the-day-what-are-the-top-3-reasons-why-students-take-a-gap-year/.